PRAISE FOR *TOKYO JUNKIE*

"A glorious love letter to the world's greatest c̶ take its place next to classics by Lafcadio Hearn, Edward Seidensticker, Donald Richie, and Ian Buruma that succeed in articulating the hold that Japan has on the hearts of so many of us *gaijin.*" R. Taggart Murphy, author of *Japan and the Shackles of the Past* and *The Weight of the Yen*

"Reads like a Japanese comic. A vivid, fast-paced paean to a great city, and Robert Whiting's emotional journey to reconciling his insider/outsider status. Wonderful!" Dan Slater, Director, The Delphi Network

"A complex, captivating portrait of a city that is both insular and welcoming, and is now one of the world's top tourist destinations." *Foreword Reviews*

"Whiting's ability to craft history lessons as narrative epics that captivate an audience and paint a stunning portrait of what Tokyo's culture and history mean to the world at large is unparalleled." Sherry Marsh, executive producer of History Channel's *Vikings* and the upcoming adaptation of Robert Whiting's *Tokyo Underworld*

"Every visitor to Japan, every student of Japanese culture, and every diplomat posted there should have a copy. . . . An essential guide to understanding the country and its people." Derek Shearer, former US ambassador and professor of diplomacy

"Whiting is the consummate raconteur, regaling readers with tales of bawdy exploits, how to befriend yakuza, and the art of hard living in a book brimming with wry humor and empathy." Jeff Kingston, Director of Asian Studies, Temple University Japan and author of *Japan* (Polity Histories)

"Seduced by its bustle and underworld hustle, Bob Whiting has spent decades exploring the hidden corners of Tokyo and the Japanese psyche. From yakuza to baseball and dirty politics to gleaming skyscrapers—he takes you on the intercultural journey of a lifetime." Joseph Shaules, Director, Japan Intercultural Institute

"What a joy!" Nicholas Pileggi, author of *Wiseguy* and *Casino* and screenwriter of *Goodfellas* and *Casino*

tokyo junkie

60 YEARS
OF BRIGHT LIGHTS
AND BACK ALLEYS
... AND BASEBALL

ROBERT WHITING

Stone Bridge Press • *Berkeley, California*

Published by
Stone Bridge Press
P. O. Box 8208, Berkeley, CA 94707
TEL 510-524-8732 • sbp@stonebridge.com • www.stonebridge.com

Names of modern-day Japanese are given in Western order, family name last, and Japanese words appear without macrons.

Front cover design by Linda Ronan using images by Sebastian Hages (alley) and Jaison Lin (cityscape).

Printed in the United States of America.

10 9 8 7 6 5 4 3 2 1   2025 2024 2023 2022 2021

p-ISBN 978-1-61172-067-9
e-ISBN 978-1-61172-949-8

Contents

Preface

The late Anthony Bourdain, renowned celebrity chef and globe-trotter, in an interview with *Maxim* in 2017, named Tokyo as his favorite city in the world and said, "If I had to agree to live in one country, or even one city, for the rest of my life, never leaving it, I'd pick Tokyo in a second." He called his first trip to Tokyo, in general, an "explosive, life-changing event" and even compared it to the first time he ever took acid, in the way it changed every experience that came after it. "Nothing was ever the same for me," he said, fascinated with the city's myriad layers and the variety of its flavors, taste, and customs. "I just wanted more of it."

I understood what he was saying because I had felt the same way when I first came to the city over five decades ago in 1962 as a raw nineteen-year-old GI from small-town America. It was a time when the United States was at the peak of its economic power under iconic new president John Fitzgerald Kennedy and Japan was still struggling to recover from the damage of defeat in World War 2.

Tokyo, at the time, was tearing itself apart and putting itself back together in preparation for the Tokyo Olympics. You could stand in parts of the city and watch as buildings were being torn down on one side of the street and new ones constructed on the other. I had arrived at what someone would later describe as the biggest construction site in the world.

I watched fascinated, astonished, as, before my eyes, the city evolved, in a few short years, from a fetid, disease-ridden third-world backwater into a modern megalopolis in what many believe to be the greatest urban transformation in history. Tokyo then staged what *Life* magazine called "the Greatest Olympic Games ever."

I was as naïve as they come. I had grown up in Eureka, a small fishing and logging town on the coast of northern California. Military training in Texas, Intelligence school in Mississippi, and a weekend in New Orleans. That was all I knew of the outside world. My knowledge of Japan was limited to Godzilla movies, dubbed in bad English, I had seen at the Eureka Theater. In fact, the first thing I did on my initial visit to Tokyo was to look for the Diet Building that Godzilla had destroyed in his debut Toho feature.

But I was hypnotized by the energy of the place—the ubiquitous neon signs, the endless nightlife—and so I chose to stay on in Tokyo. I went on to graduate from the Jesuit-founded Sophia University in the city and grew into adulthood there, surviving a self-destructive tailspin into the Dark Heart of its seductions that caused me to pack up and move to New York for three years to recover.

Finally, I settled down to become the author of several successful books over a four-decade span. Along the way I met a lot of fascinating people: newspaper barons, politicians, baseball stars, famous writers, yakuza enforcers, and other denizens of the city's underworld. I also met my wife, with whom I would spend over forty-five years, dividing my time between Japan and the numerous global capitals where she worked as a United Nations officer.

Tokyo grew right alongside me. It became the richest city in the world, riding the back of the global trade juggernaut Japan built in the aftermath of the '64 Games. It weathered the real estate collapse of the bubble era, got its choking pollution under control, covered the landscape with a succession of high-rise buildings, and became what many people regard as the cleanest, safest, most modern, most transportation efficient, most fashion conscious, and the politest city anywhere—with arguably the best selection of restaurants on the planet, boasting more than twice as many Michelin three-star restaurants as any other city, including Paris. The aforementioned Bourdain declared the food in the city superior, on "virtually every level and price point."

Robert Whiting. Tokyo, 1962.

By 2018, Tokyo had actually passed Paris as the world's leading tourist destination. Trip Advisor, the largest travel website in existence, asked its users to rank the thirty-seven top cities across the globe in terms of "the most satisfying" to visit. Tokyo was voted #1 in the world, topping several of the sixteen categories listed, including local friendliness, taxi services, cleanliness, and public transportation. I'd lived in or visited extensively many of those places mentioned in the survey and I would have voted the same.

The city may have its flaws: crushing rush-hour crowds, mindless bureaucracy (in the great typhoon of fall 2019 in Tokyo, homeless people were denied entry to a shelter because they could not provide a residence address), and certain gender-equality issues.

There are also questions about press freedom, rampant cronyism in politics, and a government that is all too often enmeshed in scandal.

But the good, in my opinion, outweighs the bad.

* * *

Tokyo is now the largest city on the planet, with thirty-eight million inhabitants in the Greater Metropolitan Area—thirteen million in the city proper. Tokyo has the highest GDP of any city at $1,520 billion, ahead of New York City, Los Angeles, Seoul, London, and Paris. Tokyo also has more Fortune 500 global headquarters than anywhere else and boasts a newly minted, awe-inspiring metropolitan skyline that ranks with that of Manhattan, Sydney, and other great capitals. The city also ranks among the highest around the globe in terms of literacy levels, with a rate of 99 percent for people above the age of fifteen, and life expectancy, with almost a quarter of the population over the age of sixty-five. Special features incorporated by the city fathers to accommodate Tokyo's aging society include talking traffic lights and ATMs, as well as ubiquitous directional tactile pavers to aid pedestrians with poor eyesight, along with special ramps accompanying steps in train stations and public buildings for the benefit of the less mobile.

In 2013 I watched as Tokyo won the bid to host another Olympics, this one scheduled for 2020, fifty-six years after the first one, if under vastly different and improved circumstances. I looked on with not a little interest as preparations began for an army of robots to help with language translation, directions, and transportation; driverless cabs; 8K TV broadcasts; algae and hydrogen as clean alternative energy sources; demonstrations of Maglev trains running nearly 400 miles per hour; and man-made meteors streaming across the sky from satellites in space for the opening ceremony. You could feel the buzz.

From my office window in Toyosu—built partially on reclaimed land at the northern end of Tokyo Bay and yet another bustling new quarter of commerce and leisure filled with skyscrapers of both the office and residential variety—I had a bird's-eye view of the Olympic Village for the 2020 Games erected under the shadow of the Rainbow Bridge. In my mind's eye I could see another Olympic Village from fifty-six years ago. Tokyo and I had come full circle. The perfect time to write a memoir had arrived, and, as chance would have it, that time would be accompanied by a coronavirus pandemic that would keep me in isolation for extended periods, allowing for total dedication to the task at hand. It also necessitated the first postponement in Olympic history.

My story is part *Alice in Wonderland*, part *Bright Lights, Big City*, and part *Forrest Gump*, among other things. It is a coming-of-age tale as well as an account of a decades-long journey into the heart of a city undergoing one of the most remarkable and sustained metamorphoses ever seen. It is also something of a love story, with all the irrational sentimentality that term entails. Tokyo and I have had our differences, our ups and downs—I once left for what I thought was good, so tired of being a *gaijin* (outsider) that I thought I would die if I stayed any longer—but as our relationship reaches the end and I look back, I must say that all in all it was the right place to spend all these years.

It is not too much to say that I am what I am today because of the city of Tokyo. It was here that I learned the art of living, discovered the importance of perseverance, grew to appreciate the value of harmonious relations as much as individual rights, and came to rethink what it means to be an American as well as a member of the larger human race.

Acknowledgments

The genesis of this book was a five-part series on the 1964 Olympics I wrote for the *Japan Times* in 2014, followed by an article in *Foreign Policy* comparing the preparations for the 1964 Games with the 2020 Games. The editors at Kadokawa Shoten, Satoshi Gunji, Tetsuya Sugahara, and Motofumi Ijuin, asked me to turn this material into a book, and since Kadokawa had published the best-selling Japanese-language editions of *You Gotta Have Wa* and *Tokyo Underworld*, I readily said yes, and Miko Yamanouchi at Japan Uni finalized the deal. I wound up with a 175,000 word manuscript, which Kadokawa published in the fall of 2017, translated into Japanese by Masayuki Tamaki, Japan's leading sports journalist, who had also worked on *Wa*. For US publication I revised and shortened the MS, removing many of the Olympic-related segments as well as chapters on my work as a military electronic intelligence analyst for the NSA and CIA, while adding new and updated material on the city of Tokyo in general and on the Coronavirus in particular, the latter having reared its nasty little head while I was working on the final version of this book.

A number of people helped me in the process of putting this book together. They include Jack Gallagher, the former *Japan Times* sports editor who commissioned the original 1964 Olympics series, *JT* writer Ed Odeven, who copy-edited it, the writer-editor Mary Corbett—my BOD sidekick at the Foreign Correspondents Club of Japan who waded through the original draft, *Nikkei Asia*

Review editor Gwen Robinson, and International Creative Management Partner Amanda "Binky" Urban. Jeff Kingston, the well-known Temple University professor and Japan author, read the MS and offered insightful comments. Peter Miller of Kamprint in Kamakura read several versions and offered trenchant analysis and encouragement. Tokyo management consultant Mitch Murata provided feedback on a number of occasions, as did securities and military affairs analyst Hiroki Allen. New York-based journalist David Roberts, the former academic physicist and diplomat who was my collaborator at *Foreign Policy* magazine, offered valuable advice, while China-based writer Don MacLaren read through the manuscript twice and corrected many mistakes. Douglas Victoria, a fellow traveler at Fuchu Air Station back in the day, offered helpful recollections. It was good to reconnect with him again. Peter O'Connor offered research materials. *FP* editor Blake Hounshell helped iron out kinks in LDP- and Olympic-related articles. *1964* author Roy Tomizawa offered advice. Bryan Dunn and Kevin Novak offered libationary guidance. David Shapiro, who edited *Tokyo Underworld* and *The Meaning of Ichiro*, did another one of his thoroughly professional edits on the MS, while *Japanamerica* author Roland Kelts, who also set this project up with Peter Goodman at Stone Bridge, did a final edit. Mark Schreiber read the final version and offered several valuable suggestions for improvement. Peter and John Sockolov did a superb job preparing the text and the photographs for publication. I thank them all for their generous help and take the blame for any other errors that may still exist.

I also want to thank Kozo Abe of the *Yukan Fuji* and Hiroshi Naito at the *Sankei Shimbun* for their help in the long, arduous task of digging out photos and express my gratitude to the following individuals: Noriko Takahashi at WAttention, Bob Kirschenbaum of Pacific Press Service in Tokyo, the Andrew Roth Gallery in New York on behalf of Katsumi Watanabe, Noriyuki Suetsugu of Getty Images Japan, Pierre-Louis Denis at the William Klein studio in Paris, Bonnie Pong Mai-wa at Hitomi Watanabe photos, and Hiroko Moriwaki and Nakajima-san at the FCCJ. Also thanks to Shoko Nakajima at Kyodo and Mark Schreiber for the photos they provided.

Finally, a big *arigatou* to my wife Machiko and my sister Margo who provided moral support as well as old photos, and thanks to everyone in my extended family in the Kondo, Hayano and Kobaysahi clans in the Tokyo area and the Noble, Davis and Gruttadauro families in the US.

* * *

Unlike my previous works, this book has no footnotes or bibliography. It is a memoir after all. However, researchers who are interested in my sources are free to contact me and I will be happy to answer specific questions. You can find my contact information on my web page:

https://robertwhiting.com/

—*RW*

The Soldier

Tokyo. Winter. 1962: "The Most Dynamic City on Earth"

At that time, the first thing that hit you on the streets of central Tokyo was the crowds. Enormous waves of people everywhere, men and women in long dark coats, bundled against the cold, bumping, jostling, a sea of black hair navigating streets clogged with automobiles and bicycles. Long queues formed on train station platforms. Commuter cars were so packed that uniformed platform pushers were required to get everyone inside and close the doors.

Then it was the construction, the level of which was simply off the charts. Everywhere you turned it seemed there was a building being put up or another one being pulled down. Crumbling sidewalks were ripped apart, roadways air-hammered into rubble, trucks whizzing by carrying dirt and building materials. Overhead, half-finished highways filled the sky, rebars and braided cables exposed. There was so much going on that it was a contact high just to stand there and watch it all.

The noise was omnipresent. A constant cacophony of auto

Construction was nonstop.

horns, jack hammers, pile drivers, and trolley cars. Honk-honk. Rat-a-tat-tat. Wham. Boom. Clang-clang-clang. An electronic billboard sign erected at a Nishi-Ginza intersection in downtown Tokyo measured the sonic damage: 79. 81. 83. 86. Beside it stood a sign that read: BE MORE QUIET! THE NOISE AT THIS MOMENT: 88. STANDARD FOR RESIDENTIAL AREA: 50 PHONS. BUSY CORNERS: 70 PHONS. But the noise, meticulously measured though it was, never stopped.

The massive congestion, the traffic jams, and the reek of setting cement produced an overwhelming assault on the senses: dust, soot, smoke, and smog were pervasive. Auto-exhaust pollution was so bad that traffic policemen carried small oxygen cylinders. Pedestrians wore facemasks and sidewalk cafes were encased in large plastic screens. There was another electronic sign near the Ginza that gave you, in addition to the time and temperature, the current sulfur dioxide and carbon monoxide levels. At a nearby police box, a first aid station was set up for citizens overcome by the toxic air.

I was a young man from rural California, nineteen years old, a mechanic's son, newly assigned to Tokyo by the United States Air Force. I was on my first foray into the city, standing in Yurakucho on a freezing-cold day in January 1962, and I was mesmerized by all the activity. I would circle the globe many times in my lifetime. I would live in many of the world's major capitals and visit many more. Yet nothing I would ever see would match the spectacle then before my eyes.

Tokyo was in the midst of a historic transformation, made urgent when the city was awarded the 1964 Olympics, the first Asian country so honored. The unsightly urban sprawl of rickety wooden houses, scabrous shanties, and cheaply constructed stucco-covered buildings that had mushroomed out of the rubble left by the American B-29 Superfortress bombings was now being razed to the ground, and in its place a brand-new city was going up. Thousands of office and residential buildings were under construction, ranging in height from four to seven stories, along with several five-star hotels and an elevated expressway network. Also being built were two brand-new subway lines to go with the two that already existed, a multimillion-dollar monorail from Haneda Airport into downtown Tokyo, and a billion-dollar 160-mile-per-hour bullet train between Tokyo and Osaka.

I had arrived in Japan weeks earlier, catching my first wide-eyed view of the country as the Military Air Transport propeller plane I was on touched down at Tachikawa Air Base on the eastern coast of Honshu, completing a forty-four-hour flight over the Pacific Ocean with stopovers in Honolulu and Wake Island. Spread out before me was an exotic checkerboard of rice paddies and farming plots that stretched out in all directions, with a snow-covered Mt. Fuji visible in the distance.

After processing, I was greeted by an older leathery-cheeked Japanese gentleman with gold teeth, wearing a dark-blue gold-tasseled uniform, who introduced himself as my chauffeur. He grabbed my B-4 bag and led me outside into the biting cold where a dark-blue Air Force station wagon waited to make the 15-mile drive to my new home, Fuchu Air Base. The ride took me over a narrow two-lane blacktop road flanked by rice fields, wooded areas, thatched farmhouses emitting smoke from narrow chimney pipes, Buddhist temples, and small roadside Shinto shrines. The road was occupied by a weird assortment of vehicles: military jeeps, big American passenger cars, Toyota sedans, motorbikes, and rickshaws. Off to one side, a packed commuter train whizzed by. I opened the window for some air and was greeted by the smell of sewage.

There was a lot to do to bring the city up to Western standards, as I would discover. Living conditions were still largely primitive in most areas outside the main hubs. The harbor and the capital's main rivers were thick with sludge from the human and industrial waste that poured into them, and drinking local tap water, we were told, was unsafe, with hepatitis a constant worry. Decades later, Tokyo would be justifiably famous for its high-tech toilets, with their automated lids, music modes, water jets, blow-dry functions, and computer analyses, that headlined an impressive sewerage. But back then, despite the frantic rebuilding, less than a quarter of the city's twenty-three sprawling wards had flush sewage systems at all, making Tokyo one of the world's most undeveloped (and odiferous) megalopolises.

This state of affairs compared unfavorably with the United States and Europe where flush toilets had been the norm in cities since the turn of the century. In statistical terms, it meant that millions of Tokyoites lacking such amenities in their homes were forced to rely on a primitive scoop and dispose system in which fecal matter had to be sucked out from under buildings by the *kumitoriya* vacuum trucks and then transported to rice paddies for use as fertilizer after processing. American troops sarcastically nicknamed them "honey trucks" because of the powerful odor they emitted. Since the trucks visited most neighborhoods only once or twice a week, there was a continual, pervasive stench in vast parts of the capital. Added to that were the *gesui,* or roadside gutters, where the kitchen and bath water effluence ran and into which late-night drunks often urinated and, not infrequently, tumbled.

At Fuchu Air Station.

Tokyo was also rat-infested. Some 40 percent of Japanese had tapeworms. There were no ambulances, and infant mortality was twenty times what it is today. Moreover, house theft was rampant, narcotics use was endemic, and it was considered too dangerous to walk in public parks at night. Yakuza (gangsters) were everywhere, their numbers at an all-time high.

Tokyo's most unlikely winning bid for the Olympics had been the result of the submission of an ambitious half-billion-dollar budget to remake the capital for the event (a figure that far exceeded the $30 million spent for the Rome Games in 1960) as well as the intensive wining and dining of the Olympic Committee during a visit to the capital in 1958. (This entertainment, according to the Andrew Jennings exposé "The New Lords of the Rings," published in 1996, included the prepaid services of Tokyo's finest call girls.) After the awarding of the games to Tokyo was announced in the spring of 1959, however, the question many people had was, "How in the world is the city ever going to be ready in time?"

The effort to redo Tokyo's urban infrastructure had been undertaken in conjunction with a massive government plan to

Streetcars were eliminated to make room to build new overhead highways.

simultaneously double GNP and per capita income by the end of the sixties through the manufacture and export of transistors, radios, television sets, and automobiles.

Tokyo was already the single most populated city in the world, with residents exceeding ten million as of February 1962 (more than doubling since the end of war, and still growing, bursting at the seams). Thousands flowed into the city every day, the bulk of them on *shudan-sha,* trains dedicated to carrying groups of job seekers, many of them teenagers fresh out of provincial junior high schools, destined for the city's factories and numerous construction sites, at salaries twice that of anywhere else in the country.

The pace of life in the city was dizzying—"double that of New York," according to *Time* magazine, which, despite the haze and smell that lay heavy over the city, called Tokyo the "most dynamic city on the face of the earth." There was so much going on that it was impossible to take it all in.

For one thing Tokyo still oozed culture—both modern and traditional. The main shopping and entertainment hubs offered grand department stores, deluxe movie theaters with 70mm screens, and *pachinko* pinball parlors jangling noisily all day long.

These crowded together with noodle stands, *yakitori* shops with their smoky grills, food marts, and discount shops, only to give way suddenly to ancient temples with serene gardens of gravel and rocks and inner courtyards where lessons in Zen archery and the tea ceremony were taught.

The futuristic seventeen-floor Hotel New Otani, with Tokyo's first revolving roof, was going up in a 400-year-old garden, once the province of a Tokugawa-period feudal lord. The spanking new Tokyo Tower, modeled after Paris's Eiffel Tower, and the tallest such structure in the world at the time, overlooked century-old geisha houses (which were just beginning to rebuild their self-esteem after having faced the tragic dilemma of the American Occupation years: close the doors quickly or welcome in the barbarians at the gate).

It was after sunset that Tokyo really came into its own, transmogrifying into a Neon City of bright, bold colors with signs in *katakana* script and *kanji* characters flashing on and off like giant insects in the sky. Tokyo gave off so much light that it was easily visible from outer space, as reported by Russian cosmonauts and American Mercury astronauts after space flights began in 1961.

There were by one count twice as many places to eat as in New York, serving just about every type of food imaginable, from the corner sushi shop to the Grill Room steaks in the Imperial Hotel. (McDonald's, Shakey's Pizza, and Wendy's were years from their invasion of the culinary scene.)

Tokyo also had more bars per square kilometer than anywhere in the world. These ranged from the cheap hole-in-the-wall places known as *ippai nomiya* (literally "one-drink" watering holes, although the consumption almost never stopped after one drink) where a Nikka whisky highball cost ¥30 (less than a dime) to the elegant high-end hostess clubs like the Crown and Queen Bee in the Ginza where you could spend a month's pay in two hours. In between were *sutando* bars, cocktail lounges, beer gardens, and *conpa* pubs (where people sat around circular tables and counters and got to know one another). There was a modern building in front of Shinbashi Station, not far from the 1,000-year-old Kara-sumori Shine, which housed a hundred different stand bars. Later during my first year, a friend from the base and I tried to have a drink at every one of them one night (a practice called *hashigo* or "ladder drinking" in Japanese), but only made it through the first twenty before we both collapsed.

"You don't know how lucky you are," Master Sergeant Korn, a crusty Air Force lifer from Tennessee with a deep tan and a corn-cob pipe, who ran the Keesler AFB assignment desk, had told me when delivering the news of my next posting. "Tokyo is the best city in the world. You'll be over there with all those geisha girls, riding around in rickshaws. Ten million people. More neon signs than you can imagine. A sake house on every corner. Makes me wish I was young again just thinking about it."

Although, as I would discover, hardly anybody used a rickshaw anymore and geisha girls were the expensive preserve of extremely wealthy men, he was certainly right about the rest.

Indeed, there were so many places to drink in Tokyo that even if you could somehow patronize them all, by the time you fin-ished, a whole new crop of establishments would have made their appearance. The spectrum of entertainments was infinite. Narrow buildings in the entertainment areas were crammed full of *mizu shobai* ("water trade" as the nightlife business was called) estab-lishments. On the first floor might be a coffee shop, the second a bar, the third a dance hall, the fourth a supper club, the fifth a restaurant, the sixth a hostess nightclub, and so on. They would be identified by a panel of illuminated signs hanging from the side of the building in one of the four Japanese writing systems: *hiragana, katakana, kanji,* and *romaji* (the roman alphabet). To get to one of them you went up a dingy elevator, inside of which a second panel listed the businesses inside and the floors on which they were located. The sheer denseness of information was daunting—too much, some said, for the Western eye to process; it took a certain kind of reckless fortitude to step onto the elevator and wade your way in. But it was also exhilarating, and I was hooked before I had a chance to fully process how I got there in the first place.

There's an old Japanese saying that you can't get drunk on sake you don't drink. But in Tokyo, not drinking hardly seemed to be an option. Issa, the great 18th-century haiku poet, when he sat by the banks of the Sumida River with sake in hand, invited even the butterflies to join him: 酒好きの蝶なら来よ角田川 ("If you're a butterfly that likes to drink, come down here to the Sumida River").

A Little History

It was not a bad thing to be an American in Tokyo back then, considering what Japanese had just endured at our hands. American B-29s had destroyed most of Japan's major cities in horrific fire-bombing campaigns, and then we dropped devastating atomic bombs on Hiroshima and Nagasaki in the only wartime use of nuclear weapons in history. Hundreds of thousands of civilians were killed. American forces occupied the country for nearly seven years, during which time they disbanded the Japanese military, instantly creating hundreds of thousands of unemployed, tried and executed war criminals, and broke up the *zaibatsu*—the old family-owned financial/industrial combines that had run the country. In the process they also helped to create massive black markets and a pervasive streetwalker culture. To cap it all off, tens of thousands of US soldiers remained on Japanese soil, a result of the United States–Japan Security Treaty signed in 1951 in San Francisco, a consummation intensely unwelcome in many quarters of the populace.

To be sure, the Occupation had its benevolent side: bulk food donations to prevent mass starvation and a new democratic constitution that eliminated the cruel and inequitable feudal family

system of Japan, gave equal rights to women, fostered unioniza-
tion, promoted land reform and, at the urging of a group of Japanese lawmakers, renounced war. Indeed, such provisions were
in stark contrast to the brutality with which Japan had treated
its neighboring countries, epitomized by the Nanjing Massacre
where Japanese troops engaged in rape, arson, and the mass murder of an estimated 300,000 men, women, and children in the
winter of 1937.

In practice, however, the Occupation blueprint proved con-
tradictory, with GHQ (General Headquarters) officials preaching
freedom of speech and democracy while simultaneously censoring
the Japanese press, limiting fraternization between Japanese and
Americans, and prohibiting Japanese filmmakers from showing
any evidence of the occupiers in their films. Then there was that
confusing change in basic policy midway through, which came to
be known as the Reverse Course, whereby the GHQ, alarmed by
the rise of Mao in China and the division of the Korean Peninsula
into hostile states, dropped its original goal of turning the country into the peace-loving Switzerland of Asia and instead opted
to make Japan a "Bulwark against Communism." That meant
rebuilding its defense systems, suppressing left-wing union activity, and putting the *zaibatsu* back together again in the form of
so-called *keiretsu* groups, a 180-degree change in direction.

Everything considered, the Occupation had been a relatively
peaceful one. The Supreme Commander of the Allied Forces,
Douglas MacArthur, had been widely respected among the Japanese. Given that several hundred thousand young American soldiers had been placed in a country where there had never been
more than a handful of Westerners at any one time (people who by
and large were traders, teachers, or missionaries), it was remarkable that things went as smoothly as they did. Tens of thousands
of American GIs married Japanese women, despite draconian
GHQ rules prohibiting fraternization. (Many, many more availed
themselves of the services of the *pan-pan* girls—young street

prostitutes—who, in Tokyo, lined the sidewalks all the way from Yurakucho to Shinbashi Station.)

The Korean War brought manufacturing out of a long depression and Japan's economy began to recover. However, thanks to a number of unpleasant incidents involving American soldiers back from duty in the Republic of Korea on Japanese R&R (Rest and Recreation—or, as some GIs put it, Rape and Revel), the American image took a hit. There were frequent reports of GIs stiffing taxi drivers, trashing bars to blow off steam, and even throwing people into Tokyo's canals, just for laughs. The most famous crime was that of Specialist Third Class William S. Girard who, while on guard duty at the firing range of a military base in Gunma Prefecture, inadvertently killed a Japanese farmer's wife who was scavenging for empty shells. The incident developed into an international scandal and Girard became the first American GI to be tried in Japanese court (which gave him a suspended sentence and allowed him to go home with his Taiwan-born wife).

Anger toward the Americans reached a postwar peak at the start of the following decade, when the pro-US government of Japan, under the aegis of the conservative Liberal Democratic Party, rammed through an extension of the Security Treaty, now putting a reduced but still significant number of 75,000 American soldiers in the country on a permanent basis (more than the United States had stationed anywhere else in the world, including Germany), causing waves of widespread, and sometimes violent, protests. "Yankee Go Home" was an English phrase that nearly all Japanese knew and understood.

By the time I arrived, however, anti-Americanism had largely dissipated. Most Tokyoites seemed quite taken with new US President John F. Kennedy and the youthful energy, optimism, and good intentions he projected on behalf of the United States. JFK's promise to put a man on the moon by the end of the decade had captured the imagination of the Japanese as much as it had the Americans. The Japanese media seemed especially preoccupied

Robert F. Kennedy at Waseda University. 1964.

with Jackie Kennedy, whose elegance and fashion sense had become a model for Japanese women to follow. As an American in Japan, you began to feel swathed in a borrowed Kennedy glow.

People also liked the fact that JFK had appointed as US ambassador to Japan Harvard scholar Edwin Reischauer, who spoke the language fluently and was married to a Japanese. The man Reischauer had replaced, the imperious Douglas MacArthur II, nephew of the famed general, had thought, like many in the foreign service, that French was the only second language a US diplomat needed to know. He regarded the idea of speaking Japanese as undignified and disparaged those Americans who did. "Going native" was poor form, as everyone in the elite American community knew.

At Reischauer's urging, JFK won further points by sending his brother, Attorney General Robert Kennedy, to Tokyo as part of a goodwill tour of Asia in 1962 in order to lay the groundwork for a planned visit by the president himself. Bobby proved to be a tremendous hit. He eschewed the usual diplomatic receptions and state dinners, choosing instead to meet with ordinary citizens as much as possible. He played soccer with Japanese children, met with women's groups and opposition Socialist Party and union leaders, sat through sumo and judo demonstrations, and sampled sake at a Ginza bar, trading toasts with Japanese customers at the counter and playing the bongos.

On a blurry black-and-white TV set in the Shinjuku Fugetsu-do coffee shop, in the company of the largely beatnik clientele, I watched live as RFK engaged angry, jeering Marxist students in spirited debate at Tokyo's prestigious Waseda University. He responded politely to charges of American imperialism in Japan and complicity with the conservative ruling Liberal Democratic Party in order to further US interests. The tousled-haired Kennedy told the students that Americans believed in having a divergence of views and the right to express them because that was the only way a country could determine its proper course.

He called the most vocal of the students down onto the stage and greeted him warmly, saying, "You are experiencing an example of democracy at its best, because never in communist-controlled lands could citizens object to government policy so vociferously." At the end, Kennedy sang the Waseda school song, which Reischauer had urged him to learn, with the assembled students.

One of the Fugetsudo denizens, a man in his thirties with a Van Dyke beard and scraggly hair, and wearing a black beret and turtleneck sweater, penned a seventeen-syllable haiku in English when it was over and handed it to me, which I submit here for posterity:

Kennedy is cool
I dig his windblown hair
Banzai the USA

Roppongi

Fuchu Air Base was a tiny island of small-town Americana in the Tokyo suburbs. It had all the accoutrements of home: manicured lawns, soda fountains, supermarkets, cheeseburgers, movie theaters playing the latest first-run hits from Hollywood. For the Japanese who had the opportunity to enter the base, it was like traveling abroad without a passport. There were BX concessions selling American goods unavailable anywhere else in Greater Tokyo at bargain basement prices, military clubs, restaurants, a bowling alley, and a basketball arena. Enlisted men lived in modern, centrally heated dormitory-style buildings. Married personnel lived at the nearby Green Park complex, a military installation with Western-style family housing, grade schools, and teen clubs. Everyone had a maid—quite often war widows who had nowhere else to go and who worked for what Americans regarded as a pittance—and that included me. Mine was an older Japanese woman with wiry hair, silver teeth, and a permanent smile who looked after my room on the third floor of a Fifth Air Force 6000th Support Squadron barracks. The room overlooked a field where old women clad in *monpei* toiled and, in the distance, young Japanese boys chased fly balls on a makeshift baseball diamond. Beyond that, Mt. Fuji rose majestically in the distance. I called my maid "Mama-san." She called me "Boy-chan."

The bars off base in a quarter known as the "Han" catered almost exclusively to American men, hard drinking, highly sexed American men, a state of affairs that may not have pleased all of the local citizenry but was certainly a boon to the local economy. The bar girls spoke foul English ("You cherry boy?" "You like play with Japanese girl?") and played 45 RPM records of the Billboard Top 40: "Soldier Boy," "Travelin' Man," and "Big Girls Don't Cry" were big favorites. Airmen bought jackets from the BX with an image of Mt. Fuji and the word "Japan" painted on the back, but few ever strayed far from the base. There were people, I would discover, who had spent three years at Fuchu and had never eaten sashimi or learned to speak any Japanese other than *sayonara*, from the Marlon Brando film, and the "Phrase of the Day" from Walt and Hiroko on FEN.

* * *

The most dynamic city on the face of the earth. Ginza, 1965.

For me, the lure of Tokyo was irresistible. If Fuchu was like Eureka, the foggy backwater in California I couldn't wait to escape, Tokyo was Manhattan. It was a half-hour train ride from Higashi-Fuchu Station on the Keio Line to the main Shinjuku Station terminal on the western rim of Tokyo, a ride that took you past rice paddies and bedroom-towns. I made the trip as often as I could, clad in a cheap three-piece navy-blue suit, custom made in two days by an off-base Korean tailor, and armed with a Japanese phrase book and a map of the metropolitan area. I also carried some extra ¥50 coins (then the equivalent of 14 cents) to give to the white-robed, disabled war veterans, some with hooks for hands, who routinely patrolled the Keio Line cars in small groups begging for money, bearing placards describing their horrible fates and singing sorrowful songs to the accompaniment of an accordion player. This was the pitiful result, I learned, of the Japanese government's neglect of its own disbanded wartime armies. Most of the Japanese passengers looked away.

There were 15,000 coffee shops in Tokyo, more than in any other city in the world, it was said, and that was long before Starbucks made its debut there. These *kissaten* featured music from classical to jazz, and you could sit all day and read and relax and no one ever complained.

I was partial to Ladies Town in the Ginza, where coffee was served by some of the most beautiful women I have ever seen, dressed in long satin bridal gowns and lacy veils, and C'est Si Bon, a little spot playing Piaf and Segovia, run by an aging ex-ballerina who told me that I looked like Warren Beatty.

* * *

There were also lots of interesting nightspots that openly welcomed foreigners. One of them was the Showboat in Shinbashi, which appeared in the movie *The Bridges at Toko-Ri* and was almost as large as a real live Mississippi riverboat. There, the customer was piped aboard a huge replica of a Mississippi riverboat and entertained by a band moving up and down an elevator shaft, as well as by a revolving squadron of hostesses. A girl driving a miniature train collected empty glasses. Also in Shinbashi was the Rendezvous, a military-themed bar where the customer was escorted by a "soldier" past a sand-bagged bandstand to his table and introduced to his hostess, who was clad in a white nurse's uniform and a pale-blue cap. Up the street in Akasaka was the Golden Getsusekai where the hostesses dressed like Playboy bunnies. In Ueno, there was the Transistor Cutie Club, where the girls were all under 5 feet tall.

A favorite place in Tokyo in those early months was the Club 88, introduced to me by colleagues in intelligence. It was a trendy night spot in Roppongi, one of the more interesting parts of the city, home to foreign embassies, internationally oriented nightclubs, and restaurants and offbeat bars. The US Military Installation Hardy Barracks, home of the *Stars and Stripes* newspaper, was also located there. The "88" stood for the eighty-eight keys on the piano, which was played by a talented African American named Larry Allen, an ex-GI from Indiana who had recorded songs for American troops during the Occupation and entertained at international and military clubs all over Asia. He was a holdover from the Golden Gate, which had occupied the same real estate in Roppongi until the police closed it down for "moral violations."

Allen, dubbed the "Clown Prince of the Keys," wrote and sang his own music. He favored deep-throated parodies of popular songs. One of them, "Shinbashi Woman," sung to the tune of "St. Louis Blues," will give you the idea:

Shinbashi woman, with all her bumps and curves
Shinbashi woman . . . those bumps and curves ain't hers . . .

The 88 had twenty tables and a long bar, in addition to a separate sushi bar. It was always packed with an eclectic crowd of people. There were diplomats, foreign correspondents, assorted businessmen, and visiting US congressmen. Officials from the police agencies came in and sat alongside yakuza bosses who sat next to CIA agents. At times, one might see Catholic priests and missionaries of other faiths sitting next to exotic dancers and hostesses from neighboring clubs who came in with their boyfriends after eleven, when the hostess bars closed.

The Club 88 was one of the few nightclubs open after 11:30 p.m. It was expensive, although not as expensive as the high-class hostess clubs like the Copacabana or the New Latin Quarter. But even on a military salary of $100 a month (the equivalent of ¥36,000) you could manage the occasional visit if you sat at the bar and nursed your drink until well after the ice was gone, a skill I

Ladies of a Tokyo evening.

readily mastered. The club had a rule that women could not enter unaccompanied; the object, supposedly, was to prevent hookers from taking over the place. Nevertheless, every night around midnight a stream of well-painted and striking young ladies would find someone to escort them in, sit at the bar, and negotiate top-of-the-line fees for their proscribed services.

The Club 88 was the brainchild of Alonzo Shattuck, one of the more accomplished and colorful characters among the stream of foreign carpetbaggers and soldiers of fortune that poured into the city after the war. Shattuck, as I would later learn, was a former Occupation-era intelligence agent who had worked for the infamous Tokyo-based black ops group, the Canon Agency, fighting North Korean agents who were smuggling heroin and crystal meth into Japan with the help of the DPRK in an effort to addict American GIs to drugs and render them unable to fight in future wars.

After the Occupation, Shattuck and a Japanese American partner, Saburo Odachi, a black belt in judo, drifted into the nightclub business, first with an American gambler named Ted Lewin, running the black-tie Latin Quarter, and when that burned down they opened up the Club 88. In 1960 Shattuck was cordially invited to leave the country by the Japanese government for certain underworld and intelligence-related activities, about which I would learn more later, but he managed to return from time to time on tourist visas and keep a hand in his business.

Lots of well-known people dropped by the 88. Nat King Cole, in Japan on tour, came in one night to have a drink and sat down at the piano to sing a few songs. I met the Hollywood actor Rick Jason there early one evening sitting at the bar. Jason was a star of the *Combat* television series, which was a huge hit in Japan, with Rick's voice dubbed in Japanese. At the time, he was more popular in Japan than in his own country, and he would appear in a number of Japanese movies over the years. He was affable and charming—"How ya doin' kid?" he said—and created the illusion that he was actually more interested in what a twenty-year-old GI was doing in Tokyo than in talking about himself.

Another time, I was astonished to see Shirley MacLaine come in. The red-haired movie actress was in town to visit her husband, Steve Parker, a dapper, mustachioed screen-and-stage producer based in Tokyo. The two had a bizarre trans-Pacific arrangement, she with a house in Malibu and he with one in Shibuya, where their young daughter stayed. Between films, she would come and visit her family.

Sometimes there was trouble. A well-known story had it that one night a member of the Tosei-kai, a powerful underworld gang, had wandered into the 88 drunk wearing a .38 in a shoulder holster. This was a violation of Japan's extremely strict Sword and Firearms Law. Shattuck asked him to leave. The yakuza refused. In a flash, Shattuck pinned the man's right arm, grabbed the gun from the holster, and dragged him out of the club. A week later, the head of the gang, Hisayuki Machii, also known as the Crime Boss of Tokyo, came around to apologize for the fuss, bringing with him the offending subaltern, who was now missing the tip of the pinky on his left hand, having been ordered to slice it off in what was the standard act of contrition in the Japanese underworld for embarrassing the gang. (I confirmed this story with Shattuck years later when I met him for the first time.)

Happy Valley

By the end of my first year, I had developed a special liking for Shibuya, a major hub on the Yamate railway line that circled the city. It was a town of young people closer to my age group— lots of students from nearby Aoyama Gakuin University and working-class types. It had a more common, quotidian feel than the Ginza playground of the rich and was also not top heavy with *gaijin* the way Roppongi was. It felt more like the "real Japan." Shibuya was an interesting mix of modern department stores, cheap cabarets and bars, street vendors, and dilapidated sake houses with corrugated tin roofs. Another feature of the town was "Love Letter Alley," a collection of makeshift stalls where Japanese young women could go to have language experts write letters in English to their boyfriends overseas—former GIs who were not likely coming back.

Shibuya was also home to the famous statue of Hachiko, the legendary canine who epitomized the loyalty so central to the traditional Japanese value system. After his owner died of a sudden stroke and failed to appear at the station where Hachiko had always waited for him, the dog stayed there, cared for by sympathetic commuters, until his own death ten years later. Today, his statue is perhaps the most popular meeting place in all of Tokyo. I was partial to the Happy Valley Dance Hall, a popular 1940s-style establishment that was packed to the rafters every Saturday night. Regulars included beauticians, secretaries, waitresses, and college coeds—nice ordinary girls whose presence helped me overcome my native shyness. A surprising number were snaggle-toothed, which was a particularly endearing quality. This feature, as a popular (if unconfirmed) belief had it, was the result of an Occupation-era policy to put more calcium in the Japanese diet, causing teeth to outgrow the mouth.

The Happy Valley consisted of a large dance floor under-neath a glittering rotating mirror ball suspended from the ceiling that cast multicolored reflections around the interior and a stage where rotating orchestras played half-hour sets. A swing band like Nobuko Hara's Sharps and Flats would play Glenn Miller and Tommy Dorsey hits from the 1940s—"In The Mood," "Little Brown Jug," and others; they would be followed by a rock and roll band offering up contemporary fare such as "Rock Around the Clock" and "The Twist"; these in turn would give way to Japanese pop singers like husky teenager Mieko Hirota, Japan's "Queen of Pops," belting out their own latest hits. Connie Francis even put in a brief appearance there one evening to sing "Pretty Little Baby" in Japanese, a version that topped the Tokyo pop charts.

When the music sufficed to put you and your partner "In the Mood," a possible destination was a "love hotel," a unique Japanese invention that came about because of the lack of privacy in most Japanese houses and apartments, with their cramped spaces and paper-thin walls. Shibuya was filled with them. You could get a three-hour "rest" or a room for the night. You "checked in" by handing over the entrance fee through a narrow slot in a wall in the lobby and were then given a key with the room number on it. When you left, you returned the key through the slot. No face-to-face contact. No uncomfortable stares. No embarrassment.

Japanese society supposedly frowned on premarital sex but that didn't seem to bother the girls I met at the Happy Valley. Not that they were sexually experienced, but then again neither was I, my lone such episode back in Eureka, an encounter with a girl named Sandy in the back of my 1955 Ford that lasted approximately ten seconds. My first visit across the street to Love Hotel

Hill was with a slender nineteen-year-old junior college student named Keiko with a cute face, silky smooth skin, and braces. She spoke a smattering of English and kept saying, "Please take care." I had no idea what she meant. When I woke up in the morning, she was gone, but she had folded my clothes in a neat pile on the tatami and left a note on top with her phone number and the words "Thank you berry much." I called her once but the older man, presumably her father, who answered the phone could not understand what I was saying using the few words of Japanese I knew, and I certainly could not understand him. So that was the end of that.

I went to the Happy Valley so often I became friends with the bartender, a tall, gaunt, morose young man with slicked-back hair and a scraggly mustache, named Jun. Jun spoke a little English and liked the chance to practice it with me when I went in. I would bring him gifts from the base. Johnny Walker Black was a big favorite. So were Napoleon Brandy, American cigarettes, Levis, and leather belts. Such items were subject to huge tariffs on the Japanese market but were dirt cheap at the Base Exchange. Jun would drink the Johnny Walker himself and then pour domestic Japanese whisky—Suntory Single Malt or Suntory Whisky Royal— in the empty bottles, and the Happy Valley would charge a fortune for it, an arrangement that ingratiated him no end with his bosses. It was a testament to the early quality of Suntory Whisky, made with pure Kyoto river-valley water, that most customers couldn't notice the difference. I found myself enjoying it as well, particularly as my consumption of it there rarely made its way onto the bar bill.

Jun did me the honor of inviting me to his home on New Year's Day 1963—his home consisting of a tiny two-room apartment where he lived with his wife and baby son. One room was a six-mat size (with a total space of 108 square feet), while the second room afforded the space of a large closet and was completely filled by a huge chest of drawers and several rolled up futons.

Communicating with a mixture of Japanese and English words and hand signals, we sat there at a low table on frayed *zabuton* (cushions), drank Japanese sake, and ate *ozoni* (soup with rice cakes) and other traditional Japanese New Year's foods. Later, after the alcohol had taken hold, he confessed that he was not a pure-blooded Japanese but rather the son of a Korean father and a Japanese mother. It was something he said he kept a secret from all but a few people, because there was so much discrimination against people of Korean origin in Japan.

Japan had colonized the Korean Peninsula in the early part of the 20th century, forcing its inhabitants to learn and speak Japanese. Two million Koreans wound up in Japan, many as forced laborers. Jun's father had been one of them, working in the coal mines in Kyushu. He wound up marrying the teenage daughter of an impoverished farming family but returned to the Korean Peninsula shortly after the end of the war and was never heard from again. Jun suspected he was in the north, where his father's parents were from. There were more than a half a million Koreans— *zainichi chosenjin* as they were called—still left in Japan. They had decided not to return home because living conditions on the Korean Peninsula were even more miserable than they were for them in postwar Japan. But since they were viewed in Japan as a lesser class of people, it was hard for Koreans to get into good schools or get jobs at good companies, or marry into respectable Japanese families. As a result, many Koreans took Japanese names and hid their identities.

Jun said that he and his wife, who was Japanese—a beauty parlor attendant whom he had met at the Happy Valley—did not want their son to suffer that kind of discrimination, so they kept his origins a secret. He said he would hide the truth from the boy for the rest of his life.

"I can tell you," Jun said, "because you're not from this country. But I can't tell others. Here my son will have a better chance in life."

Hachiko the Dog. The most popular meeting spot in Tokyo, in front of Shibuya Station.

The Happy Valley Dance Hall was a purlieu for the Shibuya-based Ando gang, the five-hundred-member underworld organization that controlled the area. Just around the corner, the Ando-gumi ran a low rent *cho-han* game, a traditional form of gambling in which patrons bet on whether a pair of dice thrown from a cup would produce either an even or an odd number. One night after the dance hall had closed Jun invited me to take part. We went down a side-street stairwell into a large tatami room behind a big steel door.

On the other side of the door we were met by a beefy man in a red Aloha shirt.

"*Nani kore?*" (What's this?), he said, a look of repugnance on his face as though Jun had just dragged in a dead cat. He had a deep half-moon scar on his badly shaven chin.

"He's okay," said Jun. "He's a friend."

The man looked at Jun as though he were transparent. Another Ando factotum pushed himself upright from the wall against which he had been slouching. He carried a carbine rifle.

Jun did not alter his expression. "He's a Happy Valley regular," he said. "He sits at the same bar as the Ando-gumi." There was magic in the name: The grim set of the gatekeeper's features relented a few micrometers and he gestured us inside.

Arrayed on either side of a long rectangular mat were a collection of *chinpira,* or low-level hoods in punch perms, *salarymen* (office workers), and local merchants. They sat with intent expressions and made bets on dice rolled by a dealer (*tsubofuri*) wearing only a *haramaki* sash around his abdomen, white pajama bottoms, and an elaborate dragon tattoo on his back. The shirtless attire, Jun explained, was to forestall charges of cheating. The centuries-old betting procedure never varied. The dealer held out the dice for all to see and, with an elaborate gesture, calling out "*Hairimasu!*" (Dice in!), placed them in a bamboo cup, which he then turned over on top of the mat, concealing the numbers. "*Hatta! Hatta!*" (Lay down your bets!) was the next cry, and the players then wagered as to whether the total of the two dice would come out even (*cho*) or odd (*han*). The thug with the rifle had gone back into his slouch against the wall. Another member of the gang lit cigarettes for the players and poured sake, much as a Ginza nightclub hostess might. I made a few small bets just to be polite, a ¥500 note ($1.38) here and there, and was surprised to discover that at the end of my desultory play I was ahead several thousand yen. But it turned out that even at this low-level game I was strictly small potatoes; not a few of the players were betting stacks of ¥10,000 notes.

By the time Jun and I wandered back into the street, the sky was just beginning to whiten in the east. Despite my coup, I had pretty well decided not to add *cho-han* to my already burgeoning list of vices.

* * *

Jun quit his job around that time and opened up a tiny bar on the second floor of a ten-story ferro-concrete building in Udagawa-cho. There was a counter with about ten stools and two tables in the back. It was like a thousand other bars in the city in that there was barely room to turn around and its survival depended on the patronage of fellow *mizu shobai* workers and other friends. He invited me to his opening party, which was attended by a handful of Happy Valley employees and some other small-timers in the Shibuya entertainment world. Jun, looking less morose than I had ever seen him, stood behind the bar mixing drinks and making conversation.

The bar struggled in the ensuing months. Jun complained he barely cleared enough to pay his rent on the place. I took him booze and cigarettes when I could. As per usual, he poured the less expensive Suntory Whisky into the empty Johnny Walker bottles and charged double. One day, months later, I dropped by and found the bar closed. I went over to his apartment and that too was empty. Jun had simply gone, no one knew where. The word was that he had borrowed money from Tosei-kai yakuza loan sharks who charged 20 percent a month and couldn't pay it back. I never saw him again.

* * *

But Shibuya retained a special place in my heart. One hot, muggy August night I had missed the last train back to the base and had no money for a taxi. I sat down in front of the station, next to the statue of the dog, actually, and prepared to stay there until 5 a.m. when the trains started running again. An elderly woman who was closing up her station-front kiosk asked me what was the matter. I told her, she listened sympathetically, and after she had finished closing up, she said simply, "Come with me." She took me through the back streets to a small first-floor apartment in a two-story wooden building, where a ten-year-old girl, apparently her granddaughter, was sleeping. She rolled out a futon on the tatami in an adjoining three-mat room and bid me good night. In the morning she made toast and coffee and sent me on my way back to Fuchu. It was a simple act of kindness that went beyond anything I had experienced before. And I never forgot it. I always remembered to stop by her kiosk when visiting Shibuya and bring presents from the base for her and the little girl. She was a nice lady.

JFK was assassinated in the morning of November 23, 1963. The next time I went to the Happy Valley I received a funeral envelope with a ¥10,000 bill inside from the Happy Valley management, which both touched and confused me. I only learned later that this was the common custom to express condolences. One of the girls at the Happy Valley went one step further. She invited me out for dinner and what would turn out to be other consolations.

Dr. Sato: The Smell of Freshly Dried Asphalt

As the countdown to the Games progressed, doubts about Tokyo making the deadline intensified. The two shiny new subway lines had opened up—Toei Asakusa (1960) and Hibiya (1961), joining the older Ginza (1927) and Marunouchi (1954) lines—but as late as January 1963 none of the target dates for road construction had been met, and Shojiro Kawashima, cabinet minister in charge of the Olympics, was forced to concede to reporters that Olympic preparations were "regrettably" behind in all aspects.

Construction on the new elevated coastal highway leading from Haneda Airport some 13 miles into the capital was late getting started because fishermen owned long stretches of the land along the intended route and were demanding multiples of the price the government had anticipated paying. In another case, speculators had bought up large plots of land the government was eyeing for development into a second inland expressway into the city and demanded exorbitant prices, which again went beyond the budget the authorities had prepared. There were eminent domain laws on the books, but the government was obligated by legal precedent to pay the full asking price, and in the above-mentioned cases the asking price was simply too high.

An even bigger problem looming ominously over the city was a dire shortage of water in the capital caused by an abnormal lack of rainfall in the wet season preceding the Games. Tokyo's reservoirs had been emptying for three months, and as the summer began the municipal government instituted water rationing. Bathhouse hours were restricted and swimming pools closed, and on narrow side streets police water trucks, usually employed to quell leftist riots, filled housewives' buckets with water hauled in from nearby rivers. *Soba* shops cut down on their cooking, while Ginza night-clubs urged thirsty patrons to "drink your whisky without water and help save Tokyo."

Drilling crews dug emergency artesian wells, while other work crews excavated canals to bring in water from nearby rivers. Japan Self-Defense Force planes dumped dry ice on overhead clouds, while on the shores of the Ogochi reservoir outside the city a Shinto priest in the mask of a scarlet lion writhed through a ceremonial rain dance. Townsmen were warned not to expect miracles. As the priest explained, "It will take two days for the message to get through to the dragon god."

As the deadline for the Games approached, there was an enormous, frantic rush to finish everything on time. Construction continued around the clock, seven days a week. Bulldozers rearranged the landscape, and dump trucks, loaded up with sand for land-reclamation projects in Tokyo's fetid harbor, rumbled back and forth in unbroken streams. In January 1964 the city government had mobilized 1.6 million residents to help clean Tokyo's streets. That's not a misprint.

At night, after the *salarymen* had gone home and the traffic thinned out, the city stepped up construction. Blinding work lights and diesel compressors switched on, traffic on Tokyo's main thoroughfares was rerouted, and new sets of air hammers and pile drivers were put to work opening up those streets. This went

Some historians called the build-up in Tokyo before the Games "The greatest urban transformation in history."

on until dawn, when the avenues were covered with temporary wooden planks and traffic resumed. Most of Tokyo's citizens stoically put up with the annoyances, using blackout curtains and earplugs to block out the light and noise. I did the same when I stayed overnight in the city. But I clearly remember a newspaper item in one of the English-language dailies about a college student who, unable to study because of the constant pounding near his rooming house, became so agitated that he marched down to the construction site, put his head underneath the offending pile driver, and ended his misery.

Three months before the Games were scheduled to begin, glimpses of the New Tokyo began to appear, including long-finished stretches of the raised expressways. You could even take a ride on a section of the new overhead highway from Shinbashi to Shibaura for ¥50 (about 15 cents), and many people did just that to see what it was like, including me, with a new acquaintance, a Dr. Sato, who took me for a spin on the 2-mile run in his brand new Nissan-Z Fair Lady roadster (his "weekend car" as he put it), oohing and aahing at the smoothness of the road, while listening to "I Wanna Hold Your Hand," by a new group called the Beatles, on the radio.

"I like the smell of freshly dried asphalt," he exclaimed, "It means progress."

Dr. Sato was my student, actually. He was a plastic surgeon who wanted a private English tutor. He had placed an advertisement on the bulletin board at Sophia University, a Jesuit institution in Yotsuya, central Tokyo, where I had started taking evening courses, and I had answered it. We met for the first time at his clinic in the West Ginza one evening after he was finishing up for the day, and after a brief interview I became his teacher. Just like that. You could do things like that in those days as there were a limited number of native speakers of English in the city—only a few thousand American civilians including businessmen, diplomats, judo students, intelligence agents, Mormons preaching the word of Joseph Smith, and ex-Occupationaires who had stayed on to seek their fortune—and countless Japanese wanted people they could practice speaking with, especially with the Olympics coming up.

Like other Americans in the capital, I found I could be sitting quietly in a *kissaten* or bar and someone would approach me asking, "May I speak English with you?" I even had people come up to me on train station platforms and ask me to correct their English pronunciation. I could stand on a street corner looking lost and in no time someone would walk up to me and ask, "May I help you?"

Most Japanese had some exposure to English, which was taught from middle school on. Missing from the curriculum built around grammar and translation, however, were conversation skills. Private English conversation schools proliferated to fill the gap. There were in fact more schools than there were teachers to staff them, with the result that ten-year-old American students at private schools in the city were also taking part-time work as English "teachers" to Japanese *adults*.

Thus, it was that, needing more funds to finance the increasing amount of time I was spending in the city, I found myself joining the ranks of those American ten year olds.

Dr. Sato was in his late forties, a slight, impeccably tailored man with slicked-back hair, who smoked Rothmann's cigarettes and carried a gold Dunhill lighter. Most of the patients in his plastic surgery practice were women, he explained, in rather good English, nightclub hostesses in the area who wanted their eyes un-slanted, their noses un-flattened, and their breasts and hips augmented in the belief that this would enhance their professional appeal.

"I want you to know that I like Americans," he said. "I remember how kind they were during the aftermath of the war. They handed out free food and candy for Japanese kids. They were a lot nicer than the Japanese militarists ever were. Imperial soldiers were arrogant. They'd hit you just for looking at them the wrong way. I'm not saying I'm glad Japan lost the war, but the problem with Japanese is that they don't know how to be equal. They either kiss your feet or sit on your face. They can learn from American democracy. I want to improve my English-speaking ability because I want to meet as many Americans as I can during the upcoming Olympics."

He said that he wanted to meet for a "conversation lesson" once a week, on a Friday or Saturday evening, for an hour at his clinic, followed by dinner somewhere, and then proceed to a club. His treat. On top of that he would pay me ¥10,000 a pop. All I would have to do was talk to him and correct his English.

I, of course, couldn't say yes fast enough. It would mean earning ¥10,000 x 4 = $111 per month (at what was then a ¥360-per-dollar exchange rate), which was more than my monthly pay and double what I made at a Ginza English conversation school where I had started teaching part time. I did stop to consider, if only briefly, why a rich doctor would want me, a twenty-one-year-old GI with somewhat limited experience of the world, as a tutor. But

I chalked it up to a simple matter of supply and demand. I certainly wasn't going to argue.

One time he invited me to an establishment down the street from his clinic to show me the results of his labors. Le Rat Mort (The Dead Rat) was an intimate Ginza nightclub that, the doctor explained, was the most exclusive and most expensive of its kind in the entire city. (Some cynics speculated that the strange name was the result of a misrendering of L'Amour—"L" being indistinguishable from "R" in Japanese. Otherwise, why a dead rat should come to symbolize dedication to elegance and pulchritude remains an unexplained mystery.)

Indeed, the place looked like something conjured up in a 1950s MGM movie musical, featuring a marble floor inlaid with mother of pearl, deep leather sofas, Picasso paintings on the walls, and gold lighters and ashtrays. Le Rat Mort, said the doctor, had the most impeccably mannered and attentive women in the city. Its owner had imposed certain ironclad rules for his charges to obey to ensure that this was so, and they went something like this: Always report for work perfectly groomed and wearing a brand-new dress. Always smile. Always flatter. Always be interested in what a client has to say. Never, ever forget a returning customer's name, his favorite drink, or his favorite song (which the piano player was expected to tinkle out immediately upon the client's entry into and exit from the club). Never let a customer's cigarette go unlit or his glass remain unfilled. Never forget the old Ginza adage: "The ideal woman is dumb on the outside but clever underneath."

In return for the perfection he demanded, Le Rat Mort's owner paid his hostesses the highest salaries of any such establishment in Japan.

The girls, with their round eyes, reshaped noses, and hourglass figures were indeed beautiful (although in my own studiously informed opinion, attractive Asian women did not need such enhancements), and they were a hit with Le Rat Mort's clientele, which, according to Dr. Sato, included politicians, movie actors, baseball and sumo stars, and other important, wealthy people who, in the pre-Olympic era, thought nothing of dropping the equivalent of $10,000 for a quiet evening of booze and companionship.

I was blown away by it all—once again a crazy trip through the Looking Glass, when all I had done was answer an ad for an English tutor. It was certainly a different level than I was used to operating on. Sumo stars, rich plastic surgeons, gorgeous hostesses. What the heck was going on?

The doctor, married with a wife and three young children, explained to me that the girls were not the sort you took home on short acquaintance. To the regulars at Le Rat Mort, the club was not a vulgar "dump" like, say, the Mikado with its twelve-hundred hostesses, where it was so easy to sleep with the girls on the first night. There, all you needed was money, although, admittedly, a lot of it was required. Le Rat Mort customers wanted the psychological chase and conquest that their club offered, one in which numerous visits were required to develop a relationship, which was not merely paid-for lust but nearly indistinguishable from true love. Sato himself had a mistress there, he said, adding that he'd even introduced the mistress to his wife, who had given her approval of the relationship because it freed her from the burdensome duties of the marriage bed and allowed her to concentrate on raising the kids. "Welcome to Japan," the doctor said with a hearty laugh.

After a number of visits I was asked if I would be willing to teach English to the hostesses there. The owner was expecting a big influx of foreigners to Tokyo because of the upcoming Olympics and he wanted his girls to be able to talk to them. Finding no earthly reason to decline, I began giving lessons every Saturday at noon at the Ginza location and it was a revelation. I barely recognized the women when they filed in wearing blue jeans, sandals, and scarves, with no makeup or perfume, chewing gum, and frequently hungover, thoroughly shattering the nighttime image they had worked so hard to cultivate.

I also discovered that most of them hated their high-paying jobs, which they deemed terminally boring, with its mindless chatter, and a pain in the neck to boot, as they had to go to the beauty parlor every day and were constantly required to buy new dresses, selling the old ones after they had worn them only once or twice. They were just making money to finance some business venture or other, they told me, like a fashion boutique or a coffee shop.

It had not yet dawned on me that with Dr. Sato I was in fact becoming the male equivalent of a Tokyo nightclub hostess, an accessory to enhance his elite status in Japan's New Order.

Yoyogi Park

The much-ballyhooed monorail from Haneda International Airport into Tokyo began operations on September 17, 1964; it would become the busiest and most profitable monorail line in the world. On October 1, ten days before the Games were scheduled to begin, the putative crown jewel of the Olympic effort, the Japanese bullet train, started operations between Tokyo and Osaka. The Shinkansen transported its passengers 320 miles in about four hours, less than half the time it had taken before, reaching peak speeds of 130 miles per hour to make it the fastest train in the world. The train followed the picturesque route of the old Tokaido Line, along the earthquake-prone Pacific coastline. The New Tokaido Line would become the busiest commuter corridor in the world, busier even than the one that ran between New York and Washington, DC. The trains' arrival and departure times were so reliable that people could set their watches by them, the average delay being half a minute.

During this period the wraps were taken off the last of the

The fastest train in the world.

shining new buildings constructed in the center of the city, among them the glamorous Hotel Okura (modeled after an ancient Kyoto temple), the seventeen-floor New Otani (the tallest building in the city), and the 1,600-room Shiba Prince Hotel. Way behind schedule for completion, the Otani builders and the ToTo Corporation (the world's largest toilet manufacturer) developed the unit bathroom: toilet, sink, and bathtub in one neat box installed by crane from the outside. Then one after another, the athletic fields, arenas, and halls to be used in the Olympics were announced ready. They included the space-age Olympic Park complex for volleyball and soccer; the bat-winged Budokan for the martial arts; the National Stadium for track and field; and Kenzo Tange's swooping, wave-shaped National Gymnasium complex for swimming and diving in Yoyogi Park. Melding modern engineering techniques with traditional Japanese forms, Tange's work would later win the Pritzker Architecture Prize and become an iconic Tokyo landmark.

Of special significance to the Japanese was the completion of the Olympic Village, also in Yoyogi Park. Located next to the important shrine Meiji Jingu, the area had been the site of a barracks and parade ground for the Japanese Imperial Army before the war. During the Occupation, the Americans had appropriated the land, renamed it Washington Heights, and made it home to the families of 2,350 US Air Force men. Now, retooled and renovated, the complex would put up the 6,624 athletes, coaches, and trainers during the Games.

Washington Heights had been perfectly situated in the heart of the city. It is remembered fondly (by Americans) as one of the best US military residential complexes ever built. Respective gates led you to the key hubs in Tokyo. One exit took you to Shibuya, another to Harajuku and the tree-covered ground of the Meiji Shrine, and still another to Yoyogi. It was a short, cheap taxi ride to Shinjuku or Roppongi. Washington Heights was also home to the Meiji Club, the best military club in the Far East, with a large bank of slot machines and top Stateside talent. I spent a lot of time there warming up on my way to the Happy Valley.

For many Japanese, however, the fact that Americans had occupied this particular territory had been humiliating enough. What made it even worse was the alarming manner in which some of the foreign barbarians living there had behaved, right next door to the sacred Meiji Shrine, no less.

In 1956, for example, there had been the widely reported case of five teenaged American boys accused of raping an eighteen-year-old Japanese girl. Instead of being forced to face justice in Japanese court, however, the five youths were merely sent back to the United States, no questions asked. Japanese domestic maids working on the base complained in one magazine piece that they were expected to cook, clean, launder, answer the telephone, and be a governess to the family's children, all for $24 a month, while the provocatively dressed ladies of the house were over at the officer's club getting tanked up and flirting with other women's husbands.

Then there was the case of the sexually liberated family in which every single member, including the maid, caught the same dose of gonorrhea. I personally knew the hapless father, who worked at Fuchu. He had slept with a bar girl off base and contracted the disease, which he gave to his wife, and then to their maid, who turned around and gave it to the sixteen-year-old son and his high school buddy who, in turn, gave it to the daughter. They were all sent packing to the United States.

The Americans returned the Yoyogi Park land in 1963, relocating near Fuchu, all expenses paid by the Japanese government. It was an act of American generosity considering the value of the real estate they had willingly vacated, a gesture toward the Olympics that was welcomed all across the political spectrum, as both left- and right-wing groups had long wished for the day when *all* the Americans, starting with those based in central Tokyo, would pack up and go home. It was yet another step on the road back to self-respect. Shortly thereafter the Americans closed down other military sites such as Jefferson and Pershing Heights. The Sanno military hotel in Akasaka and Hardy Barracks, with its heliport, were regarded as too important for the US Embassy to give up. Both are still under US control today, the Sanno having been moved since to another prime Tokyo location in Minami-Azabu.

But not quite everything was finished. Yet to be completed were six of the planned expressways, as well as the fleet of mobile public toilets the government had ordered built at the last minute over the summer and spring, after some alert bureaucrat discovered there were not enough public restrooms in the original plans. In an effort to put a stop to the common male practice of relieving the bladder on side streets in the city—"a habit grown too much," as Hamlet would say—that might offend the tender sensibilities of Olympic visitors, signs in the subways were put up that said, "Let's refrain from urinating in public."

* * *

A full week before the Opening Ceremony, Olympic athletes began arriving at Haneda Airport—the Russians via Aeroflot, the

Americans via Pan Am, the British via BOAC—with welcoming press conferences arranged right on the tarmac. Along with the athletes came the first waves of international tourists.

It was the first time in the history of Tokyo that this many *gaikokujin* from around the world had gathered there (in Japan, much less in one city), with the exception of the early Occupation when several hundred thousand mostly American soldiers were in the city—not exactly what you would call welcome guests, however. Many Japanese appearing on man-in-the-street interviews said they were seeing *gaijin* for the first time in their lives.

The city that had newly emerged was almost unrecognizable compared to what it was when I first arrived. Construction had halted, and everywhere you looked you saw a glistening new building. There were flags all over the city honoring the ninety-four nations participating in the games—7,000 of them said the papers, each one of them tended to by a Japanese boy scout. The Hotel Okura displayed the flag of every participating nation outside its main entrance

Menacing yakuza had virtually vanished from the streets. At the request of the government, gang bosses had ordered the more "unpleasant looking" mobsters in their ranks to leave the city for the duration of the Games and undergo "spiritual training" in the mountains or seashore. The beggars and vagrants who had occupied Ueno Park and other parts of the city had also magically disappeared, as had the streetwalkers who normally populated the entertainment areas. As an added bonus, the city's 27,000 taxi drivers had been persuaded by the authorities to stop honking their horns, all in the interests of making Tokyo sound as sedately refined as a temple garden hung with wind chimes. At many intersections were containers of yellow flags, put there at the pedestrian's disposal by the governor's office, for use in safe passage across the street, a necessity given the humongous traffic jams that clogged Tokyo's main avenues.

The citizens of Tokyo had been trained to accord the highest courtesy and hospitality to the athletes, officials, journalists, and spectators who converged on the capital. Smiling interpreters, organized by the municipal government, roamed the city in special cars, searching for bewildered-looking foreigners to help— and they were not hard to find. In the Ginza, at the big shrines like Meiji Jingu, at cafes, clubs, and restaurants, there was never a shortage of loud-talking foreign tourists anxiously poring over their guidebooks and maps, attempting to decipher Japan's arcane chronologically based address system and quite evidently in need of assistance. During that time, I found it nearly impossible to walk down a street in any of the main shopping and entertainment areas without being stopped by someone and asked if I needed help finding my destination.

Even when no volunteer raced up to offer you guidance, it was still hard for the foreign visitor to get lost. No matter where you were, on the sidewalk, at the train station, in Japan's labyrinthine underground pedestrian walkways, there were signs posted in English pointing the way.

There were also signs in Japanese reminding the citizenry to be on its best behavior, along with others warning young girls not to be taken in by the ladies-first etiquette practiced by foreign men. "Do not mistake this as an expression of love," said one that I remember with particular fondness.

On October 9, one day before the start of the games, as if ordained by the Shinto gods, a heavy rain visited Tokyo and washed away all the dirt and dust and air pollution, cleansing the city for the big event.

October 1964: "The Greatest Olympics Ever"

I watched the opening ceremony at Dr. Sato's luxurious new Western-style Harajuku apartment, on the seventh floor of a brand new ten-story residential building that had just opened up, one of the most desired spots in the city. The National Stadium was visible from the bay window in the living room, which was the size of a hotel lobby. Present were the doctor's wife, his two pre-school daughters, and two Japanese movie actresses, both wearing trendy Mary Quant miniskirts. Rounding out the entourage was a Japanese *nisei* business executive from Hawaii named Harry.

We sat on expensive leather couches in front of an enormous Toshiba color television eating *fois gras* and drinking Napoleon brandy. What I remember most about that day was the aura of pride that pervaded the room; my hosts and their other guests were bursting with it; it was in their misty-eyed faces, if not in their otherwise mostly restrained reactions to the on-screen ceremony. For them, for the whole of Japan, it was plain to see that this was a transformational moment.

Emperor Hirohito, the man in whose name the attack on Pearl Harbor and the invasion of Southeast Asia were undertaken by the Japanese Imperial Army some twenty-five years earlier, the man who was saved by MacArthur, if stripped of his power and divinity, performed the welcoming duties for the visiting athletes—not as the head of state as normally required by the IOC but in his capacity as "patron" of the Tokyo Olympics, to use the term concocted by the Organizing Committee with the assistance of the Ministry of Education.

He stood there in a special box wearing a simple black suit, a thousand riot police guarding the grounds outside, as the athletes marched into the shiny new National Stadium before a crowd of 75,000: American athletes in their big cowboy hats, Indians in purple turbans, Ghanaians in saffron robes, and the Japanese contingent, coming in last, in red blazers and white slacks, carrying the Hi no Maru flag, which was, along with the emperor, another symbol of Japan's imperial past. Trumpets blared and cannons roared as Yoshinori Sakai, a nineteen-year-old student athlete born in Hiroshima just hours after the atomic bomb fell on the city (and dubbed the "Atomic Bomb Boy" by the press), carried the Olympic torch up a flight of 179 steps to deposit it in its cauldron, the five-ring Olympic logo on his white T-shirt set fashionably beneath the red-ball logo of the Rising Sun. Takashi Ono, a Japanese gymnast, took the athletes oath on behalf of the 5,151 participating athletes—4,473 men and 678 women.

Through it all the emperor stood there alone, a diminutive 5'2", looking for all the world like a neighborhood accountant without his wartime military uniform, medals, and white stallion, watching with a demeanor that was notably more respectful than imperial. The *Chicago Tribune*'s Sam Jameson, who sat in the press box on the other side of the stadium, later wrote, "I don't think I ever saw the Emperor being the only person standing before that. I imagined in my mind that he was thanking the world for readmitting Japan into international society."

The broadcast of that opening ceremony, on October 10, 1964, which ended with the JSDF (Japan Self-Defense Forces) aerobatic skywriting team Blue Impulse tracing the five rings of the Olympic symbol in the sky with their F-86 Sabre Jets (without the benefit, one might add, of an electronic guidance system for the pilots), was watched by over 61.2 percent of the viewing public in Japan and was the first such Olympic event to be telecast live internationally. It was also the first to be telecast in living color.

(The only thing that marred the event was the release of 8,000 doves from their cages. Intended as a symbolic finale for peace and friendship, the spectacle instead rained droppings on the athletes, causing them to run their fingers through their hair in disgust—except for the Americans who were thankful they were wearing those big hats.)

I was already enamored of the country, and in my own way I shared in the emotion, but at the same time, a little voice inside me was starting to make itself heard. "What are you doing here?" it asked, as I took another swallow of the superb cognac. "You're a simple GI from a small town in California. What have you to do with movie stars and the super-rich?"

Adding to this discomfit was my excoriation at the hands of the Hawaiian *nisei*, Harry—once for my failure to recognize two such famous actresses, a faux pas not taken lightly in elite social circles, and once for giving a facetious answer to a question put to me by one of them. She wanted to know if I was there in some capacity related to the games. I told her yes, I was running in the 400-meter relay with Bob Hayes as a warmup to the pole vault event. She flushed, evidently supposing she had asked me an inappropriate question. Harry weighed in immediately with the scowling admonition that Japanese people did not take well to sarcasm.

"Mr. Whiting is my best friend," announced the doctor, as though to allay my qualms. "*Besuto furendo.* He is my personal tutor."

The other guests were suitably impressed, which was of course the doctor's intention.

(It should be noted that while the term "best friend" was imported *in vivo* into the Japanese language, the range of its usage was considerably broadened in the transfer. At a time when ten-year-old American children were being asked to serve as language tutors, for a grown-up native speaker it was not hard to find offers of best friendship, even under the most casual circumstances.)

"*Sugoi,*" gushed the actresses in unison, embarrassment forgotten, using a popular Japanese word that means "wow" or "cool" or "awesome."

In fact, one could say that having a personal American tutor *was* an indispensable accessory for the discerning well-to-do Olympic-era Japanese. (It wasn't long afterward that the indispensable accessory morphed into a blond American female tutor.)

Dr. Sato was himself the son of a very rich doctor with connections to the Imperial Family, born with the proverbial silver
spoon in his mouth. (I found out that he had spent the entire war
in the family villa in the resort town of Karuizawa, watching the
B-29s bomb Tokyo from afar.) In addition to his Ginza clinic he
was now building his own hospital outside Shinjuku. He was in
the top 1 percent in terms of income. He traveled around the city
in a chauffeur-driven Lincoln Continental Limousine, dressed in
expensively tailored English suits, and, as we have seen, spent his
evenings cavorting in plush Ginza nightclubs. He was comfortable
spending more money in one day than most Japanese *salarymen*
did in a year.

Ordinary Japanese company workers, such as those that I had
gotten to know through my other tutoring jobs, could not imagine the doctor's lifestyle. They commuted for an hour or more
each way on uncomfortably packed trains, worked twelve-hour
days, drank cheap Nikka whisky at discount stand bars in the
entertainment hubs, and had one suit that they wore daily until it
was shiny, pressing it by laying it out under the futon each night
in their small and gloomy apartments, which were often little better than hovels and where it might take several hours for the gas
heater to warm the bath.

But, as I came to understand, Japanese on all levels of the economic scale shared certain beliefs. These might be summarized
as follows: The war had been bad, but Japan was not entirely to
blame for it. Japan had done a noble thing in attempting to throw
off the white man's yoke in Asia.

Japan's wrongdoings in war were no worse than those of other
countries. They had hated the idea of foreigners occupying Japan
and had mixed feelings about the Western-style constitution that
had been imposed on them by the Americans. They were on a collective mission to restore Japan's face in the world and hosting the
Olympics was the first big step. The pride they felt in that achievement was beyond description.

1964 Tokyo Olympics

3

1. Trumpets blared and cannons roared as Yoshinori Sakai, a nineteen-year-old student-athlete born in Hiroshima just hours after the atomic bomb fell on the city (dubbed the "Atomic Bomb Boy"), carried the Olympic torch up a flight of 179 steps.

2. Opening Ceremony of the 1964 Tokyo Olympics.

3. Japan loses the silver medal.

4. Anton Geesink of the Netherlands takes the open-weight judo gold from Akio Kaminaga.

5. "'Witches' save Japan's national honor."

4

5

We all tend to look at the way other people live through the prism of our own set of values. I certainly wouldn't have wanted to be a corporate warrior in Tokyo. Your life was simply not your own. Yet, I came to admire them for their dedication to their firms—and to their country. To many Japanese, that gritty all-consuming struggle out of the dust and the ashes was a kind of life fulfillment. There was a certain beauty in it.

Alien Demons and Witches

As expected, the Americans took the most gold medals—so many in fact that Tokyoites took to whistling the American National Anthem unconsciously and the medals ceremony band began truncating it at "... so gallantly streaming."

Japan wound up with sixteen gold medals for third place over-all, taking five golds in gymnastics and five in wrestling. It would be their best showing ever until the Rio Olympics in 2016.

More memorable, perhaps, for students of Japan, were events that offered a view into the Japanese psyche at the time.

One was the marathon, run on Wednesday, October 21, in the persistent rain and fog that had plagued the second week of the Games. Marathons were extremely popular in Japan, and the 26-mile race, which went from National Stadium to a halfway point near Fuchu on the Koshu Kaido highway and back, was watched by energetic crowds of people nine and ten deep on each side of the road, many of whom had staked their spots the night before. Helping swell the throng were airmen from Fuchu Air Station and nearby Tachikawa Air base, among them a certain bleary-eyed kid from California just coming off an all-night shift staring at radar signals.

The event was won by Ethiopia's Abebe Bikila, gold medal-ist of the Rome Olympics, making him the first man to win two

Olympic marathons. I remember just catching a glimpse of him as he flashed past, not an ounce of extra flesh on his frame, striding along the pavement with an ease that was almost disrespectful. At least the famed "barefoot runner" was wearing shoes this time.

But the marathon contained another story that gripped the nation as well. It involved Japanese runner Kokichi Tsuburaya, who had entered the stadium in second place with such a substantial lead he seemed guaranteed the silver medal, which would have been an Olympic first for Japan.

By then, I had retreated out of the mist to a small wood-front coffee shop near the Higashi-Fuchu train station with colorful wax replicas of food and drink displayed in the window, among them an appetizing banana, tomato, and cucumber sandwich. I sat there at a rickety Formica table in the corner, beneath a poster showing the Olympic rings below the Rising Sun, sipped oolong tea, and watched the end of the race on the 21" Sanyo TV the proprietors had bought for the Games, cheering along with other customers whose ranks included a local rice farmer and a couple of puffy-faced off-duty bar girls in jeans and blouses with bandanas wrapped around their heads, chainsmoking Winston cigarettes. The cheering for Tsuburaya was building to a crescendo—*I-ke! I-ke! I-ke!* (Go! Go! Go!)—when suddenly the UK's Basil Heatley heaved into view and proceeded to put on one of Olympic track and field's greatest all-time spurts. He steadily closed the gap in the last 200 meters, passing Tsurubaya shortly before the wire and turning the wild cheering in the coffee shop, and in the stadium, and no doubt in the rest of Japan, into one huge collective groan.

Tsuburaya was visibly mortified at the seeming ease with which he had been overtaken. After the race, he was quoted as saying to fellow marathoner Kenji Kimihara, "I committed an inexcusable blunder in front of the Japanese people. I have to make amends by running and hoisting the Hinomaru in the next Olympics, in Mexico."

But Tsuburaya, a First Lieutenant in the Japan Ground

Self-Defense Force, suffered back problems (lumbago) and, four years later, in January 1968, while training for the Mexico City Olympics, would commit suicide by slashing his throat in the Defense Force dormitory. He was found in his room holding his Bronze Medal.

A suicide note found at the scene is still remembered today. To his parents he said he was "exhausted to the bone" and couldn't run anymore. Then he apologized to his high school principal and a JOC (Japanese Olympic Committee) official for being unable to "keep my promise."

Another event obsessively anticipated across the nation was the judo open-weight class, held two days after the marathon on a Friday afternoon. The Japanese sport of Judo, developed in the late 19th century by Jigoro Kano, who had based it on the ancient martial art of ju-jitsu, had been included in the 1964 Olympics for the first time ever at Japan's behest. The Japanese had dominated the sport in international competitions following World War II. It was a martial art that symbolized the Japanese way of approaching all athletics (including baseball) with its special focus on endless training and development of spirit (accomplished, among other things, through special winter camps where athletes had to arise at four in the morning and run barefoot through the snow in freezing temperatures).

For the Tokyo Games it had been decided to award medals in lightweight, middleweight, heavyweight, and open-weight classes. As expected, Japanese *judoka* took gold medals in all of the first three classes. Some fifteen thousand people packed the hall for the final open-weight match between national champion Akio Kaminaga and Dutchman Anton Geesink, who was 6'7" and 270 pounds to Kaminaga's 5'11" and 230 pounds. Geesink had crushed Japanese opponents for the gold medal at the 1961 World Judo Championships in Paris. But many in the crowd and watching on television, believed that Kaminaga would prevail on his home ground given the momentousness of the event, where national pride was at stake, and Kaminaga's assumed superior fighting spirit because he was Japanese. After all, the whole point of judo from its inception was that a small man could defeat a larger man with proper technique and attitude.

But it was not to be. Geesink, a former soccer and basketball player, had speed and agility as well as size. He dominated the match from beginning to end, pinning Kaminaga to the mat in just nine minutes and twenty-two seconds. It raised the question in everyone's mind, including mine, of just how far an athlete can go on *konjo*, or fighting spirit, alone. The lopsided win by the big blond foreigner was a bitter disappointment for millions of Japanese fans. It was doubly painful because Geesink had humiliated his Japanese opponent in front of the entire planet, via satellite television. I could see that pain firsthand when I watched the match, standing in front of a big TV on display in the show window of an electronics store on the Ginza. Around me was a large crowd of grim-faced Japanese men in suits, some of whom looked to me to be on the verge of tears.

Author and Japanologist Ian Buruma would later write in a memorable essay:

> Sports, like sex, cuts where it hurts the most, that soft spot where national virility is at stake. And at no time was it more delicate than in the 1960's, when the nation was beginning to crawl away from the shame of the greatest humiliation of all: defeat in war and subsequent occupation by a superior foreign power. The Tokyo Olympics were supposed to have put the seal on all that. The revival of national virility, already boosted by the accelerating economic boom, was at hand, the Judo Open Weight gold medal was meant to have clinched it: the shame of defeat would be wiped out and Japanese face would finally have been restored.... [But instead it] was as though the ancestral Sun Goddess had been raped in public by a gang of alien demons.

Still, unlike some victorious American athletes whose effusive celebrations knew no bounds, Geesink had shown restraint and respect to Japan in his triumph. He had bowed to Kaminaga after the match, as was required by judo form, and had behaved in a dignified manner throughout. With a gesture of his hand, he had stopped his jubilant coach and teammates from running onto the sacred mat. The moment was captured in national newspaper headlines and has never been forgotten by the Japanese.

Unfortunately, in his later years he moved to Japan to become a professional wrestler and did much damage to his image not only because of the tergiversation but also because of his surprising inability to perform in his new sport. Said Giant Baba, owner of the All Japan Pro Wrestling association to which Geesink belonged, "With a *judogi* on, there was nobody better. In wrestling trunks there was nobody worse."

It was left to the maniacally trained and wonderfully adept Japan national women's volleyball team to salvage the nation's pride. Their gold medal victory over the taller, stronger Soviet Russian squad on the final evening of competition at the four-thousand-seat Komazawa Olympic Park Gymnasium would set television viewing records.

According to Video Research, 66.8% of all TV-owning households in Japan were tuned in to the match from the beginning, making it the second-most-watched television program in Japanese history—a position it still holds today (first is an NHK New Year's Eve songfest). As the final point was scored the rating had gone up to 95%. (This raises the question of what the other 5% were watching.)

The "Witches of the Orient," as a Russian newspaper dubbed them, would go on to become a metonymy for the Games and the subject for a raft of academic treatises spanning the next fifty years. Their bruising eleven-hour-a-day practice regimen over a period of two years was seen to symbolize the dogged resurgence of the Japanese economy, short on resources but full of fighting spirit. Their gold medal victory would go down in Japanese sport-ing lore as one of the Top Ten great sporting achievements of the 20th century, reaching #5 on a list compiled by the *Asahi Shimbun* at the end of 1999.

* * *

The Olympics were a resounding success, making, in just about everyone's opinion, the madness of reengineering an entire city worthwhile. Japan had originally been designated as host of the 1940 Olympics, but when war appeared on the horizon, the event was canceled. Now, after twenty-four years of catastrophic events, Tokyo came to host the first Olympic games in Asia, and all sorts of records were set. They were the first Games in Olympic history that used computers to keep results, introducing new electronic timing devices, variations of which are still in use today. Innova-tions included a new timing system for swimming that started the clock by the sound of the starter's pistol and stopped it with touchpads, and a photo finish using an image with lines on it to determine the sprint results. Such advances thrust Japan into the forefront of global technological development, literally overnight.

The Olympics put the Seiko Watch company, the official time-keeper of the Games and owner of the iconic Hattori Building in Ginza 4-chome with the famous clock on top, on the map. More-over, a major Hollywood film, the Cary Grant movie *Walk Don't Run*, would be set in Tokyo during this time.

I could not get tickets to any of the glamor events but did man-age to see a soccer game between Iran and Romania. I remember that the stadium was packed and very enthusiastic, although few in the stands had any serious rooting interest in either team. But just being in Tokyo and soaking up the atmosphere was enough. It was impossible to walk into any coffee shop, restaurant, or bar without finding a new TV set tuned to the NHK telecast of the Games. More than once, I was taken for an Olympic athlete and asked which event I was participating in. "Beer drinking" was my stock answer. (Evidently, I had still not fully processed Harry's warning about the use of irony.)

When it was over, *Life* magazine, citing the emotion-filled opening ceremony, the high quality of competition, and the pervading goodwill, called the 1964 Games "the greatest ever." *Sports Illustrated* noted that, to the very end, Japanese kept their manners toward their foreign guests. During the two weeks 194 pickpockets were arrested in Tokyo, but only 4 in the Olympic area had copped a foreign wallet.

For the Japanese, all of this was a source of pride. A new Japan had just been introduced to the world, and it was nothing like the old. No longer a militarist pariah shattered by war, it had successfully reinvented itself as a peaceful democracy on its way to becoming a world economic powerhouse. The Games had demonstrated to the West that Japan was now their equal and was going to be a force to be reckoned with. The emperor, the flag of the Rising Sun, the unofficial anthem "Kimigayo," and the use of Japanese soldiers (even if they were now members of the so-called Self-Defense Forces), once symbols of the menace Japan had posed to its Asia-Pacific neighbors, now stood forth in an entirely different and far more salubrious light.

That this had been accomplished in a mere two decades served as an example to other countries in Asia and the developing world seeking to modernize their own societies. For the citizens of Tokyo, the Olympic success was doubly important because their city had now been transformed into a shiny international metropolis that would be a magnet for foreign tourists, businessmen, scholars, and others.

Indeed, as if to put the final stamp of approval on the place, the most popular franchise in screen history would choose Tokyo the following year as the central location for one of its most famous films, *You Only Live Twice*, produced in 1966 and released in 1967, becoming a global smash hit. The Hotel Otani would appear as

You Only Live Twice, filmed in Tokyo in 1966, was a huge global hit. The Hotel New Otani management gave the 007 crew carte blanche to shoot in their five-star hotel. They were deeply disappointed to hear 007 respond to a question by a SPECTRE operative in the film—"Where are you staying in Tokyo, Mr. Bond?"—by saying, "The Hilton."

the Osato Chemical and Engineering Co. Building, Tokyo headquarters of the infamous SPECTRE. I was able to watch some of the filming between classes at Sophia, which was ten minutes up the hill. Also featured was the adjoining garden, as well as the Tokyo subway system, the Kuramae Kokugikan sumo hall, and the neon-lit Ginza nightscape. In the film, that keen Japanologist, James Bond, also gave out the secret of the precise temperature to which sake had to be warmed to please the demanding palate.

Dark Side of the Olympics

If for the citizens of Tokyo the Olympiad was a blaze of glory, it also cast some shadows. The transformation of the metropolis from a war-ravaged city into a major international capital, seemingly

The Nihonbashi river culture disappeared in the rush to rebuild.

overnight, had a dark side that was rarely talked about. The Games were in fact responsible for a great deal of environmental destruction and human misery in the city and its environs. As one who was there and paid attention to what was going on, I can attest to that.

There was absolutely no reason to have a high-speed train connecting Tokyo to Osaka just for the Games, since there were no events taking place in Japan's second-largest city. Yet the Shinkansen project was rushed through by JNR executives in the name of "urban improvement." The goal was to impress the rest of the world with the high level of Japanese technological achievement while the global media focused on the Tokyo Olympiad. Thanks primarily to the haste (and also to dirty politics and graft), the project wound up costing a billion dollars, twice what the original budget called for (and roughly one-third the total cost of the Games), and the JNR president was compelled to resign.

The funds diverted to cover the expanding costs of the Shinkansen took money away from other projects, like the monorail, which had originally been intended to link Haneda Airport to the city center. Instead it wound up terminating in sleepy Hamamatsucho, a less-convenient station several stops away and far from the top hotels. There was simply not enough capital to buy the land and extend the line to a more logical location like Tokyo Station or Shinbashi, for which the monorail company had acquired a license.

Moreover, in order to avoid buying expensive privately owned land for the monorail, its builders constructed

And a national treasure was ruined.

it over water on a route provided gratis by the municipal government, covering the rivers, canals, and sea areas below with landfill and concrete in the process. Fishing permits held by local fishing cooperatives in these districts were revoked by City Hall and many local fishing jobs were lost. A seaweed field in Omori in the city's Ota Ward from which a prized delicacy, *Omori nori*, had been harvested since the Edo period, simply disappeared. (The tradition itself, however, is still preserved at the Omori Nori Museum, founded in the same district in 2008.)

The lack of funds affected highway construction as well, as it also became necessary to build overhead expressways above the existing rivers and canals to avoid purchasing land. Among the many eyesores that resulted from this arrangement is that of the iconic Meiji-period bridge at Nihonbashi, a historic terminus for the old Tokaido Road footpath to the economic center of the old city—and the zero point from which all distances are measured in Japan. The bridge had been built back in Meiji times so that it would provide a view of Mt. Fuji for anyone crossing from the east side to the west.

I remember taking a walk along the canal to see the famous bridge, shortly before the Games began. I was dismayed to see its once charming appearance completely ruined by the massive highway just a few feet overhead, like a giant concrete lid, obliterating the sky. The smell from the toxic water in the canal was so offensive I had to cover my nose. I imagined Mt. Fuji, looking on from afar, doing the same.

The reconstruction effort for the Olympics cost Tokyo much of its navigable waterways and put an end to what had been a vibrant, commercial river culture in and around Nihonbashi. Planting the support columns of the highways and other structures in the water below had rendered many river docks useless, costing even more jobs. Water stagnated, fish died, and biochemical sludge, known as *hedoro* in Japanese, formed in the previously unpolluted Tokyo estuaries, creating increasingly putrid cesspools. Some were simply buried with debris from construction and the tearing down of World War 2–era structures. Others were filled with concrete and turned into roads. Life did not return to the Kanda River, the Sumida River, and other connected waterways for several years, and when it did it was in the form of unsavory pathogens.

Then there were the highways themselves, clogged as they were with stop-and-start traffic. As *Chicago Tribune* correspondent Sam Jameson put it, "Building an expressway system based on a mathematical formula of a two-lane expressway merging into another two-lane expressway to create . . . a two-lane expressway was not the smartest thing to do. It guaranteed congestion. The system had to have been designed by someone who had never driven."

Another casualty of the 1964 Olympics was the trolley lines, which had been a cheap, reliable, and pleasant way of getting around the city. The elimination of two major lines in street-widening schemes caused a corresponding increase in vehicular traffic and a worsening of air quality in Tokyo and set the stage for the removal of almost all the other trolley lines in the city. With their dedicated traffic lanes, they were the most dependable passage through the traffic congestion.

Corruption, in the form of bid rigging (*dango*) and price collusion, a well-known fact of life in postwar construction in Japan, also reared its ugly head during the pre-Olympic years. Many construction firms were fronts for organized crime, as one organized crime figure told me later, and yakuza gangs were a fixture at most construction sites. They brought in the laborers, supplied temporary lodging, ran the food concessions, the afterhours gambling dens, and brothels, and, of course, provided "protection." With taxpayer money siphoned off to line the pockets of corrupt politicians and underworld bosses, the subsequent cost-cutting often resulted in shoddy work. The use of sand from the sea when mixing concrete, for example, caused the internal rebar and steel beams used in highway construction to rust prematurely.

The staging of the Olympics provided an opportunity to reward Tokyo's underworld gangs for their devoted efforts in helping the conservative (and CIA-backed) ruling Liberal Democratic Party pass the 1960 extension of the US-Japan Security Treaty, which kept US soldiers in Japan over widespread opposition in the country at large. Yakuza bosses had deployed their minions to suppress protests and were in the Diet building on the night the treaty was passed in a special Diet session, successfully barring the doors to opponents of the ratification massing outside.

It took Japan over thirty years to repay the money it borrowed from the World Bank to build roads for the 1964 Olympics.

The Student

You Speak That Shit?

The Olympics and its aftermath made for a culminating moment in my life as well. Even after the athletes departed and the stadiums went silent, the buzz and the energy remained. Per-capita GDP continued to rise steadily to more than triple over the course of the decade. The "economic miracle" was in full swing, and I had a ringside seat to the metamorphosis taking place at all levels of the society.

I had been in the country for nearly three years and was due for a discharge the following March. I had decisions to make.

In the course of my visits to places like the Old Imperial Bar and the Okura, I had on numerous occasions overheard foreigners disparage Japan and its people as odd, quirky, inscrutable, and hard to trust. Knowing this to be untrue, I seized upon the conceit that I would become the one American to deal with Japan free of bias, becoming a voice of reason in uncovering and extolling its virtues (and feel virtuous myself in assuming so generous a stance). I would be the one Yankee who didn't go home, earning instead a positive welcome to remain. But around the time of the Olympics, the climate began to change.

Not too many days after the closing ceremonies, I dropped in at a bar, a little out-of-the-way place in Shibuya I had frequented before, to nurse a quiet beer and ponder what other entertainments the evening might hold. Nearby sat a group of men in business suits. Several looked up when I walked in and sat down. The looks were not friendly; they seemed resentful that I was intruding on their private preserve when by all rights I should have left with the rest of the Olympic tourists.

No one spoke to me, but it was clear that they were speaking *at* me. A capsule of the snatches of the conversation I caught included such endearments as: "too many *gaijin*" . . . "Americans acting as if they owned the place" . . . "time for them all to pack up and leave." They were willing to make an exception, however, "for any of their good-looking babes they wanted to leave behind." The chortles ended in a toast: "Here's to Japan, the greatest country in the world!"

The incident brought home a realization that had already begun to dawn. I was no longer going to find automatic hospitality just because I was an American. On the contrary, it was becoming plain that my entree into the world of Ginza clubs and high society was not something merited by my personal charm and accomplishments but rather the sort of treatment that might be accorded a pet monkey.

My "best friendship" with Dr. Sato was by then already on the wane.

The number of lessons declined and, soon after, completely ceased. I later learned that I had been replaced by a pretty blond exchange student from Minnesota who had answered a "tutor wanted" ad on the Sophia bulletin board placed by an emissary from the good doctor. In fact, I heard about this from the tutor herself, who, as chance would have it, turned out to be a classmate of mine at the university. Shortly after, she resigned the position because, she said, her pupil was more interested in her curves than in his verbs.

In truth, I was relieved. I was ready for something a little less shallow and more grounded in reality.

One thing I knew for certain was that I was not going to pursue a career in the military. I had worked for three years in what was called the Elint Center, a highly classified electronic spy operation that was under the joint direction of the National Security Agency and the Central Intelligence Agency. Its mission was to detect Soviet and Chinese defense systems in case the Cold War should ever turn into a hot one. The CIA ran high-altitude U-2 reconnaissance missions while the NSA ran lower-level surveillance operations. I was an analyst, trained to read out the magnetic tape recordings the pilots brought back.

As my enlistment wound down, I was approached by a higher-up, who asked if I might be interested in going to officer training school. Around the same time a National Security Agency official whom I had also worked for in the same building proposed to sponsor me for a job in Fort Meade, Maryland. Both offered the opportunity of completing my college education while working. I did not hesitate in turning down both offers. It seems the military had made enough of a man of me so that I could be decisive about what I didn't want for myself and what I did want. And what I did want was to stay in Tokyo. All that remained for me now was to decide what I did.

I decided I was going to stay on in the city and see what it was like living on the local economy. I had my eye on a small Japanese-style apartment—an unheated, cold-water flat of two tatami rooms in Komagome in the old eastern part of the city. It was within walking distance of the Yamate Line train station and the public bath I would have to use. I would enroll at Sophia full time, make a serious attempt to learn *kanji* characters, and see where it took me.

It wasn't just the Olympic spectacle that Tokyo had put on for the rest of the world, although it had been something to see. The city was making it clear it was going to be a force to be reckoned with from now on—in industry, commerce, culture, sports, and entertainment—why wouldn't I want to hang around and watch the show?

I was already heavily addicted to Tokyo. I liked the incredible energy, the activity, the politeness, the orderliness, the cleanliness, the efficiency, the trains that always arrived on time, the mix of the old and new, the temples, the shrines, the crowds, the bright neon lights, the charm, and the uniqueness of it all. Tokyo was a city where umbrellas appeared as if by magic at the very first raindrop. It was a city where taxi doors opened automatically for you. It was a city where if you lost your wallet or purse, you could go to the police station, and the cops as a matter of policy would loan you a thousand yen so you could make it back home. And it wasn't so unusual they would call the next day to report that the wallet had been found with all the money inside. There was nothing like it in Eureka.

At the same time, I had also come to savor the unknowns life kept throwing at me while in the city. And if you were a callow young man from Eureka searching for an identity, Tokyo was not a bad place to start looking. As I would soon discover, after three years on its fringe I had barely begun to scratch the surface.

* * *

The possibility that I might stay confounded a number of my colleagues at the Elint Center, most of whom were counting their wakeups until they could return home.

"America is the greatest country in the world," they would say. "Why the hell would anyone want to live in a place like this?"

Some of the comments I received flew in the face of the high principles embedded in the constitution America had bequeathed to its new democratic ally and were delivered in characteristically colorful terms:

"You a Jap-lover, Whiting?"

"You like those slope-head women?"

"You got a thing for slanted pussy, Whiting?"

It was with the same sort of high regard for international friendship and understanding that they had greeted my attempts to speak the local language with the Japanese nationals on the base:

"You speak that shit, Whiting?"

Elint Center Staff Sergeant Richard Saunders, a big, beefy Kansan and Air Force lifer who was on his third assignment to Japan since the Occupation, took it upon himself to lecture me about my future.

"Don't do it," he said. "Japan's no place for a young man. You'll get involved with a Japanese girl and you'll be screwed. Your life will be over."

It turned out that Sergeant Saunders was speaking from hard experience, as he had married a Japanese woman not long after he first arrived and it had not turned out well.

It was jaundiced advice that was easy to ignore. If they could not see the possibilities offered by life in Tokyo—a city about to blast off into the stratosphere—it was their problem, not mine. I wasn't about to miss the ride.

Komagome: Life in the Low City

I come from a lower-middle-class family of five, with an older sister Margo and a younger brother Ned. My parents, originally from New Jersey, had moved to California after the war. My father was a plumber, a mechanic, a jack of all trades who served in the Navy during World War 2, including a stint with the second wave at Guadalcanal, where he was cited for bravery. He did not particularly like the Japanese, although he raved about their cameras. My mother was abandoned at the age of twelve by her parents—a race-track hustler and a bar floozy—who left her to care for her five younger siblings. She never got over the trauma and spent her life perpetually angry. My father was seldom home, partly I suspect to avoid her temper. I grew up scrawny and pimpled, morose and depressed, wishing I were somewhere else—wishing I were *someone* else. I was, for a time, an honor roll student at Eureka High School until one day I just stopped studying. I had gotten a C in Algebra and took it again to raise my grade but flunked it. I was, I am sure, the only person in the history of Eureka High to do that. I joined the Air Force at age eighteen, after a semester at Humboldt State University, to get away from it all, which is how I wound up in Japan, a country I barely knew existed when growing up.

There were no Japanese among Eureka's mostly lily-white— and red-necked—population of approximately 30,000, most of whom drove pickup trucks and had never seen a subway. There were no Japanese restaurants and I can't recall any Japanese movies ever playing at the local cinema, with the exception of the aforementioned horribly dubbed *Godzilla* flicks and another monster movie named *Rodan*, which I paid 25 cents to see at the Eureka Theater. I knew of Mt. Fuji only from a brief scene in the 1958 film *Around the World in 80 Days* and geisha only from the Jerry Lewis film *Geisha Boy*.

I began my life as an official resident of Tokyo on April 1, 1965, one day after my military discharge. I had my student visa and settled into my new lodgings in Komagome, which was located in the "Low City," or Shitamachi, as the older eastern part of Tokyo was called. The area was known for its traditional neighborhoods of merchants and artisans and its working-class culture. Komagome Station was one of the twenty-nine stops on the Yamate Line that circled the core of the city.

A new Tokyo may have emerged from the debris in the post-Olympic era, but away from the Ginza, Roppongi, and the New Otani, the city, particularly the eastern side was, even under the best of circumstances, difficult for the casual observer to understand. It was a confusing, haphazard sprawl lacking any discernible semblance of city planning, an accidental mishmash of old and new, of what survived the earthquake, the bombings, and the fires and what didn't—and what was designated to stay, move, or face the wrecking ball in the continuing building fervor.

The address system was chaotic. I had needed a detailed hand-drawn map to find my way from the station to the apartment and still had to stop periodically and ask directions. That's how difficult it was to locate, which was par for the course for the city. House #1 in a given neighborhood might be next to House #17, while House #2 was 100 yards away, the result of a policy in which buildings are numbered in the order in which they are built, rather than where they stand. With Tokyo's narrow, meandering, and unnamed streets (save for the main arteries), unrelated to basic concepts of north-south or east-west, taxi drivers needed precise detailed instructions or maps to find their destinations—until GPS came along decades later to make their lives easier.

However, there was a certain method underlying the madness, as I discovered in my studies at Sophia. Tokyo had been designed in a special *uzumaki* or whirlpool style, thanks to legendary shogun Tokugawa Ieyasu who, in 1603, had moved the seat of government to Edo, then a small castle town subsisting primarily on fishing, ending a long period of civil war. He set out to make it intentionally confusing to potential invaders, with the castle—comprising the heart of the city—protected by a swirling 5-kilometer inner moat that itself ran into a larger 15-kilometer outer moat spiraling around the castle's perimeter, and eventually connecting with the Sumida River. The result was a maze-like pattern of canals and stone walls, similar in effect to the defensive layout of many ancient walled towns of Europe, with three dozen different gates that restricted visibility and movement. It was the largest castle complex in existence.

By the mid-18th century, Edo had become one of the largest cities in the world, with a population of over a million. Fifteen generations of the Tokugawa clan ruled Japan from Edo Castle under a feudal system that strictly limited foreign contact, as well as travel between different regions.

The coming of American Commodore Matthew Perry and his Black Ships in 1853, seeking trade concessions and use of ports, forced Japan to open its doors and triggered the collapse of the old samurai order. Fifteen years later, forces loyal to the Japanese Imperial Court in Kyoto deposed the Tokugawa shogunate and elevated the seventeen-year-old Emperor Meiji from a mostly ceremonial role in Kyoto to head of state. The throne was moved to Edo, whose name was changed to Tokyo, its *kanji* denoting "Eastern Capital," and Edo Castle became the Imperial Palace. The Meiji Restoration marked the beginning of Japan's transition from a feudal society to a modern industrial state. The samurai clans were abolished.

Through it all the distinct layout of the city remained, surviving the Great Kanto Earthquake of 1923 and World War 2 basically intact, although most of the structures of the Imperial Palace compound were laid to waste in the Allied fire bombings and had to be rebuilt (Emperor Hirohito declared the capitulation of Japan from the basement of the concrete library in the palace compound). The original stone walls and canals of the central core, along with nine gates and three watchtowers, formed a course around which joggers ran every day.

* * *

I had uncovered my new lodgings with the help of a certain Kazuhiko Kusaka-san, a kind-faced man in his late twenties who was an employee of the Toda Construction Company in Kyobashi where I taught English once a week, courtesy of the Sophia University bulletin board. The digs were a fifteen-minute walk from the station on the second floor of a cheaply constructed two-story stucco building in a nondescript residential area of wooden houses, many of which looked as though they could not withstand a strong wind, and gray utilitarian ferro-concrete structures. The agent said the landlord would not ordinarily accept foreigners, but since the Toda Construction Company was my rent guarantor, they would make an exception in my case.

My apartment, to use the term loosely, was laid out in terms of tatami mats, the traditional floor panels woven with straw, which remain today as the standard measure of space, even as the city sees fewer and fewer of them. It consisted of a six-tatami room (about 100 square feet), a three-tatami room, a tiny kitchen area with a two-burner gas cooking stove, a small refrigerator, and a cramped flush toilet of the squat variety in a tiny commode barely big enough to stand up in.

I slept on futons that I pulled out of the closet and unfolded every night (and aired out my window in the morning like everyone else in the neighborhood). The closet also held my wardrobe of two pairs of Levis, two worn sportcoats, three shirts, and one cheap suit. There was no telephone and no hot running water. If I wanted a bath I had to go to a nearby public *sento* (bathhouse) and scrub down with everyone else in the neighborhood. Heat in the winter would be provided by a tiny gas heater. Relief from Tokyo's unbearably hot and humid summers would come in the form of a small fan. My desk was a low coffee table in one corner of the room, requiring me to sit lotus style when I used it. The rent was the yen equivalent of $40 a month, which I would be able to afford by teaching English. It was about one one-hundredth of the rent for posh Western-style residences in the Roppongi–Azabu area where foreign executives on lavish expatriate expense packages and their families lived.

"Rabbit hutches" was a term later coined by a visiting European diplomat to express his amazement over the relatively poor quality of housing in Japan's so-called high-tech society. Some Japanese were offended by his less-than-diplomatic remark, but most recognized the rueful truth behind it. Mr. Kusaka's room in the

Toda Construction Company's Komagome dormitory across the street was about the size of a prison cell at Alcatraz. In the wake of the Olympics, such comparisons with the West were awakening many to the wide gaps in the standard of living, but it also provided impetus for hard work and savings that would one day deliver a family's dream home.

According to an article I had read in *Time* magazine, almost once a week a Tokyo infant was accidentally smothered to death in an overcrowded communal futon. Newspapers reported that a taxi driver nabbed by police for making love to his wife in the public plaza of the Imperial Palace was given a sympathetic release when he pleaded that he could simply not perform his husbandly duties at home—home being a 9-foot-by-9-foot room inhabited by a family of six. This was why there was such an institution as love hotels. And it was one reason, I came to believe, that Japanese men gained a reputation as hopeless workaholics. They preferred to loiter in the office until the late evening hours and then hit the bars with colleagues on company expense rather than go home to impossibly cramped quarters.

* * *

I commuted to Sophia University by train every day—taking the Yamate Line to Shinjuku, the busiest train station in the world, then transferring to the Chuo (Central) Line, which took me to Yotsuya in the heart of the city. I battled my way through rush-hour crowds, stood in lines at ticket machines, had my ticket punched by a uniformed employee of Japan National Railways, and was then helped onto packed cars by professional platform pushers. The station floor around the wicket was inevitably blanketed with thousands of tiny round paper dots: train-ticket confetti. The entire trip took an hour and cost the equivalent of a dime.

The Olympics were over, but the engine of the Economic

Miracle was just reaching maximum speed. There was still construction everywhere you looked in the city—large sections of road were covered with planks and work still continued on two of the overhead new highways. According to Kusaka-san, many of the city's wooden residential houses were built to last only about twenty to thirty years, not because of the earthquakes and typhoons that periodically ravage the capital—after all there are thousand-year-old wooden temples and other structures that are still standing—but because of government policy to boost construction: by annually decreasing a wood structure's book value they could keep construction workers, architects, and bank loan officers employed, creating an endless loop of building and employment. Now that was organization. To cite one telling statistic, provided by Kusaka-san, there were four times as many architects in Tokyo as in New York and twice as many construction workers. They helped make Tokyo what some people liked to call "the most transitory megalopolis" in the world, a city in a constant state of home rebuilding.

Tokyo was also arguably the most polluted city in the world. Photochemical smog created by vehicle exhaust still engulfed the streets, making walking and bike riding at times unpleasant, especially in the summer. Factory emissions from around its perimeter added to the car exhaust. On certain hot, muggy days the air became so polluted it caused headaches and watery eyes, and the city government found it necessary to issue alerts and advisories for children and people with asthma to stay indoors. I took to wearing a facemask like everyone else and waited for the rain to wash it all away.

I led a frugal existence as befitting my modest means from teaching English and the fact that I no longer enjoyed the stability of the military life, with its free lodging and easy access to American amenities, which were now luxuries in the local economy. To avoid frequent trips to the barber shop, I let my hair grow out from the military buzz cut I had sported at the ELINT Center.

Not much one for cooking, I always ate out at low-priced eateries. The daily menu might feature: coffee and a 2-inch-thick slice of toast for breakfast at a coffee shop in front of Komagome Station, lunch at a *soba* (buckwheat noodles) street stall, and for dinner *cha-han* (fried rice) at a working-class Chinese restaurant with torn vinyl seat covers near the university.

I took baths at a public bathhouse two to three times a week, scrubbing down my body while squatting on a stool in front of a low, tiled row of spigots and mirrors, alongside a couple of dozen other men from the community,

Platform pushers were employed during the morning rush.

who were staring in wonder at my white skin and my foreign genitalia, which I tried modestly to hide with a towel, as per the Japanese custom. Then I would rinse myself off and step into a large communal pool of agonizingly hot water and soak until I couldn't stand it anymore. Often, Kusaka-san would invite me to use the

Toda Construction dormitory bath, which afforded a little more privacy and a little less embarrassment.

The *sento* or public bath in Japan was like the well in other societies, a place for exchanging local news and banter. So people would strike up conversations with me there from time to time— "We hear you are from California. Is it cold there?" It was amazing how much they already knew about me.

"Your rent is expensive," said one of my fellow bathers shortly after I had moved in, a man I had never seen before. "You must make a lot of money for a student."

I smoked Hi-Lite cigarettes—a harsh but very popular Japanese brand similar to French Gitanes—which I purchased from a little old lady at a tiny kiosk on the corner. I bought fruit and vegetables from the stand across the street from my apartment and sundries from the other family shops in the neighborhood, which stayed open for business from early morning until late at night.

I had a favorite neighborhood *shokudo*, a restaurant serving sushi, grilled fish, *ochazuke* (tea poured over rice, usually taken with Japanese pickles), and other common dishes. Named the Sakuranbo, it occupied the first floor of a concrete building down the street, windows guarded by bamboo bars and a big red paper lantern hanging in front of its sliding doors. Inside was an oak wood counter with eight stools, and along one wall was a raised tatami section with four tables and partitions made of rice paper. Behind the counter was a smiling middle-aged man with buck teeth, a white *hachimaki* towel wrapped around his head, and a permanent smile, whom everyone called "Masutaa" (Master), as was the common appellation for shop proprietors, and who called me "Bobu-san." His wife, a thick-set middle-aged woman, waited on the tables.

I spent many a pleasant summer evening there watching the nightly telecasts of Yomiuri Giants games over a bowl of *ochazuke*. Sometimes I would simply drop in for a glass of beer around 11 p.m. and catch the evening sports news. Masutaa was a Giants fan,

as was seemingly everyone else in the city—in the country actually—and I learned you could start a conversation with just about
anyone in Japan by asking how the Yomiuri Giants—the Kyojin—
did the night before:

"Kyojin kachimashita ka?" (Did the Giants win?)

At the Sakuranbo, however, I could tell whether the Giants
had won or lost that evening just by looking at the expression on
Masutaa's face when I walked in.

Other evenings I hung out with Kusaka-san and his colleagues
from the Toda Construction dormitory. Kusaka was a graduate of
Chuo University. A member of the college English-Speaking Society, he spoke English quite fluently despite never having been outside Japan. He professed to like Americans, even though he had
spent his childhood amidst the ravages of war. Several years older
than me, he remembered seeing, as a boy, the B-29 Superfortresses
flying overhead dropping firebombs.

Still, he also remembered getting gifts of chocolate and chewing gum from the invading American soldiers and, later, his family
getting free supplies of food from the Occupation, which helped
them avoid starvation.

"Life is complicated," Kusaka would say, with some
understatement.

One time, Kusaka played host and guide, taking me along
with two architects visiting at the Toda Company, one from
Bangkok and the other from Dallas, Texas, who were studying
Japanese architectural design. He showed us the assorted small
shrines and temples in the neighborhood, as well as shops selling
old-fashioned Japanese ceramics, antiques, and folk crafts. The
tour also covered public parks and gardens, including one dating
back to the 17th century, the beautiful Rikugien, built around 1700
for the fifth Tokugawa shogun. The garden's name refers to the
six elements of traditional Japanese poetry, and tucked away in

Rikugien, Garden of the Daimyo, a short walk from my tiny apartment.

the garden are eighty-eight miniature scenes from famous poems. You couldn't take it all in in one day.

Kusaka also introduced us to a couple of small Japanese bars and restaurants in the neighborhood, where we sat on tatami floors and ate such delicacies as octopus, broiled eel, seasoned seaweed, and sashimi, and got drunk on Kirin beer and sake. It was a Japanese drinking party custom to get up and perform something—to show your *kakushi gei*, or hidden talent, as the Japanese said. So when my turn came, I sang the only songs I knew the complete words to: "The Star-Spangled Banner" and Elvis Presley's "I Can't Help Falling in Love with You." I sang them badly, which, I discovered, was the idea. If you made a fool of yourself, it relieved everyone else of the pressure to look good. The general idea of such drinking parties in Japan was to dissolve individual differences into a general friendly rapport; attempts to put on airs or show one's superiority were looked on as breaches of harmony and did not go over well. The Nail That Sticks Up Gets Hammered Down, as the old saying went. I was happy to learn that the quality of my singing kept me well within acceptable range.

Water for Tea

Needing more funds to finance my daily life, I found myself answering a help-wanted ad in the *Japan Times*, Tokyo's leading English-language daily, that went: "English Conversation Teacher wanted. American Native Speaker. Twelve-hundred yen an hour. Evenings and weekends. No experience necessary." The pay was what a twenty-year-old Japanese might earn working a full day.

The school was the Thomas Foreign Language Institute located in Ochanomizu in the eastern part of the city. Ochanomizu was a bustling university town, home to Meiji University, among others, and famous for its many used bookstores, usually crammed with students, teachers, and local company workers, standing and reading in the aisles.

It was also the location of the domed Holy Resurrection Cathedral, popularly known as Nikolai-do, an Eastern Orthodox Church founded by a Russian archbishop in the 19th century and designed by famed British architect Josiah Joseph Conder, where the Russian community of Tokyo, many of them descendants of refugees from the Russian Revolution, would congregate for weekend services.

The name Ochanomizu literally means "water for tea" and references the nearby Kanda River from which water was extracted to make the shogun's tea during the Edo period. But in 1965 the river was so polluted that anyone drinking the water was taking his life in his hands. Breathing was also an issue: such was the toxic, sulfurous odor and photochemical smog from interminable traffic jams that facemasks were de rigueur for Ochanomizu pedestrians.

* * *

My school, also known in Japanese as the Gaigo Gakuin, was

established by the Dominican Order in Japan and was in a six-story ferro-concrete structure on busy Suzuran-dori. There was a sign up on the lobby wall next to a painting of Jesus Christ gazing up at heaven that said, "Those interested in studying the bible are invited to free lessons."

I was greeted by the superintendent of the school, Father Arthur Beaulieu, a young, cherubic, endlessly cheerful French Canadian from the famous town of Charlevoix in Quebec on the St. Lawrence River, who conducted one of the shortest job interviews in history.

"Are you an American native speaker?" the Father asked me in a thick French Canadian accent.

"Yes, I am," I said. "I was born and bred in the United States."

"Good," he said. "When can you start?"

There were four hundred students enrolled in the school and a dozen teachers of various nationalities who taught classes in one of fifteen classrooms on floors two through five. But there were no other American native speakers, which made me somewhat of a novelty—and a prize.

The purpose of establishing the school was to attract Japanese high school and college students of English, offer them Bible lessons on the side, and then, hopefully, convert them to Christianity, a minuscule minority religion in Japan. Only about 1 percent of the population was Christian. So little was known of Christianity back then that some Japanese confused Jesus and Santa Claus, which made for some interesting department store window displays: Santa on the cross, Jesus in a sleigh with reindeer. For most Japanese, Christmas was just another day on the calendar. Years afterward it became what New Year's is in the West—an occasion for parties—which then evolved into a romantic time to spend with one's significant other. It later came to be said that more women in the capital lost their virginity on Christmas Eve than any other time of the year. Condom sales spiked during this period.

Father Beaulieu had come to Japan in 1958 at the age of twenty-eight, when, to hear him tell it, the city was a cheerless, unpleasant place. "There was great poverty," he recalled. "The houses were wood and corrugated tin. No paint on them. Very drab. You read Japanese literature about the cherry blossoms. But it was hard to spot cherry blossoms anywhere because so many cherry trees had been destroyed during the war. It was dangerous to walk in certain parts of Ueno Park. There were a lot of criminals and lots of homeless lived there. We were forbidden to walk across it because there were too many dangerous people."

When the school first opened, Bible-class attendance and the conversion rate had been good. At one point there were as many as ninety Bible-class students, and many wound up as converts.

That religion does have a history in Japan, dating back to the 16th century, when it was introduced by Portuguese and Spanish priests and then ruthlessly suppressed by the Tokugawa government. It enjoyed a second flourishing during the Meiji period when assimilating all things Western was seen as the key to modernization. The faith received yet a third boost during the Occupation when General MacArthur recruited 10,000 Episcopalian ministers from the United States to counter what he called the "low morality" of the people. The General was alarmed by the prevalence of open prostitution, driven by Japanese poverty and GI demand, as well as by growing drug use. It was reported that the general vowed to convert 70 million Japanese to Christianity. However, the final count of approximately 600,000 by Occupation's end fell well below expectations.

There were a few famous Christians in Japan. Six of the postwar prime ministers would be baptized. Yomiuri Giants baseball star Shigeo Nagashima had attended Rikkyo University, a Christian school where the players had to recite Christian prayers before each game. He and his wife had gotten married in the Dominican church on the Rikkyo Campus. But Father Beaulieu was skeptical that he had ever seriously read the Bible.

For Father Beaulieu, religion in Japan was more culture than anything else. He wasn't sure the Japanese people really believed in any of it. Historically, Buddhist temples were the census bureaus for the government and the center of village life in much of old Japan. There was no shortage of Shinto and Buddhist priests, whose main function was presiding over events, festivals, and exhibitions, which were an integral part of social life. People went to the Shinto shrine for weddings and for blessing newborn children. They went to the Buddhist temples for funerals. In the postwar era, however, Japanese also adopted the white wedding dress and the black tuxedo because they thought it looked "cool." It was a fashion statement. They would have a service at a Christian chapel, then change into formal Japanese dress for a Shinto ceremony. Sex before marriage was a moral issue related to social mores, not Christian-style guilt. Yet, at the same time, there was an underlying respect both for the many animistic deities, which Shinto holds are everywhere—in the lakes, the forests, the mountains—and are part of the mystery of existence, as well as for the Buddhist belief in reincarnation and the endless cycle of life.

"You have to understand the Japanese mindset," a friend of mine would later put it. "There is more chance of converting the entire Middle East to Christianity than there is of converting Japan. This is not just because of the prevalence of Buddhism and Shintoism, but because the Japanese already have their own religion: Japan and the idea of being Japanese."

This was reflected, he said, in beliefs or practices that came so naturally and subconsciously to the Japanese that most people never thought about them. They were—and are—part of everyday life, like saying *"itadakimasu"* before a meal. Although the phrase is not recognized as a religious act, it is actually meant to thank the *kami* or gods for the food. There are myriad other such verbal expressions scripted for a definite time and place: *"gochisosama"* after a meal, *"otsukaresama"* at the end of the workday, *"ojama-shimasu"* when entering someone's house or office, and so on.

From the year-end house cleaning to removing shoes on entering a house and pointing them toward the door, to laying out the futons so that nobody sleeps with his or her head to the north, to sweeping the front of the home every morning, or putting out salt mounds in front of homes or restaurants, Japan's everyday rituals have their roots in Shinto. Take them away, said my friend, and Japan might break down.

The emperor, in the Shinto scheme of things, was one of many deities, although he ranked at the top. He could be described as a kind of rice shaman, given to the people by his ancestors, duty bound to see that the rice harvest was a success each year. His divinity was inherent—a status that was not his to renounce regardless of how fervently MacArthur had wished him to do so.

In the face of all this, the Gaigo Gakuin forged on. The teachers were a motley crew. There was Dr. Aun Kyu Ki, a Burmese doctor doing advanced medical studies in Tokyo, who wanted to supplement his income by teaching English. Dr. Ki was a short, round-faced man from Rangoon who bubbled with excitement whenever he talked. But he was not fond of his Japanese hosts, he said. He remembered the war years in Burma when the Japanese had occupied the country and, he said, their brutality had been unmatched. Nearly two decades later, he still hadn't forgotten it. What bothered him was that he didn't think the Japanese felt any remorse about the way they had behaved.

"These people are bloody racist," he said to me one summer evening as we stood on the sidewalk outside the school during a break. "They are the most racist in all of Asia."

"Why do you say that?" I asked, taken aback at the intensity of his anger.

"I'll tell you why," he said, puffing on a Hi-Lite cigarette. "I was educated at Oxford. I speak perfect King's English. Yet, many students do not want me as a teacher and transfer out of my classes because I don't look like a Westerner. My skin is too dark."

On the other hand, he told me, he thought very highly of

Japan's medical schools and its pharmaceuticals, which of course is why he came to the country.

"So, it's not all bad," he said, with a shrug.

There was Jurgen Beck, a young German who was traveling around the world and earning money for a ticket to his next destination, Vladivostok, by teaching English. Jerry, as he was known, spoke English extremely well, albeit with a thick German accent.

"*Ve are gung to get vet,*" he would say when it started to rain.

Jerry pretended to be American, because it got him more teaching jobs. He was also a muscled weightlifter and a womanizer, whose tall, dark good looks attracted an inordinate number of young Japanese female university students to the school. Father Beaulieu had allowed him to stay in a room on the top floor, or rather, the attic, rent-free. It was where Jerry conducted most of his extracurricular activities, although such were strictly against house rules.

"There are five million girls in this city," Father Beaulieu would say. "Pick any of them you wish. You don't need girls from the school. They are here for other reasons."

But Jerry ignored the proscription and as far as I know Father Beaulieu never pressed the issue. The worst comeuppance the ersatz "American" experienced was when an angry waitress at a coffee shop in the neighborhood, one of his ex-paramours, doused his tea with Tabasco sauce.

Father Beaulieu himself was one of the happiest men I have ever met. He always had a smile on his face. Every time I saw him, he positively beamed with benevolence and good cheer. I never saw him frown. He said he was happy because he was doing God's work.

But he also staunchly advised against involvement with young Japanese women, not only students at the school. He thought that those who sought out foreign men had ulterior motives, that they just wanted a ticket to the richer West.

"Come to Japan, have fun, and make money," he told me. "But

don't stay here. It's a backwater. Don't waste your time. Go back to your own country and make a life. Japan is no place for a young foreign man. It's a place for old people to come to when they retire. Don't stay. You will lose yourself."

* * *

I taught English to a variety of students. I use the word "taught" very loosely here because I had no idea what I was doing. I had absolutely no qualifications and little experience save with Dr. Sato and the group at Toda Construction, where all we did was talk. But nobody seemed to care. I was a native speaker. It was enough that I sit and talk with them and correct their own attempts at speaking the language, as Father Beaulieu had instructed.

None of my students seemed remotely interested in being converted to Christianity. There was one chubby, rosy-cheeked student, a sophomore at the elite Ochanomizu Women's University, whose English was quite good and who was forthright in expressing her skepticism toward the church.

She would ask me questions like, "Why do Americans capitalize 'God' when they don't even know he exists? What kind of father would send his son to die? It doesn't make any sense. Neither does the Virgin Mary."

She told me that she admired Bertrand Russell for his reasoned rejection of Christianity and could simply not agree with Thomas Aquinas's view. She gave me a copy of Russell's 1935 book *Religion and Science* with a leaf from the summer mountain resort of Karuizawa to use as a page marker and asked me to read it so we could have a discussion, which I did. I had never heard of Bertrand Russell until then.

Some days later she elaborated her secular opinions in what turned out to be a fairly one-sided discussion about the Dark Ages, the Inquisition, and the weakness of beliefs founded solely on blind faith. I had been raised a Presbyterian but had stopped going to church in junior high school and had never really considered the issues that she was raising, although after wading through Russell's cold logic and heavy prose I found myself agreeing with her. Nevertheless, given who my employer was, I was compelled to add to the discussion.

"Well, then," I said, my brow furrowed as if in deep thought, "do Japanese really believe Emperor Hirohito is descended from the Sun Goddess?" This was one of the very few things I knew about the Japanese Imperial Throne.

"The Emperor is a war criminal," she replied. "The Americans should have put him in prison instead of keeping him on the throne as their puppet."

* * *

The Ochanomizu students were my window into the heart of the culture that had come to fascinate me. I realized I had much more to learn from them than the other way around. My encounter with the jarringly frank Bertrand Russell acolyte made me want to learn more about Japanese history, and so I starting reading Occupation-era journalists like Mark Gayn (*Japan Diary*) and Russell Brines (*MacArthur's Japan*), coming to understand, among other things, the reasons that GHQ officials had decided not to charge the emperor along with Tojo and others but instead to keep him on his throne as a continuing "symbol" of the nation.

My experience teaching employees at Mitsubishi Heavy Industries, which I also began around that time, was equally instructive. The company, famous for its wartime production of Japan's Zero fighter planes, was one of the world's leading shipbuilders. The lessons took place at 5 p.m. Saturday afternoon because that was the only time their work schedule would allow.

My students were the elite soldiers in the Japanese *salaryman* army, the vanguard of the emerging economic miracle. They were all dressed in the uniform of the era: dark suits, white shirts, and

Japanese students in Ochanomizu survived my attempts to teach them English.

understated ties. One of them, a Mr. Suzuki, a polite, soft-spoken diminutive man in his mid-thirties with rimless gold-frame spectacles and hair combed flat, was a designer of oil supertankers. It was Japanese attention to detail, Mr. Suzuki told me, that accounted for the extraordinary quality of Japanese supertankers. Suzuki-san had been offered the job of chief designer by a Scandinavian shipbuilding company, at a salary four times what he was making in Japan. They would move him and his wife and two children to Oslo, set them up in a beautiful new house in the suburbs (a vast improvement over the small and cramped quarters he and his family shared in the Mitsubishi housing complex), and put his kids into the finest school in the country. He would go to and from work in a chauffeur-driven car. What reason could anyone find to turn such an offer down?

"I'm Japanese," he explained. "I belong in Japan. I want Japan to be the country that manufactures the best products in the world—TVs, automobiles, cameras, and supertankers. That's why I am staying. If I went to Norway, everyone would say I am a traitor."

Evidently my surprise showed on my face.

"You're an American," he said. "A young American. So you probably can't understand what I am talking about."

Ryogoku: Sumo Town

My education in things Japanese took another big leap in the summer of 1965 when the Ochanomizu school passed on to me a request to teach English conversation to a group of bankers at the Fukagawa Branch of the Fuji Bank near Ryogoku train station. That was in eastern Tokyo, in the heart of old Edo—Shitamachi— as the Japanese called the older neighborhoods. The place reeked of history and Japanese culture. Located on the banks of the Sumida River, Ryogoku was where in 1703 high-ranking shogunate official Kira Kozukenosuke, the villain of a legendary tale known as *Chushingura*, was slain by forty-seven samurai to avenge the death of their master before they committed ritual suicide (*seppuku*) by order of the authorities. Part of Kira's mansion is preserved there in a public park.

Ryogoku was also the heartland of sumo, the ancient sport of Japan, dating back almost to mythical times. It began as a religious Shinto ritual, performed in the Imperial Court, in which calling down and wrestling with the gods had something to do with prospects for a bountiful harvest. It morphed into a popular spectacle in the Edo period, with out-of-work samurai, or *ronin*, manning the lists. Kuramae Kokugikan, the National Sumo Stadium where three of the six annual tournaments took place, was just across the Sumida River from the Ryogoku train station on the Sobu Line. The area was home to a number of sumo wrestling stables, as well as factories, small-scale workshops, and frail-looking wooden houses with paper window shades where workers and craftsmen lived.

The area had been leveled in the horrific American B-29 fire-bombing raids of March 9–10, 1945, that claimed 80,000 lives, as I discovered from reading a book called *I Saw Tokyo Burning*, a riveting eyewitness narrative by French journalist Robert Guillain. Generated by the rising heat of the flames, violent, hurricane-force winds sent sparks flying, igniting everything in their reach. People, houses, pets burst into flames on the spot. Those who made it to the nearby canals or rivers were asphyxiated from smoke inhalation or boiled alive in the steaming water.

One of my bank students, a polite, soft-spoken middle-aged executive who had lived through that terrible experience, said, "I would rather have died in the atomic bomb. That's how bad the Tokyo firebombing was. At least in Hiroshima or Nagasaki, you died instantly."

"The next morning, there were blackened corpses littered everywhere," he went on matter-of-factly. "The river was filled with them and so were the streets, which blocked bicycles from riding through. You couldn't even walk. The smell was horrible. The wind was still blowing, and the air was thick with swirling ashes from the corpses. All my relatives died. The local authorities picked up body parts, bones, and ashes and assembled them all at the shrine. Those who wanted bones could come and pick them up, but nobody knew which bones belonged to whom."

As an American, I was mortified. I didn't know what to say. Sensing my embarrassment, he said simply, "It was war. What can you say? It's in the past."

The area was rebuilt after the war, new sumo stables going up to replace those leveled in the bombings. Since the bank was a sponsor of the sport, bank employees, my "students," had access to the sumo stables, or *beya*, as they are called, and they were kind enough to arrange for me to attend a practice session at one nearby. They led me to a large nondescript wooden building with the name and crest of the stable on the front door. Inside was a small dirt-floor ring (*dohyo*) used for daily practice. We were ushered in and seated at a slightly raised tatami floor adjacent to the ring, where we were served tea and cakes while we watched young sumo wrestlers, clad only in sashes called *mawashi*, grapple with one another. I was astonished at the sheer size of them.

"They eat a special stew called *chankonabe* [a compilation of every source of every kind of nutrition] to help them gain weight," said my guide from the bank. "They also drink a lot of sake and beer. . . . Some of these *sekitori* are so obese they need help from an assistant when they go to the toilet," he added helpfully. "Their arms can't extend all the way to the rear to clean themselves."

A senior wrestler, or *sekitori*, corrected the young wrestlers' form by issuing violent blows across their backs and thighs with a *shinai*, or bamboo sword, eliciting cries of pain from the participants.

"Thwack, Thwack," followed by grunts of pain. "THWACK!"

"Physical punishment is part of their education. It makes them better wrestlers," said one of my students, with a certain amount of perverse pride.

I was invited to several tournaments at Kuramae and became a fan of the top two grand champions of the time, Koki Taiho and Kashiwado. Taiho was already being hailed as the greatest sumo wrestler of the postwar era. He was twenty-three at the time, standing 6'2" and weighing 300 pounds, and had already won eleven tourneys. His name meant "Phoenix" or, loosely, "Giant Bird." Or "Big Bird," a name that predated the Sesame Street character by five years. The son of a Ukrainian refugee from the Russian Revolution and a Japanese woman, he had been born on the northern island Sakhalin but moved to Hokkaido in 1945 after the Soviet Union took control of the territory. Taiho was raised by his mother and never again saw his father, who had returned to Moscow.

Taiho entered sumo in 1956, recruited by a sumo scout while working as a lumberjack. He joined the Nishonoseki stable. At the time he weighed only 155 pounds. He rose quickly through the ranks and won his first tournament in 1960. It was the first of his record thrity-two tournament championships and earned him promotion to second-highest rank of *ozeki*. A year later, following two more tourney titles, he was promoted to *yokozuna*, becoming the youngest grand champion in the history of sumo. By then, thanks to a lot of *chankonabe* and beer, his weight had increased to 330 pounds. He trained four hours a day, pounding a wooden pillar with his hands, slamming into it with his chest and head, and doing countless knee bends. His forte was the *yorikiri*, or straight forward force out.

He was also fair skinned and handsome, with jet black hair, and had a flood of marriage proposals from female fans.

Taiho's archrival was Kashiwado, a 6'2", 310-pound mountain of muscle from the northern prefecture of Yamagata. Born as Tsuyoshi Togashi, he was recruited by the Isenoumi stable in 1954 at the age of sixteen and promoted to *yokozuna* at the same time as Taiho.

Sumo was a difficult sport with a long tradition, one of carefully graded hierarchies. It took time to advance, which made the dual promotions of Taiho and Kashiwado all the more remarkable.

Kashiwado, whose own specialty was also the *yorikiri*, had bested Taiho in individual competition up until that time. But he had only one tourney championship under his belt, finishing runner up in a number of others. He sat out four tourneys in a row from January to July 1963, earning the nickname "the glass yokozuna." But he made a spectacular return in September, winning his first fourteen matches in a row and setting up a finale with Taiho that sumo fans talked about for years to come. Taiho had won so many tourneys by that time (fifteen) that most people wanted to see Kashiwado win, including an NHK TV commentator, a retired sumoist, who said as much on the air. Kashiwado prevailed, forcing Taiho out of the ring in a matter of seconds, to thunderous cheers.

Not everyone was celebrating, however. Famed novelist

Shintaro Ishihara (a future Diet man and governor of Tokyo) had watched the match and, in a contentious newspaper op-ed published the next morning in the *Nikkan Sports*, deemed it a fake. A *yao-cho* as the term for a fix went in Japanese. He charged that Taiho had intentionally lost to help further the rivalry between the two wrestlers and generate more interest in sumo, which had waned somewhat in the onslaught of championships by Taiho, who had won eleven of the previous twelve tournaments.

Ishihara was no ordinary writer. Two months before graduating from Hitotsubashi University he had won the Akutagawa Prize (Japan's most prestigious literary award) for his novel *Taiyo no Kisetsu* (Season of the Sun). His brother Yujiro had played a role in the screen adaptation of the novel and become Japan's hottest movie star. He and Shintaro, who by then had a number of best-selling books under his belt, became the center of a youth cult in Japan. An indication of Shintaro's lofty opinion of himself could be found later in life in an interview with *Playboy* magazine (1990) where he said, "If I had remained a movie director, I can assure you that I would have at least become a better one than Akira Kurosawa."

Ishihara would later become an ardent ultranationalist, famous for his controversial remarks about foreigners in Japan. Some observers speculated that he had singled Taiho out for criticism because of his Russian heritage. The combative Ishihara's charge infuriated Taiho, and he protested to the sumo association so vigorously that the sumo elders prepared a lawsuit against Ishihara. Ishihara was given a choice: apologize or face a civil lawsuit in court. Ishihara chose to write a letter of apology, one of the few times in his colorful career that he was forced to eat his words.

The irony of this notorious incident was that it drew Taiho and Kashiwado close together outside the *dohyo*. They developed a genuine friendship, which continued until Kashiwado's death in 1996. Taiho would go on to win a total of thirty-two tournaments before retiring in 1971, including six in a row twice. Kashiwado won only five, but he was runner-up fifteen times and appeared as a *yokozuna* in forty-seven tournaments, a feat that put him sixth on the all-time list.

My friends in Ryogoku related the Ishihara contretemps to me in great detail, but little did I suspect that the man himself would one day set his sights on me as well, but that is a story that comes later.

Izakaya Nights

I had a girlfriend in Ryogoku. My first real Japanese girlfriend. She worked at an *izakaya*, one of those vibrant working-class smoke-filled pubs you see all over the city, red lantern outside, thick wooden beams inside, tables on raised tatami platforms, and waiters and waitresses wearing kimono and *yukata* (a light cotton robe). The students and I always went to this one particular *izakaya* after class. We'd order beer and dried squid and *konomiyaki/tamagoyaki*. One of the waitresses was a perpetually laughing, flirtatious girl of around twenty, with rosy cheeks, named Chako. She was quite fetching in her work kimono, with her hair pinned back and flashing white teeth. Her father, a bald-headed man behind the counter, owned and ran the place. He approached our table one night and asked if it might not be possible for me to come to his residence on the second floor of the *izakaya* every Saturday afternoon to teach his daughter English. It wasn't difficult to say yes.

So the following Saturday I began the "lessons" as I euphemistically called them. Chako had some proficiency in English, which she had studied at university. She liked to talk about "the" Pat Boone, Elvis Presley, and the Ventures. After each lesson, her father would prepare a dinner of steak and vegetables, served in the upstairs parlor where the lessons took place.

It was quite clear to me that she was interested in more than

Red-lantered *izakaya*, one of the great Japanese inventions. A cross between an Irish pub and a tapas bar.

just learning English. She dropped hints about how she liked to go out to clubs at night to dance with her friends.

So one evening, after a few weeks of lessons, I asked her out to dinner at the Sands Club in Roppongi on the top floor of the Hardy Barracks, where the Far East headquarters of the *Stars and Stripes* newspaper was situated. When she showed up at the appointed place, the Shitamachi girl was gone and a *moga*—"modern girl"—was in her place. She had her hair down, below her shoulders. She was wearing a tight red dress that was obviously uncomfortable for her and was teetering on high heels. She looked like a completely different person.

We drank a few cocktails, danced to the music of the touring Liverpool Beatles, a Beatles cover group, ate dinner, then went up on the roof to look at the Tokyo night sky. Tokyo Tower was lit up in bright orange just a few blocks away. A few more such dates ensued. One was at Nicola's Restaurant in Roppongi where she had a pepperoni pizza for the first time in her life, and the insouciant

Italian American proprietor Nicola Zappetti (a man who later become the central character in my book *Tokyo Underworld*), walked by and said, "Nice broad you've got, kid." On another date we went to Anne Dinken's Jewish Kosher Deli, the first of its kind in Japan, in Akasaka. It was run by a brash and sassy divorcee from New York who trained her Japanese waiters to be just like their Carnegie Deli, New York counterparts: surly and sarcastic and prone to slam your food on the table in front of you. She berated us for not eating our enormous pastrami and rye sandwiches fast enough. On our third date we went to a dance hall in Asakusa where we did the twist. Then we took a boat ride on the Sumida River passing under the Ryogoku Bridge. This in turn led to a fumbling romantic encounter in a back-street Asakusa *ryokan.*

By the following Saturday, instead having of our usual lesson, Chako left word she wanted to meet at the Senso-ji temple in Asakusa, nearby. Senso-ji was Japan's oldest and grandest Buddhist temple, dedicated to the goddess of Mercy. And pigeons.

When I arrived to find her waiting at the famous giant red Kaminarimon—Thunder Gate—with its massive paper lantern painted in vivid red and black to suggest thunderclouds and lightning, the *kuki* (air), as the Japanese say, had changed.

Instead of her usual English-lesson garb of jeans and T-shirt, she was clad in an elaborate, expensive kimono and wore a solemn expression instead of her usual cheerful smile.

She led me inside the Nakamise-dori with its small shops and stalls, selling all sorts of souvenirs—fans, woodblock prints, Buddhist scrolls, Godzilla T-shirts—and fortune-telling stands. It was about the length of two football fields and jam packed with visitors.

She stopped at one of the good-luck-charm stands and bought me a small *omamori*, wrapped in a small, silky cloth attached to a string.

Then we walked down to the five-story pagoda and main hall at the vast, open center of the grounds, filled with pigeons. Standing there she turned and said she wanted to ask me a question. A serious question.

"Fire away," I said.

"I have a boyfriend," she began, nodding in the affirmative at my raised eyebrows. "He asked me to go to Europe with him. I said yes. He bought the tickets. But this was before I met you. What should I do?"

It was the last thing I had expected her to say. A boyfriend? A trip to Europe? What should I do? Whoa. Wait a minute. I was a little taken aback by her confession. On the other hand, I was going regularly to the Happy Valley—nothing serious, but that was information that I had yet to share with her. So I guess she wasn't the only disingenuous one in the relationship.

It was late November and a chill filled the air. A gust of wind blew the autumn leaves across the square.

A few steps away, people were bathing themselves in holy smoke emanating from a large incense-burning vat in the inner courtyard, smoke that would supposedly cure all manner of physical and mental ailments. I felt like jumping in.

I hemmed and hawed and finally opted for humor.

"Foreign travel is a great way to expand your horizons," I said, lamely. "You should not miss out on this opportunity. It will be a good for your education."

It was obviously the wrong thing to say because a dead, cold silence followed. Then she suddenly turned and, bowing ever so slightly, walked away, leaving me alone with the pigeons.

After the next week's session at Fuji Bank, the students and I went as usual to the *izakaya*. Judging from the way Chako slammed the glass of water on the table in front of me, splashing water all over the front of my cheap suit, she was obligated to serve. I guessed she was still mad. When we got up to leave, she handed me a note in English that I read on the train ride back to Fuchu.

"I will stop your lesson from now. Sincerely Chako."

And that was the end of that. She managed to be absent every single time after that the Fuji Bank class visited her restaurant.

Holy smoke at Asakusa Kannon complex, or Senso-ji, as it is also known.

Her father still spoke to me though . . . and why not? He was probably very relieved not having to contemplate a *gaijin* son-in-law.

In Father Beaulieu's view of the world, I was lucky. Liaisons between young Japanese girls and young foreign men, he reminded me, were doomed to failure.

"Be grateful that you emerged unscathed," he said. "You're one of the fortunate ones."

"Meet Me at the Hour of the Horse"

Kusaka was a practitioner of the martial arts; he had a black belt in aikido and was an aficionado of samurai lore. It was he who turned me on to Miyamoto Musashi, the famous 16th-century swordsman, taking me to a day-long marathon showing of a five-part Toei film series based on his life, produced in the early 1960s. We sat, the two of us, in the back row of a dingy side-street theater in Ginza and he explained to me what was going on. It was an eye-opening experience.

Miyamato Musashi was one of the most accomplished swords-men of all time, but one who also mastered art forms like calligra-phy, painting, sculpture, the tea ceremony, and flower arranging. Before his death he wrote *The Book of Five Rings*, a contemplation on the life of a samurai that has endured to this day (and for a time in the 1980s, during the great Japanese Bubble, became required reading in Wall Street boardrooms). Throughout the book, Musashi implies that one who follows the Way of the Warrior must also set out to master art forms apart from the sword and seek higher consciousness as well as skill in combat.

The film series, based on the epic novel by Eiji Yoshikawa, traces Musashi's exploits starting at the age of fourteen in the his-toric battle of Sekigahara in 1600. This conflict set the stage for the Tokugawa shogunate, the reign of the family that ruled Japan from 1603 to 1868. Musashi seeks perfection in swordsmanship, inventing a style of wielding a long sword (*katana*) and a short sword (*wakizashi*) together. He bests one opponent after another, climaxing in a famous duel on Ganryujima, an island between Honshu and Kyushu, with archrival Sasaki Kojiro, whom he defeats using a boat oar that is inches longer than Sasaki's sword. He also seeks spiritual enlightenment, spending three years in a castle repository reading books containing all of man's knowledge.

The Musashi series is filled with cultural touchstones: a flower-arranging master who relies on *ki*, an important Japanese word that means heart, mind, spirit, and a number of other related things, and whose work Musashi identifies by noticing that the stems are cut with a sword, not scissors, unlike the work of other flower-arranging *sensei*; a watercolor print Musashi so admires that he refuses to take as a gift when offered because he considers himself unworthy of possessing such beauty; a craftsman spinning a perfect bowl from clay reminding Musashi he still has far to go in his quest for personal excellence; Musashi preparing to write with a black ink brush, but following the principle of Zen Buddhist calligraphy where one must first clear one's mind before executing the stroke.

The films also featured traditional Japanese music—the *shakuhachi,* the *koto,* and the *shamisen*—as well as the beautiful silk tapestry and the striking period costumes. I was made aware of the old class structure of the society during the long feudal Tokugawa period: samurai, farmers, artisans, and merchants in descending order. I learned about the Chinese zodiac hours ("Meet me at the hour of the horse," Musashi says in arranging a duel with a rival), and the penchant for incessant formal apologies—including one or more used by samurai before they lopped off a rival's head.

Then there were all the lines expressing samurai philosophy:

"A warrior is ready even while sleeping."
"The sword is without compassion."
"My death will be a testament to the life of the sword."

Some of these were delivered while Musashi is picking flies out of the air with chopsticks.

In one incredible scene that ranges across snow-covered rice paddies near Ichijo-ji temple outside of Kyoto, Musashi dispatches no fewer than seventy-three samurai seeking revenge for the defeat of their master in battle. He has accepted their challenge, he says, because "I am a samurai and I cannot run away. If I did it would bring shame upon the name of Musashi. The path of the warrior is severe."

At one point he says, "I have given up all desire. I live only for the sword." But after his defeat of archrival Sasaki, confirming his indomitability in all of Japan, he lays the sword down and returns to his paramour, the lovely Otsu, who has been waiting for him with the patience of Odysseus' wife.

As my friend Kusaka-san put it at the end of the last scene, "If you want to understand Japan, know the way of Musashi."

Inspired by all this, I asked Kusaka to teach me something of his martial art, aikido. In our first lesson, conducted at the hour of the horse, he threw me halfway across the Toda Construction Company dojo, even though at 5'11" and 155 pounds I was 3 inches taller and 20 pounds heavier than he.

"I am a samurai and I cannot run away," I said, getting back up for more.

Then he threw me across the *dojo* again.

"The path of the warrior is severe," he said solemnly.

It was great stuff. I ate it up.

* * *

Musashi was the trigger for the addiction to Japanese movies that I developed during this period. I particularly liked the all-night movie showings at the Shinjuku Toei Gekijo, which featured yakuza films such as the highly popular *ninkyo* (chivalry) series, which began in 1964. The storylines usually centered around a loyal old-school yakuza avenging the honor of a murdered *oyabun* (boss) by purifying his sword and doing battle with sneering, gun-toting villains in rival gangs, often amidst falling cherry blossoms and background *enka* (traditional ballad) music. The brooding, stoic Toei star Ken Takakura was usually the main attraction, as he made over ten films a year. Never did the blood flow as much as when he was on screen, the climactic battles always filled with severed limbs, geysers of red shooting from sliced carotid arteries, and other gore. I sat there taking it all in, drinking cans of Kirin beer sold at the concession stand and munching dried eel. It certainly fueled my fascination for the world of yakuza.

The Takakura films, as with the Musashi feature, offered important insights into the nation's psyche—something that was not often understood. In the post-Olympic era, entry into the ranks of corporate Japan was seen as something to aspire to. It was everyone's dream to go to Tokyo University and ultimately

make department head in a publicly listed company or government ministry. At the same time, however, people idolized the
Lone Wolf characters played by Takakura and others because they
rejected established societal paths in which individuals had to
subsume their identities to the group and instead went their own,
independent ways, living outside the box and often outside the
law. In history and folklore these men were often the ones who
saved the village, the culture, and the country at large. The biggest
hero of the Meiji period was the samurai Sakamoto Ryoma who
led a revolution to topple the feudal *bakufu*—the government that
supported the Tokugawa shogun—and modernize Japan, before
he was attacked by assassins and murdered at an inn in Kyoto. His
story has been told and retold in films, TV dramas, and books.

While many Japanese resented the strictures and excesses of
corporate life and were envious of those who succeeded outside
the Establishment, for the most part they were in fact deeply risk
averse. Not many were willing to defy the system. Parents would
rarely encourage a son who rejected the elite path to organizational success and instead aspired to start his own company, or a
daughter willing to risk throwing it all away to become a singer.
This is a gross generalization, of course. Takakura was applying
for a managerial post at Toei Studios after graduating from Meiji
University when he auditioned for a role on impulse, and the rest
is history. Japan's most popular actor today, Koji Yakusho, once
worked in the Chiyoda Ward municipal office in Tokyo and quit
to become an actor. But you get my drift. I hope. People seemed to
feel a certain safety in the idea of Japanese homogeneity, of a faceless majority, with everyone going forward together "at 35 miles
per hour," as former *Time* Tokyo Bureau Chief Frank Gibney once
put it. And it is still true today to a great extent.

Other celluloid attractions were the Saturday afternoon features at the Toho Theaters in Shinjuku, starring Yuzo Kayama
(known as Japan's Pat Boone), singing and playing his *eleki gitaa*
(electric guitar), and the action-romance films of Nikkatsu Studios

Toei top stars Koji Tsuruta [left] and Ken Takakura [right].

star Yujiro Ishihara, the so-called James Dean of Japan. Second-run houses offered up classics like Akira Kurosawa's *Stray Dog, Yojimbo,* and *The Seven Samurai* and Yasujiro Ozu's *Tokyo Story* and *An Autumn Afternoon.* My Japanese was still a work in progress so the film reviews in the English-language *Japan Times* by Donald Richie helped me understand the sometimes-confusing plots and put things in context. Such films gave me insight into the optimism and despair of postwar culture. One interesting fact they revealed was that under MacArthur's GHQ policy Japanese film-makers were not allowed to depict any evidence of the Occupation presence. That meant no American people or signs in English on screen. Later, after the GHQ had gone home, films like *Gate of Flesh*, *Red Line Base*, and *Battle Without Honor and Humanity* made up for lost time by portraying Americans as brutal thugs and drunken rapists. (French films, I might add, were also extremely popular in Tokyo. *Plein Soleil*, *Le Samourai*, and others featuring Alain Delon were huge hits. I could understand the gist of the dialogue using my high school French, and the *kanji* I was studying at Sophia helped me to read the subtitles.)

In addition to film, I immersed myself in Japanese novels like Yasunari Kawabata's *Yukiguni* (Snow Country) in Japanese, with the help of a dictionary. There was that famous first line:

国境の長いトンネルを抜けると雪国であった。
"The train came out of the long border tunnel—and there was the snow country."

I could actually read and understand the damn thing, although it took me three months to get through it. Subsequently I went on to *Kikkyo* (Homecoming) by Jiro Osaragi, in English, as well as *Kagi* (The Key) by Junichiro Tanizaki—alternating them with novels by Tolstoy, Dostoyevsky, and Turgenev, which I was also discovering. For the first time in my life I was taking my education seriously.

* * *

Kusaka-san liked to patronize one particular establishment, a bar near the station where he had a thing going with the *mama-san*. (In fact, he would later marry her.) The lady in question was a pleasant, attractive woman in her late twenties. The same could not be said of her stable of hostesses of various shapes and sizes. Unfortunately, Japanese proprieties dictated that I sit there and buy them drinks, let them pour my beer, and engage in mindless chatter all evening while Kusaka talked with his loved one. Then at the end of the evening, the *mama-san* would produce a bill of unsparing size, which I was expected to split with my friend. We both had jobs and money in our pockets. It was only right that we spend it on others less fortunate, like the women who worked in the bar. They were not there to serve us, I discovered. It was the other way around. That was the way things were done in Tokyo's *mizu shobai*, or "water trade," scene.

I did this for a while—to be polite and to repay Kusaka's kindnesses. Despite his sixty-hour-plus workweeks, he did not make a whole hell of a lot more than I did as an English-conversation teacher. But in truth, I was rapidly depleting my funds, and, as I had begun to discover, there were more satisfying (and cost-effective) ways to spend my leisure time. In those days, a favorite sport among foreign men was the exchange of stories about quirky encounters with Japanese women. Listening to the Lotharios describe their adventures, I was given to doubt either their veracity or the taste in men of the women they described—until I had my own stories to tell.

Often young women would come up to me in a coffee shop and ask if it would be okay to speak my native language in front of me. One junior high English teacher read out the request from a piece of paper she had carefully inscribed in advance. I never found occasion to say no.

Then there was the girl who knocked on my door one evening, introduced herself, and presented me with a fifth of Johnny Walker Black. She was the maid to a wealthy family, as it turned out, who had been out shopping, seen me on the train, and followed me home.

I could not bring myself to turn the poor girl away. Besides, it had been quite some time since I had any prime whisky in the house.

A couple of enterprising young ladies, sisters, would

circumvent the difficulty of my not owning a telephone by calling the red coin-operated public telephone at the fruit and vegetable stand across the street and having the proprietor, a plump, jovial middle-aged lady with gold teeth, shout up to me and ask if it was OK for the girls to visit. It was from my acquaintance with the sisters, whose primary interest seemed ostensibly to be practicing their limited knowledge of English, that I began to suspect the presence of an apartment-cleaning gene in Japanese women. More than once in my absence these girls somehow got the key to my apartment from the landlord—a man whom even I did not know how to contact—and washed the dishes (or should I say the lone dish), swept the tatami, and took out the garbage.

Kusaka-san told me the whole neighborhood knew the details of my comings and goings, including my social life, thanks to the lady at the fruit and vegetable stand, who, I later discovered, held the title of Neighborhood Watchperson—an important position appointed by the local *chonokai*, a neighborhood association formed to keep the community operating at peak efficiency and help out in times of trouble—to fight fires, to organize funerals and festivals, to aid the sick, the disabled, and the elderly, and so forth—and to keep an eye on strange foreigners. It was a feudal tradition that dated back centuries. I would be coming back home from school, and *oba-san* would wave and say, "You had visitors today." I would go up the stairs and open the door to find my little abode spotlessly clean and perhaps a little cake from the bakery near the station waiting for me on my solitary table.

Times have changed, of course, and the novelty surrounding foreign men has largely worn off. Today's more independent and liberated women might understandably take offense at the above account, related here solely in the interest of accurate reporting. Many, many years later, in fact, I would anger the Japanese staff members in the American Chamber of Commerce in Japan by publishing a story in the ACCJ magazine about the Tokyo-based American lawyer and renowned netsuke collector Raymond

Bushell. Bushell had first come to Japan as a Merchant Marine captain immediately after the war, arriving at the small port of Shiotsu in southern Honshu, where he was given a teenage concubine by the town mayor and chief Shinto priest for the duration of his stay. The priest even "married" them for appearance's sake, conducting a ceremony at the town shrine but putting the groom on the left-hand side of the bride as opposed to the customary right, a sleight of hand, as it were, which, according to the priest, technically invalidated the whole affair. The women at the ACCJ took offense at this depiction of Japanese womanhood and demanded it be removed from the *Journal* website, which it soon was.

"Japanese Politics Is All about Money"

Sophia was a leading Japanese university established by the Jesuits in 1913, with a campus near Yotsuya Station and the new Hotel New Otani, all built on what had been samurai ground. It had a substantial international division with an eclectic student body—sons and daughters of diplomats, businessmen, journalists, and missionaries based in Tokyo, overseas exchange students, transients, scholars, world travelers, and a couple of ex-military people like me. Alumni included a future prime minister (Morihiro Hosokawa) and a hugely popular singer named Judy Ongg, who would have one of the biggest pop songs in Japanese musical history "Miserarete (Love is Talking to Me)."

My personal favorite on the faculty was a political science professor named Kan Ori, a homuncular PhD from Indiana University who taught courses in Japanese political history, the Japanese constitution, and the postwar Occupation. Few students I knew at Sophia were interested in this field of study, but Professor Ori, who habitually closed his eyes and smiled when he began to speak, had a way of making what many thought a dry subject extremely interesting. One example was his discussion of the internecine war within the GHQ for the future of Japan.

One faction, Ori told us, was led by Colonel Charles Kades, of GS1, an Ivy League lawyer and FDR New Dealer who led the movement to make Japan the Switzerland of Asia. He had a principal role in drafting the new democratic postwar constitution, which gave women equal rights, redistributed land, and supported unions.

Opposing him was General Charles Willoughby, one of SCAP head General Douglas MacArthur's "Bataan boys" and head of the G-2 Intelligence division. His goal was to make Japan a "Bulwark against Communism," for which purpose he hired Japanese yakuza from the black markets to suppress communist "agitators," who were then quite active in Japan.

Kades, who thought Willoughby a fascist, and Willoughby, who regarded Kades as a "pinko commie," did not form a mutual admiration society. Willoughby hired a Tokyo police detective to spy on Kades and chronicle his private life. It turned out that Kades, a married man whose wife was in New York City undergoing treatment for cancer, was carrying on a passionate love affair with the wife of a member of the aristocracy, one who was indirectly implicated in a massive bribery scandal that brought down the Ashida socialist government supported by Kades. Willoughby used this evidence to ruin Kades's GS career and foster the success of what came to be known as the Reverse Course, which helped put Japan's conservatives in power for the next half century and more. Scandals, intrigue, spies, and sex—whoever said that political science was dull? It was astonishing to learn how the fate of postwar Japan hinged, in significant part, on an illicit romance.

It was Professor Ori who approached me about tutoring the well-known political reporter for the mass-circulation daily *Yomiuri Shimbun*, Tsuneo Watanabe. Watanabe needed an English-conversation teacher to prepare for an assignment in Washington, DC, he told me. Intrigued, I immediately said yes.

The *Yomiuri Shimbun* was Japan's largest daily with a staggering circulation of about twelve million copies counting morning and evening editions. That was double the combined circulation of the *New York Times*, the *Wall Street Journal*, the *New York Daily News*, the *New York Post*, and the *Washington Post*. It was a conservative newspaper whose top rival in Japan was the liberal *Asahi Shimbun*, with a circulation nearly as wide as the *Yomiuri*'s. (Watanabe contemptuously called it the *Akai Shimbun*: The Red Newspaper.) Nine out of ten Japanese households had breakfast with a newspaper, and most commuters traveled the distance to work buried in its pages. Delivering that paper into the household mailbox every morning was a full-time, fully grown employee of a newspaper sales company. The stop-start whine of a newspaper-laden motorbike at 5 a.m. served as a familiar wake-up call in Tokyo's neighborhoods, including my own. In Japan, unlike in the US, there were no amateur part-time paperboys (who could go on from there to become self-made men as in the Horatio Alger epics).

Watanabe, then in his early forties and silver-haired, was one of Japan's leading journalists. He wrote a twice-a-week column that also appeared in the English-language version of the *Yomiuri*. He interviewed the high and mighty in the Japanese political world, as well as important visitors from the United States. He was soon going to be transferred to Washington, DC to take over the *Yomiuri Shimbun* bureau there and needed to brush up his conversation skills and knowledge of political terms in English before going.

Over the course of nearly a year I went to his deluxe third-floor apartment in the posh residential area of Sanbancho in central Tokyo, where he lived with his beautiful wife, a former model and actress, and young son, two or three times a week at ten in the morning. We would retreat to his den and seat ourselves on tatami across a low table, surrounded by stacks of books on government and politics in various languages. We would drink tea and talk about the affairs of the day in English, which Watanabe-san was, in fact, quite good at. Occasionally we would be joined by his friend Sam Jameson, the famed correspondent for the *Chicago Tribune* (and later the *Los Angeles Times*), who was a member of a regular study group, or *benkyo-kai,* that Watanabe had organized for his associates to discuss politics and play mahjong. The group included rising LDP star, future PM Yasuhiro Nakasone. I felt I had entered into the inner circle of the ultimate insider.

I did my best to help Watanabe-san improve his English. The education he gave me, in turn, was priceless.

Tsueno Watanabe had had a remarkable life. A banker's son and nephew to a real estate magnate, he was no stranger to wealth. However, he did not grow up as a typical Japanese conservative. As a junior high school student in 1939, he had openly criticized the Japanese Imperial Army and teachers who promoted militarism. In high school he was called to work in a factory making airplanes, a task he resisted by making defective parts, he told me. He passed the entrance examination to elite Tokyo University, but during the last stages of the war, in 1945, he was drafted into that same military he had criticized, and as a lowly private he suffered physical abuse at the hands of his superiors and watched his friends sent off on suicide missions as *kamikaze* pilots.

"They were trembling in fear," he told me once, recalling the experience. "There was no bravery. No joy. No yelling, 'Long Live the Emperor!' That was all a lie. Some of them couldn't even stand up. They had to be lifted up bodily and pushed into the cockpit."

He told me that he had hated the militarism of Japan with every fiber of his being.

After the war, in September 1945, he re-entered Tokyo University and applied for membership in the Youth Communist Federation. He distributed pamphlets and fliers and encouraged people to attend Party lectures. By 1947, he was acknowledged as a regular member of the Communist Party. He belonged to one of the cells in the university and delivered speeches at other universities to recruit new Party members.

But he came to find the movement as dogmatic as the Japanese military, and in December 1947 he submitted his resignation, calling the JCP "impractical."

After graduation he passed the difficult entrance examination to the *Yomiuri Shimbun* and became a political journalist, cultivating contacts in the newly formed (1955) conservative Liberal Democratic Party, which would go on to rule the country for the next several decades. The LDP was a merger of two groups, the Liberal Party of largely former bureaucrats and the earthier Democratic Party of professional politicians, with backgrounds in agriculture, fishing, and local government. Watanabe gravitated toward the latter group, becoming captain of the *kisha* (Reporter's) club covering powerbroker Banboku Ono, one of the few who had opposed Tojo and the war, and developing a relationship with the aforementioned Nakasone, the up-and-coming political figure whom many were comparing to JFK—for his youth, vigor, and a fashion style that featured tailored suits and designer silk ties.

Watanabe produced scoop after scoop, based on information fed to him by his LDP allies. By the late 1950s he had become the paper's star reporter, writing articles on Japanese politics and giving paid speeches on the side to select audiences.

* * *

Watanabe was gruff and blunt. He absolutely hated Emperor Hirohito and the imperial system, which was, of course, an amalgam of state and religion (Shinto). In particular, he blamed the emperor for allowing the war to happen and thought the Imperial Palace should be torn down and the grounds paved over and turned into a parking lot. He was also an outspoken opponent of the Yasukuni Shrine, the controversial shrine for Japan's war dead—the grounds there were an unabashed memorial to the last war, with a pavilion dedicated to its weaponry, an interment burial site for Class-A war criminals, and a controversial place of worship for

The most powerful man in media in Japan. We had a special relationship.

rightist politicians. Watanabe told me he thought Shinto was a mumbo-jumbo creed.

It was from Watanabe that I first learned how corrupt politics in Japan was, that the graft, fraud, and other funny business that characterized the run-up to the Olympics was just a small sample of what went on.

"Japanese politics is dirty," he liked to say. "It's all about money. Not policy. Only money."

Watanabe supported the LDP, as did his newspaper, for he believed it was better than the alternative, but he absolutely despised Eisaku Sato, the big-eared prime minister of Japan at the time. Sato, son of a samurai turned sake brewer, was the younger brother of Nobusuke Kishi, the former Class-A war crimes suspect turned American puppet and CIA favorite. (Kishi, had been a member of Hideki Tojo's wartime cabinet, responsible for forced labor and sexual slavery policies in China as well as the expansion of the opium trade, before selling out to the Americans in the postwar era. He was released from Sugamo Prison, where he had been held for three years as a war crimes suspect, on December 23, 1948, the same day that General Tojo and six others were hanged. As prime minister in 1960, a position he attained with the help of donations from the CIA, he oversaw the approval of the Security Treaty extension that would keep American bases in Japan, using yakuza manpower to overcome massive resistance from protestors. Kishi was also grandfather to Shinzo Abe, who would go on to become Japan's longest serving PM decades later (in case you were wondering if family connections mattered in Japanese politics).

Watanabe thought Sato was venal and corrupt to the core, and indeed the PM's tenure was engulfed in a string of corruption scandals erupting in 1966 that earned him the nickname the "Black Mist." Among the more celebrated malfeasances were the arrest of a lower house LDP MP on charges of bribery; Sato's transportation minister arranging for an express train to stop at the tiny station in his home town; the head of the Self-Defense Forces taking private trips on YS-11 planes; the speaker of the lower house dealing in fraudulent bank drafts (*tegata*); and LDP Diet members extorting businessmen for money.

Public opinion of Sato was low. Were it not for the parliamentary system of Japan, in which the head of the ruling party becomes prime minister, a result of the factional power play of LDP kingmakers behind closed doors, there is little chance he could have ever been chosen prime minister. He certainly could not have won in a direct election such as that held for the presidency of the United States.

Watanabe once described to me in detail how he thought Sato won the post of prime minister. In 1964 former Prime Minister Hayato Ikeda, suffering from throat cancer, had been compelled to resign because of his failing health. It was decided by party officials that, rather than endure a difficult intraparty factional battle over his successor, it would be better for Ikeda to choose the next party president—who would automatically become PM—himself. The logical choice was Ichiro Kono, the man who had organized the 1964 Tokyo Olympics and who was close to Ikeda. The PM, who was unable to speak because of his illness, wrote down the name of his successor, Kono, on a piece of paper, folded it, and handed it to an aide.

"Somewhere along the line," said Watanabe, "the paper was intercepted, made to disappear, a large amount of money changed hands, and a new piece of paper appeared with Sato's name on it."

"I'm not joking," he continued, seeing the incredulous look on my face. "I am deadly serious. Maybe I could not prove it in court, but I know it happened."

Corruption in the Sato regime was a frequent target of Watanabe's columns, and he told me that Sato's wife had once visited his wife with a gift—an envelope full of money. It was a not-so-subtle hint that she might suggest to her husband to ease off on his attacks on the PM's office. Watanabe's wife, an endlessly good-natured and kind-hearted lady, of course refused.

"Sato should commit *harakiri*," said Watanabe with contempt in his voice.

Instead, in November 1966, Sato went on television and announced his candidacy for a second term as party president, on the theory that only he could best correct the unsavory situation. "It is regrettable that my administration and party have invited public distrust for lack of moral standards," he said. "The main thing is that I, as the responsible person, fully grasp the implications."

No one doubted that he would win, which in fact he did in the December party election.

Sato was the one responsible for Watanabe's transfer to Washington, DC. The *Yomiuri Shimbun* had wanted to buy land for a new building and a government official agreed to facilitate the purchase in exchange for *Yomiuri* getting Watanabe out of Sato's hair.

Watanabe left for the American capital in 1968, but not before helping Professor Ori arrange an interview for me with Yasuhiro Nakasone, something I needed for my graduation thesis on the LDP. In return, I introduced Watanabe to an ex-military friend

Watanabe's nemesis "Black Mist" Prime Minister Eisaku Sato and US President Richard Nixon.

of mine and fellow Sophia student who had a Japanese wife and lived and worked in Washington, DC, with the US Civil Service. My friend and his wife both saw to it that the Watanabe family was well taken care of during their time in the United States.

The Sato government stayed in power helped by an overall feeling of tranquility and satisfaction among the populace. The country had never been better off, percolating along with an annual growth rate of 13.6 percent and near full employment. In 1966, Japan had overtaken Britain to become the world's fourth largest industrial power. A new car, a Toyota, became the status symbol of the up-and-coming family, with many saving to buy a new home.

There was nowhere to go but up, or so it seemed.

Particularly galling to the PM's foes, including Watanabe, was the subsequent awarding of the Nobel Prize to Sato in 1974. He received it for proffering his three non-nuclear principles—non-production, non-possession, and non-introduction of nuclear weapons on the archipelago—as well as for entering

Japan as a signee to the Nuclear Non-Proliferation Treaty. The award prompted many people to suspect that the Nobel Prizes were fixed, given Sato's support for the US in the war in Vietnam. In fact, it would be revealed in a document released in 2009 that Sato, in exchange for breaks in the US textile market, had secretly agreed to let US President Richard Nixon keep nuclear weapons in Okinawa once it was restored to Japanese sovereignty,

A popular critic named Fujio Akatsuka was then moved to remark, "When Sato was awarded a Nobel, I lost my faith in mankind." Some observers called it the worst mistake in the history of the Nobel Prizes, including Oivind Stenersen, principal author of the official Nobel Peace Prize history.

Watanabe, in a later meeting, was so disgusted he could barely bring himself to discuss the subject.

"He must have paid a lot of money for that," he said.

* * *

The post-Sato government was led by lower-house member Kakuei Tanaka, a real estate and construction baron who had risen from poverty and a sixth-grade education to defeat Sato's handpicked candidate, Takeo Fukuda, for LDP president in 1972. Watanabe's close friend Nakasone was a key member of the Tanaka cabinet, and this helped bring Watanabe, and his newspaper column, back into the thick of the fray.

Kakuei Tanaka would later be ousted from office in 1974 in a land scandal. However, by then Watanabe had developed his own dark connections. Among other things, in 1973, he became a member of the operations committee of the new billion-dollar Celebrities Choice Club, a posh private membership organization with a cabaret, disco, assorted deluxe restaurants, and large Picasso painting decorating the lobby. Housed in a brand-new six-story building of polished Italian marble and stone, it had been established by ex-Tosei-kai crime boss Hisayuki Machii in an attempt to become respectable, along with the ultranationalist fixer (and LDP founder) Yoshio Kodama (also known as "the Godfather" for his connections to various yakuza bosses). It would become one of the busiest social spots in the city, limousines arriving every night carrying government leaders, business executives, entertainers, diplomats, and US military officers, not to mention yakuza bosses eschewing traditional skirt-like *hakama* for tailored three-piece suits.

"Yankee Go Home"

My own interest in politics, fostered in great part by my experience with Watanabe, was manifested in many forms: additional university courses and my graduation thesis on the factions of the Liberal Democratic Party among them. Then there was an art student from Waseda University who introduced me to the Japanese political left. Akemi was her name, and I first met her one evening in the Village Gate, a popular jazz coffee shop in Shinjuku, where she was passing out fliers announcing an upcoming demonstration over the war in Vietnam, protesting the United States' continued bombing of Hanoi and Haiphong. She was a member in good standing of the Zengakuren, the leftist student protest group that had led many an anti-American protest, including the famous 1960 million-person march protesting the Security Treaty extension and the continued stationing of American troops in Japan.

Akemi had almond eyes, a black ponytail, and long legs, all of which helped pique my interest in her politics. In the interest of politeness, I inquired about the demonstration.

She asked me if I was against the war. Then, without waiting for a reply, she answered for me, switching fluently to English.

"Of course you are," she said. "American soldiers must get out of Vietnam. American soldiers must get out of Okinawa. America soldiers must get out of Japan."

"Why?" I asked ingenuously. "We are protecting the world from communism."

She looked at me with mixture of disgust and exasperation.

To tell the truth, I had never stopped to examine my political philosophy in any sort of depth. I wasn't sure I had one, in fact. My father was an Eisenhower Republican and so, by default, was I—back home, that is. I had spent over three years working for the CIA and the NSA, secretly spying on the communist regimes in Russia and China, surviving the Cuban Missile Crisis in the process, which certainly put me in the conservative camp. At the same time, like everyone else, I had become a big fan of John F. Kennedy, who was a Democrat, but also a hawkish one who had famously said, "We will bear any burden, pay any price, meet any hardship, support any friend, and oppose any foe to assure the survival and success of liberty."

Wasn't that the American way? And who could argue with it? Certainly no one who was a US ally.

I had automatically assumed that going into Vietnam was the right thing to do and that Japanese people necessarily agreed with me. After all, the Japanese government under Sato was donating millions of dollars to the Saigon regime, while Japanese industry profited hugely from sales to the US military there. Accompanying those assumptions was my belief that Japan was—and should be—eternally grateful to the United States for stationing soldiers on its soil to protect it from the communist threat. Because of the US bases in Japan, the country only had to spend 1 percent of its annual budget on defense, which allowed it to concentrate on industrial development and international trade.

I had just finished reading *The Green Berets*, a book about US involvement in Vietnam by Robin Moore, who had himself served in the Green Berets. It was the inspiration for the John Wayne movie of the same name a few years later and should give you some indication of my sophistication—or lack thereof—in regard to the subject.

"If the communists take over from the north," I told Akemi, "they will overrun Southeast Asia. And maybe Japan as well. Haven't you ever heard of the domino theory?"

"Americans kill innocent people," she responded with a sigh, "bomb villages, bomb Hanoi. Same as Hiroshima. All war is bad."

"Then why did your country start one? Remember Pearl Harbor?" I asked, stupidly.

"I was not born yet in Pearl Harbor," she said, her eyes flashing. "All Japanese today hate war. And we don't want the American war machine in our country."

The crux of the issue for Japan at the time was Okinawa, the southernmost island chain in Japan. It was where three-quarters of the US military bases in Japan were situated, primarily because of Okinawa's strategic location next to the China Sea. The Okinawa bases occupied about a fifth of the main island. During the Vietnam War, Okinawa was a key waystation and staging ground for heavy B-52 bombers and troops headed for Vietnam. (Okinawa would revert to Japanese control some years later in 1972, but the American bases remained and were suspected to be a secret storehouse of American nuclear weapons—a suspicion that in later years proved well founded.) All of this did not exactly endear the US military to the local population.

* * *

The following weekend, in cool October weather, I participated in my first antiwar demonstration when I marched along with Akemi and her friends in a parade to commemorate International Anti-War Day, as it was called. Setting out for Shinjuku, there were thousands of people on hand, singing antiwar songs, exuberantly mouthing the words of Bob Dylan and Peter, Paul, and Mary. Among them were many long-haired hippie types in jeans and bell-bottomed trousers, some calling themselves "folk guerillas." As we reached the station, some of the marchers began throwing Molotov cocktails in the direction of the trains, forcing them to stop. The riot police showed up. Tear gas filled the air. There were pockets of hand-to-hand combat. I stayed and watched on the fringes, keeping well away from the noxious tear gas, but with grudging admiration for those on the front line who were so willing to engage. Eventually the tear gas got so bad that the crowd was forced to disperse and the police, wearing gas masks and brandishing wooden clubs, restored order. Separated from Akemi and the group I started out with, I went to a bar in Kabuki-cho and washed my eyes out. I heard later that she had taken a friend, injured in the melee, to a hospital, and I did not see her for a while after that. Some of her other friends had been taken in for disorderly conduct but then released. Only the makeshift bomb throwers remained in jail.

It was a revealing experience. Somewhere along the line, in the years after the Security Treaty, the once-rampant demonstrations died down and the Japanese people got a stereotypical reputation of being passive robots, pathetically focused on study and work. But such was not the case in my experience, certainly not on that day and that evening. The revolutionary cultural and political ferment around the globe in places like Columbia University, Berkeley, and the Sorbonne (turmoil that would be intensified further by the 1968 assassinations of Martin Luther King Jr. and Bobby Kennedy) was mirrored on university campuses in Tokyo, including Sophia, where student agitators caused management to reinforce the front and back gates and add more security guards.

The Japanese media during that era were diverse and outspoken, in my opinion, much more than they are today. The popular commercial TV network TBS hosted riveting live student debates every Saturday afternoon. The quality of such public discussion would, unfortunately, go downhill after that, as the LDP solidified its power and discouraged political discourse.

Japanese students were not only fed up with the government's support of the US in Vietnam, as well as American control of Okinawa, they also hated the autocratic Japanese university system, which was based on tortuous entrance exams and served only to prepare students for entry as foot soldiers into the corporate world. Student protest would reach a peak in January 1969 when radical student groups took over Yasuda Auditorium in the nine-story clock tower on the campus of Tokyo University. They barricaded classrooms, heckled and assaulted professors, and boarded up the windows, dropping chairs and desks on anyone who came near, wielding poles made out of lumber, which were often spiked. School authorities compared them to yakuza (and indeed, according to Manabu Miyazaki's 2005 tome *Toppamono*, some of the leftist students claimed later they had employed underworld gang techniques of intimidation). It would take over 2,000 riot police with water cannons, tear gas grenades, and helicopters to get them out. Prime Minister Sato would close the campus for a year and there would be no graduations that spring. There were also confrontations at Shinjuku Station where riot police had to forcibly clear antiwar groups numbering in the thousands. Students would occupy the West Exit Plaza and declare it a "liberated zone."

It was a heady experience. The one constant through all of it was my relationship with Akemi. The more I got to know her, the more I was fascinated. She read Goethe, loved the Beatles, knew the words to "All You Need Is Love," and smoked French cigarettes.

But I had competition. Kyoko, a sullen, bookish girl, with stringy hair, who wore horn-rimmed glasses and a black beret, always seemed to be around whenever I saw Akemi. Kyoko, I would later discover, belonged to the activist antiwar group Beiheiren, which helped US soldiers desert, providing them with false passports and other documents that enabled them to escape to Sweden through Russia. Kyoko was also in love with Akemi, or so it clearly seemed, judging by the way she was always hanging onto Akemi's arm, and Akemi seemed to reciprocate. On the one evening Akemi deigned to visit my place of residence to inspect the books I was reading on Vietnam, Kyoko suddenly appeared at my threshold to fetch her, although I did not recall having given her my address.

"Where is Akemi?" she asked in a peremptory tone as I opened the door. She marched right past me without even saying hello.

My relationship with Akemi, such as it was, continued sporadically for the next few months. We would meet at the Village Gate, and hit other Shinjuku night spots, with Kyoko usually tagging along and holding hands with Akemi. It was surreal.

"She needs me," Akemi told me at one juncture. "She doesn't have any other friends."

Together we attended gatherings of antiwar groups, and women's liberation groups as well, usually at Shinjuku coffee shops where photos of Joan Baez and Bob Dylan adorned the walls. People made impassioned speeches and food and drink were served; *onigiri* (rice balls) and Nikka whisky were staple items on the menu. My Japanese was not good enough to understand all the diatribes, but the general meaning was clear enough. On occasion someone had a joint to pass around. That took some courage because under Japan's strict antidrug laws anyone caught smoking marijuana could wind up arrested and spending months in jail.

Then it all came to an end. Without warning Akemi disappeared and I never saw her again. I called the number of her Waseda dormitory and was told that she had moved out. I searched the Shinjuku coffee shops but there was no sign of her.

One day early the following spring, the proprietress of the vegetable shop across the street yelled up that I had a call on the red public telephone in front of her store. It was Akemi. She was in Kagoshima. She had graduated from Waseda and her father had ordered her home. She was calling to tell me that her father had also arranged a marriage for her and that she was preparing for the June wedding by attending cooking and sewing classes. Her future husband worked in her father's import-export company

1960s Protests and Demonstrations

1

2

3

4

1. Anti–Vietnam War protests in Shinjuku were common in the late '60s.

2. The Battle of Yasuda Hall at Tokyo University, 1968.

3. Injuries were common.

4. A million people demonstrated in front of the National Diet Building on June 15, 1960, protesting against the signing of the Mutual Security Treaty, which kept American bases in Japan.

5. A massive riot-police force was mobilized to do battle with the protestors.

5

and was anxious to start a family. The wedding would be held in Kagoshima, and Akemi wanted me to attend.

"Please come," she said. "Kyoko is staying with me. It will be a lot of fun."

"What about the global peace movement?" I asked.

She hesitated for a moment, then replied, "It's time for me to grow up."

I expressed my regrets that I would be unable to attend due to work and study commitments, but I wished her well, and got her address so that I could send a wedding gift: a copy of *Quotations from Chairman Mao Tse-tung.*

* * *

As strange as it might have seemed to me at the time, Akemi's sudden conversion from raging activist to housewife was not uncommon in Japan. It happened with men too. Yesterday's Marxist became tomorrow's corporate warrior. The student battling police in front of Shinjuku Station would graduate, cut his long hair, put on a suit and tie, and join the ranks of the obedient *salarymen*. Inside every ideological brave-heart was a pragmatic seeker of *wa*, Japan's prized social harmony.

I didn't know it at the time, but the same thing would be happening to me.

The Degenerate

Zen Cathedral

It was baseball, a quintessentially American sport, that gave me my first true connection to Japan and its people. Many foreigners who had made their way to this country were already Japanophiles with Bunraku, *koto*, classical dance, martial arts, or any number of Japanese cultural interests to pursue. For me, having arrived from the US knowing little about the country, and initially not particularly pleased to have been sent here, the game was a real entry point, a conversation starter with Japanese, a common passion that could transcend differences and create rapport.

It seemed that there was no one in Japan who was unfamiliar with baseball, with either its rules or its particular culture.

It was by watching popular nationwide telecasts of Yomiuri Giants games every evening and listening to the commentary, sprinkled as it was with American baseball terms, that I began learning conversational Japanese. It was by going through the morning sports news dailies that I learned to read the language. Each morning I dragged myself out of the futon, put on my jeans, T-shirt, and sandals and, brushing my long hair out of my eyes, headed for the station kiosk, armed with my *kanji* dictionary.

There I picked up a copy of the *Nikkan Sports*, one of the top million-selling sports papers, and proceeded across the street to the Sakura coffee shop. For the next couple of hours, I would sit in a booth with the paper spread out before me on the polished oak table, sipping my morning roast and smoking my Hi-Lite cigarettes as I made my way through the stories. I would become aware of the curious stares bent in my direction as soon as I began deciphering the front-page headline with its colorful array of Chinese characters.

王、長島アベックホームラン、巨人は阪神に勝ち３連勝
(Oh, Nagashima Pair Up to Slam Home Runs, The Giants
Beat the Hanshin Tigers for Their Third Win in a Row)

Patrons passing by my table would stop and ask if I could really read what I was looking at and exclaim to others in wonderment when I said I could.

"Sugoi kono hito. Hora mite. Nihon no supotsu shi wo yonde iru."
(This guy is something else. Look at him. He's reading a sports paper.)

The morning sports daily was a treasure trove of information that far exceeded what US daily newspapers offered in the pre-digital era. It had all the professional baseball news—extended box scores, inning-by-inning accounts, interviews, the latest standings, the schedule, the top-thirty batter and top-twenty pitcher listings, and lots and lots of photos. Through these papers I got to learn not only the players' names and statistics, but something about their lives as well.

There was also high school and college baseball news, as well as articles on sumo, professional wrestling, judo, karate, and fishing. Then there were the daily mahjong lessons, political stories, entertainment news, celebrity scandals, and arrests of well-known people for assorted transgressions. Included also were the TV and movie schedules, want ads, and the sex pages—yes, the sex pages.

These might include interviews with leading porno starlets from Nikkatsu studios, which had lately become a hotbed of soft-porn flicks to counter the loss of regular cinema revenues due to the rise of TV. Such interviews would probe the cloistered secrets of erotic technique and other information of penetrating interest. Lending credence to these revelations were photos of the subject in the buff, pubic hair airbrushed out in accordance with Japan's blue laws. Down at the bottom of the page were assorted ads for Turkish baths and other establishments providing amatory services, complete with phone numbers, photos of the top hostesses, and prices. Want some companionship delivered to your home? Pick up the *Daily Sports* and it will tell you whom to call.

You got a certain sense of community through the sports dailies.

* * *

I had always loved baseball, growing up a fan of the San Francisco Giants, and that interest had continued in Japan. There were twelve professional teams in two leagues, the Central and the Pacific, drawing millions of fans a year. The Giants were the oldest and winningest and by far the most popular, thanks to the presence of their two great stars, Sadaharu Oh and Shigeo Nagashima, who were called the Babe Ruth and Lou Gehrig of Japan. There was a well-known saying that the three things Japanese children liked most were the Kyojin (the Giants), Taiho (the reigning sumo champion), and *tamagoyaki* (a savory-sweet egg dish), in that order.

The Giants, founded in 1935, were owned by the *Yomiuri Shimbun*, the world's largest newspaper. The paper also owned the country's oldest commercial TV network, NTV (Nippon Television), which aired the Giants home games nightly. Enter any coffee shop, sushi shop, *izakaya*, or bar after seven at night and there would be a TV tuned to the Giants game. It was a citywide obsession. It was a nationwide obsession. Surveys showed that one out of every two adult Japanese was a Giants fan. You could compare their popularity to that of the New York Yankees, Boston Red Sox, and Los Angeles Dodgers combined. But that would be understating the case.

If baseball was the national religion of Japan and the Giants the leading practitioners of the faith, then Korakuen Stadium was its cathedral. There were two other ballparks in the city: Meiji Jingu Stadium in the Meiji Shrine complex, where Babe Ruth and visiting MLB all-stars had played in 1934, and Tokyo Stadium in out-of-the-way Arakawa-ku. Korakuen, built in 1937 and located in the middle of a downtown amusement park in the eastern part of the city, was the only one that actually looked like a Major League stadium. For one thing, it had grass in the infield, unlike the other facilities used by Japanese professional baseball. For another, it was a double-decker stadium, also an anomaly in Japan, one that seated 45,000 of the faithful. It measured 288 feet down the lines and 360 feet to dead center. Some said that it resembled Detroit's Briggs Stadium.

Korakuen had been partially damaged by B-29 bombers during the war. It was used as an Occupation-armaments dump until the GHQ deemed it desirable to have baseball played there again and promoted a tour of Japan by the 1949 San Francisco Seals of the Pacific Coast League. The two-league system, Pacific and Central, started in 1950, and it was off to the races.

I was a guest parishioner, so to speak. From time to time, I would put on my Levis, polo shirt, and baseball cap (bearing the insignia of Kyojin's archrival Hanshin Tigers), head out to the stadium, and, with a ¥150 ticket in my pocket, make my way to the upper-deck extension known as the "jumbo stand" overlooking left field, with its panoramic views of the city. Korakuen had many charms—among them the roller coaster and the parachute drop ride visible next door, the various concession stands selling *yakitori, yakisoba* (fried noodles), sushi, dried squid, and hot dogs (made of fish meal), and the young females in hot pants

Korakuen Stadium was Tokyo's Zen cathedral.

who navigated the vertiginous upper-deck stairways like mountain goats, dispensing Kirin draft beer from the enormous tanks
strapped to their backs. There were tightly permed yakuza scalp-
ers patrolling the outer concourse, selling tickets if you wanted a
more expensive seat in the infield area.

The jumbo stands were a great place to be on a summer night,
looking out at the neon signs and the Chuo Line trains rum-
bling by in the distance. Signs in *kana* and *kanji* lined the outfield
walls, advertising a myriad of products: Suntory Jun Nama Biiru,
National Color TV, Morinaga Chocolate, Sakura Color Film, Yokohama Tire, Fuji Color Film, Nihon Fire and Marine Insurance,
Toshiba Color Terebi, Daiwa Securities. Many of the ads featured
Giants stars Nagashima and Oh.

What struck me first was the difference in crowd ambience. I
had been to Major League games in San Francisco. I had seen the
Giants play the Cardinals with Stan Musial at Seals Stadium and
again against the Dodgers with Duke Snider. San Francisco was a
free-for-all of rowdy fans. There was lots of screaming and yelling,
even cursing at times; every fan seeming to have his own shtick. In

Tokyo, by contrast, fans behaved as if they were watching a piano recital. It would have been considered crude behavior to stand up and scream "Kill the ump!" or "You bum!" as an American might. The lone exception was the organized group cheering in the outfield stands, led by well-practiced cheerleaders, who provided a constant stream of chants to the accompaniment of drums, trumpets, and other noisy devices. If you wanted to yell, that was where you went. Otherwise you kept quiet and didn't bother anyone.

The endless rote cheering combined with a succession of sacrifice bunts, 3-2 counts, and coach-player conferences created, at times, a numbing effect, much like the alpha waves that emanate from performances of Noh plays.

I went to quite a few night games at Korakuen during the latter half of the 1960s. I was fascinated to watch slugging first baseman Oh, who hit from a bizarre one-legged stance, the likes of which had never been seen in professional baseball anywhere to my knowledge, and who was leading the league in home runs.

Oh would raise his right foot, his knee at groin level and stand there in the batter's box on his left leg, motionless, looking like some Lake Nakuru flamingo as he waited for the pitch. His hands were back so far so that the barrel of the bat touched the peak of his cap. At the very last microsecond, as the ball sped toward the plate, he would step into the pitch and make contact, often sending the ball into the outfield stands.

My initial fascination with Japanese baseball had been triggered in part because, when I first arrived, it was the only thing I could remotely understand on Japanese television. Many of the words were English derivatives: *sutoraiku* (strike), *boru* (ball), *kabu* (curve), *homu ran* (home run), *picha* (pitcher), *cacha* (catcher), *shotostoppu* (shortstop), etc. You get the idea.

But gradually, I also began to see the cultural differences at work. In Japan, the focus on group ethic, the constant talk of hard training and samurai fighting spirit lent to the game something of the aura of a martial art.

Giants manager Tetsuharu Kawakami, who meditated Zen-style daily, was famous for saying that "Baseball is Zen." Sadaharu Oh practiced his swing with a samurai longsword, slicing pieces of paper suspended from the ceiling in perfect halves. Third baseman and national heartthrob Shigeo Nagashima, the most popular sports figure in the land—Joe DiMaggio's popularity squared—reportedly slept with his bat in his arms every night. He swung so fiercely and fielded his position so aggressively the shortstop was almost unnecessary.

While most teams had one or two Americans, mostly ex-Major Leaguers on the downside of their careers who still performed well enough and were valued for their power, the Giants had none. Kawakami wanted to win with a pureblooded team to show the superiority of the Japanese system. As he put it, he also wanted a "Real World Series" with the American champion to show how good an all-made-in-Japan team could be.

But there was another factor as well. The Giants were seen not only as winners but as the epitome of good manners. "May the Giants always be strong, and may they always be gentlemen," their founder Matsutaro Shoriki had decreed. Foreign players, however, often had deportment problems that would not be considered good for the Giants image. They spit chewing tobacco on the dugout floor. How disgusting. They slid hard into second base, a nasty habit practiced by American import Daryl Spencer, who was all of 6'4" and 220 pounds and was seriously dangerous, putting more than one opposing infielder on the disabled list. Americans liked to fight. Their pitchers liked to throw brush-back pitches. And they hated to practice, at least in the all-out, intense fashion of their Japanese teammates. "Crazy Japanese!" and "Fucking Jap!" were English expressions added to the baseball lexicon by the Americans and duly reported in the newspapers (ファッキング ジャプ—*fahkkingu jappu*—was how the latter would appear on the printed page).

"The Devil's Vest"

When American missionaries first introduced baseball to Japan in the 19th century, the idea of sport was not widely known outside of garden games enjoyed by the aristocracy, the religious ritual of sumo, and the martial arts of the samurai, none of which were considered de facto sports in the Western sense. The most successful early practitioners of the new sport were high school and university teams that grafted the philosophy of the martial arts onto the game, emphasizing the virtues of discipline, loyalty, dedication, endless training, development of spirit, and absolute execution of instructions delivered by the manager (*kantoku*) or coach, all inherited from the vanished world of samurai.

Left out of the equation was any suggestion of having fun.

Nowhere was this better exemplified than in a hugely popular manga and animated TV show, *Kyojin no Hoshi* (Star of the Giants), which aired every Saturday evening at seven o'clock on NTV during the late 1960s, just before the baseball game telecast. It was an account of the travails of a young boy who grows up in the dire poverty of the postwar era and, thanks to years of brutal, sometimes sadistic, training conducted by his disciplinarian, if alcoholic, father, develops the physical skills and spirit necessary to become a star pitcher for the Kyojin. (The word *hoshi* is Japanese for "star," but in the saga it stands for one particular star shining in the nighttime sky, which the father calls the "Star of the Kyojin." Hoshi is also the protagonist's family name.)

It was a gripping tale of the utterly merciless pursuit of perfection. I was transfixed.

Highlighting family, duty, perseverance, and honor, it touched a national nerve, which made it one of the most highly rated TV programs of the 1960s and 1970s. For millions of Japanese, it was a soaring paean to the power of *konjo*, or fighting spirit, and *doryoku*, or effort, to prevail over the most daunting odds. They are the values that, not coincidentally, helped lift Japan from the ashes of defeat in war to become an economic superpower.

It was the stuff of blood and guts that was thought to have brought the nation otherwise unattainable success in the Olympics. Superior mental strength and willpower could overcome any perceived physical deficiencies, and no measures were too extreme to inculcate that desired stick-to-it-iveness. This included physical beatings, for they helped an individual, especially an athlete,

The animated film series *Kyojin no Hoshi,*
Star of the Giants, was the inspiration for *The
Chrysanthemum and The Bat.*

overcome what Giants manager Kawakami liked to call a "natural predilection for laziness."

I used to watch *Kyojin no Hoshi* every Saturday evening at my aforementioned neighborhood *shokudo,* the Sakuranbo, and stay on to catch the telecast of the Kyojin *naita,* or night game. I would order a beer and a slice of grilled salted fish and settle in for the evening's entertainment along with the other customers. I noticed that the place's waitstaff, Giants fans like everyone else, were as riveted to the screen as I was.

Later I saved enough to buy my own TV set, but it was always more fun to watch *Hoshi* and the game in a bar or restaurant or coffee shop to soak up everyone's reaction.

I had mixed emotions about *Kyojin no Hoshi.* I was both moved and repulsed by it and its impact on the populace. To fully explain why, some detail is necessary here.

The hero of *Kyojin no Hoshi* is a young boy named Hyuuma, who is eight years old when the story opens. His father Itetsu is a craggy-faced day laborer whose once-promising career as a third baseman for the Yomiuri Giants was destroyed after he was wounded in the war. Itetsu ekes out a living in construction and is barely able to afford the rent on a ramshackle house in one of the poorest districts of Tokyo's Shitamachi, where the family—including Hyuuma's mother and sister Akiko—resides. The *shoji* (paper screens) are patchwork and the tatami are ragged.

The family faces further adversity when the mother dies of tuberculosis—a common disease in postwar Japan—and Hyuuma's older sister, now in high school, is forced to take her place running the household while still keeping up with her studies.

The father decides to make his ten-year-old son into the ballplayer that he was unable to become. For the next several years, he forces Hyuuma to wear a torturous contraption called "The Devil's Vest"—a harness of leather with tightly coiled steel springs clamped to his son's arms so that any movement from a simple task like lifting a pair of chopsticks to throwing a fastball becomes extremely arduous. Hyuuma is not allowed to take it off—not even in the bath or in bed at night. He is ordered to hide it under his clothes when he goes to school.

"Never show anyone that you are straining," said his father.

At night, after a day of digging ditches at construction sites, the father puts Hyuuma through a series of grueling drills: frog hops, pushups, pitching exercises, and fielding hundreds of ground balls—hard grounders that hit Hyuuma in the jaw, nose, and stomach, leaving him bleeding and at times even unconscious.

A calligraphy painting on the otherwise bare wall of the Hoshi home bears the ideograph for *konjo* (根性), or "guts." It is the Hoshi family motto.

Hyuuma is made to wear the harness for five long years. When he is finally allowed to take it off, he is by far the strongest baseball player in his school. But his tale of suffering has only just begun.

In high school he practices six hours a day after school with the team and even more on the weekends, ending each session bloody and bruised from batting and fielding exercises known as "Death Drills" and exhausted from endless running (or sometimes squat jumping) up and down the stairs of a nearby shrine.

Then, at home in the evening, there is still time for truncated sessions with his father, who has now taken to whacking Hyuuma with a *shinai*, or bamboo stick, to correct poor form. Before going to bed each night Hyuuma religiously polishes his glove—a sign of respect in the Shinto world, which holds that all inanimate objects, even baseball gloves, have souls to which thanks must be conveyed.

The father, for his part, sacrifices for his son by working seven days a week. Hyuuma's sister Akiko, now out of school, takes a job at a gasoline station but breaks a leg in a fall and is hospitalized. Before her accident, there was barely enough money to put food on the table. But now, the ensuing medical bills are more than the family, lacking insurance, can afford.

Hyuuma tells his father he wants to quit school and work with him as a day laborer in construction in order to supplement the family income. The father explodes in anger. He slaps his son across the face and tells him he has to stay in school at all costs and play in the all-important national championship tournament at Koshien Stadium in Osaka, the mecca of high school baseball. It had been his mother's dying wish. Hyuuma complies and stays in school, and the father takes an additional nighttime construction job. (Adding this in to his already extended workday, along with time for meals, transportation, and other *quotidiana*, would have left him with about fifteen minutes a night for sleeping, but I wasn't one to quibble.)

The sister, meantime, returns to work on crutches, her leg in a cast, anxious to do her part. The father is angered again when he discovers that Akiko has been doing Hyuuma's homework and rips the pages she has written out of Hyuuma's workbook.

Scenes of Hoshi pitching are shown in a split screen with his father wielding a pickaxe and his sister pumping gas on crutches. For an animation series about a boy playing baseball, it was pretty heavy stuff. What I knew of the game up until then had been strictly American style—meaning, basically, playing the game for the enjoyment of it. But the moral code running through the story, the sense of family sticking together through thick and thin, the willingness to sacrifice everything for what is perceived as the ultimate good, and to always do the right thing, was fascinating to me.

A key lesson comes early in the story. One day, the father gives Hyuuma, still in elementary school, ¥40 to go buy a pack of cigarettes for him. On the way, Hyuuma passes by a carnival and wanders inside. He sees a game where customers can win cartons of cigarettes by knocking down stacks of them with a baseball. He pays ¥40, knocks down all of the cartons and races home, his arms filled with half-a-year's supply of cigarettes. His father is furious and demands his ¥40 back.

"I don't want cigarettes obtained in such a manner," he says. "I am not teaching you baseball so you can make money. There are other more important reasons."

It was heartbreaking. But, as the Japanese said, there was beauty in suffering and in *Kyojin no Hoshi* the suffering was so beautiful—because of the love behind it—that it made you want to cry. And I did cry, in spite of myself, sitting there in the Sakurambo drinking my beer, tears rolling down my cheeks, asking myself what the hell was going on—Was I turning Japanese?—and hoping Masutaa would not look over and notice the *gaijin* weeping over a children's cartoon.

* * *

Hoshi elevates his game and becomes a star in high school. His fastball is blinding, raising puffs of smoke from the catcher's mitt on every pitch. Batters recoil in fear. He leads his team to victory in the summer tournament at Koshien Stadium for the National High School Baseball Championship and then turns pro, intensifying his already extreme work ethic.

In spring training, he is subjected to the grueling 1,000-fungo Death Drill and is asked to throw 300 pitches his first day. That is two-to-three times what any American coach would allow for fear of the damage it could cause to the arm. Another day he throws 1,000 pitches.

All this time he has not had a girlfriend. "Baseball is my lover," he says.

On his own, Hyuuma devises a drill with two small abandoned boats and a fishing pole in the middle of nearby Sumida River. He stands the fishing pole up in one of the boats and suspends a ¥5 coin from it on a string. Then he stands in the other boat 90 feet away, both boats rocking in the water, and attempts to hit the coin by throwing baseballs at it. After much practice, he is able to hit the coin every single time.

"I can see the heart of the coin," he says.

He develops a pitch called the Dai-Riigu Boru (Major League Ball), one that spins viciously as it moves in and out and up and down. By studying *kendo* (Japanese fencing) he learns to read the movement of the bat in the batter's hands, so that his pitch winds up on weakest part of the bat and is therefore impossible to hit solidly.

With his mastery of this pitch, Hyuuma goes on to fulfill his destiny and become the Star of the Giants.

* * *

I often asked myself if other Americans could suspend their own cultural values long enough to become as deeply caught up in the excruciating journey of the *bushido* hero in *Kyojin no Hoshi* as I was. I didn't know the answer. I only knew that I was hooked.

The series took to extremes the spirit of sacrifice and perseverance, even by Japanese standards. Much has changed since then,
of course, but at the time, it struck a deep chord in its audience.
The spirit depicted in *Hoshi* could be seen at work in other
aspects of Japanese life—in the school system with its focus on
uniforms and endless study, including the evening, weekend, and
summer vacation *juku* (cram tutorials) that so many students were
compelled to attend. It could be seen in the corporations, where
impossibly long hours were the norm and "death by overwork" a
familiar everyday term. (The government as of this writing is cur-
rently pushing a new labor law to moderate work practices; its first
draft included the proviso that overtime for discretionary workers
would be capped at *100 hours a month*!) And that spirit was very
much alive in the nonfictional baseball world, nowhere else more
clearly than in the Kyojin system of the sixties and seventies under
manager Kawakami.

Kawakami had been a drill instructor for the Japanese Imperial Army during the Pacific War, at an installation in Tachikawa,
later a US military base. Kawakami was a demanding taskmaster
by all accounts and was widely hated by those under him. Soldiers
grumbled that if he led them into battle, he would be the first to
die, not by enemy fire but by a hand grenade thrown from behind
by one of his own men. But Kawakami never saw action. He stayed
where he was until 1945 when Japan surrendered.

As a player, at 5'9" and 165 pounds, Kawakami developed into
a taut, muscled, level-swinging hitter whose trademark was low
screaming line drives to the outfield fences. He was also a perfec-
tionist who did shadow swings late into the night at the team dormitory and, as mentioned, took up Zen, spending days on end at
unheated Buddhist temples in winter, meditating, chanting, reading scriptures, burning incense, and doing supplicant drills, all in
an effort to conquer his inner self and perfect his concentration.

As manager, Kawakami ran the team as if it were a unit in the
Japanese Imperial Army. He established a strict system of fines and

condoned the systematic use of physical force on younger players to keep them in line. Those who broke curfew in the Giants dormitory, where the young and single players stayed, were punished by the dormitory superintendent's *tekken*, or "iron fist," as it was called. Discourteous players were smacked on the back and legs with a bamboo stick. Underage players who were caught smoking had to write a hundred times every day for a month, "I will not smoke until I am twenty years old."

Such practices prompted some players to compare life on the Kawakami Giants to a prison camp. Yoshimasa Takahashi, who would join the Giants in 1973 from the Toei Flyers, had this to say about his experience: "The atmosphere on the Giants was something else. The mood in camp was very tense, much more so than it was with the Flyers. Everyone had to stay so focused that you never heard anyone even crack a joke. It was forbidden to drink alcohol at dinner and there were bed checks at curfew time. Break the rules and you were fined. At the Flyers' camp when practice was over, we would sit down and play mahjong with our uniforms still on. Sometimes we would drink all night and then go play the game. It wasn't that rare a thing. Under Kawakami *kantoku* that would have been unimaginable. They controlled you on the field and in your private life as well. They believed you couldn't be strong otherwise."

While I found aspects of the moral code of *Kyojin no Hoshi* appealing—I even found myself wondering what my life would have been like if my own father had rigged me up to a Devil's Vest, the obvious psychopathology notwithstanding—there was a strain of xenophobia running through the story that struck me as decidedly unhealthy.

The program depicted many actual characters in the Japanese baseball world. Stars like Oh, Nagashima, and Kawakami were all portrayed as well-groomed, polite, pure-hearted, sincere human beings, but the foreign ballplayers were another matter, most notably in the case of Daryl Spencer.

After nine relatively successful years in the Major Leagues, Spencer signed on with the Hankyu Braves of Japan and played for several more seasons. He failed to win a title, facing pitchers who walked him intentionally (eight times in a row in one doubleheader) to stymie his bid for the home run crown in 1965. However, he was a feared presence in the Japanese game and was acknowledged as such in the *Kyojin no Hoshi* series, although in a not very flattering way.

In one episode, Hoshi faces Spencer in a key at bat in the Japan Series. As Spencer steps in, he might have been taken for a refugee from the movie set of *Planet of the Apes*, the extreme dark-brown hairiness of his arms extending right down to his fingers. He takes his stance, chewing tobacco and spitting it out in gobs, then glares at Hoshi with murderous hate in his eyes.

"Come on, Baby!" he growls.

Hoshi winds up and throws a Dai-Riigu ball, which Spencer blasts down the line, but foul, into the stands.

"Take Hoshi out!" scream the fans. Anxiety fills the stadium.

Spencer doesn't move. He yells, "Hey, come on, Baby!" wagging his finger in a mock come-hither gesture.

Hoshi trembles in fear, but then a vision of a ¥5 coin swinging on a stick, illuminated in the dark by a burning torch, appears to him. Memories of his practice on the river return and his resolve strengthens.

Spencer continues to yell out his by-now monotonous challenge, obligingly following the scriptwriter's notion of English vernacular. He is nearly frothing at the mouth. Hoshi winds up and fires. Spencer unleashes a monster swing—and sends a dribbler down the third-base line, which Nagashima scoops up on the run and fires to Oh at first for the final out.

Hoshi wins. The Giants wrap up yet another Japan Series title. Spencer can be heard muttering in English, "Oh, terrible. God Damn!"

The crowd at the Sakuranbo lapped it up.

Salaryman

It was in Tokyo working as a corporate *salaryman* during the economic boom of the late 1960s that I learned how to drink. Really drink. Blasted. Blitzed. Blotto. Night after night, because that is what my Japanese colleagues did. It was their way of blowing off steam after toiling ten hours a day in cramped offices, forced to obey button-down rules, then facing a ride home on jam-packed commuter trains. The stress level was off the charts. From 7 p.m. to 11 p.m. every evening, some eight million people jammed into the 30,000 places to eat and drink in the city. Most of them were men, as they made up the great bulk of the workforce, with women being relegated to secretarial or administrative work until it came time to get married and stay home with the children. The negative consequences of drinking in the West—DUI, ostracism, overnight stays in the clink for drunk and disorderly behavior—were mitigated here by an excellent public transportation system and a lack of social stigma against public drunkenness. So drink is what they did, without apparent limits.

Until I began the job, I was not aware that the samurai ethic also encompassed alcohol consumption. It took me a while to become acclimatized, but I gradually built up my stamina until I could hold my own with the best of them and close down any bar in Shinjuku. By necessity I became a connoisseur of the popular hangover cure drinks sold at train station kiosks. My preference was Lipovitan D, an energy drink containing taurine and nicotinic acid, manufactured by Taisho Pharmaceutical. It was certain to wake you up and give you the *Faito!* (Fight!) promised in the product's cliffhanging TV ads, which featured a rugged outdoor protagonist holding on by his fingernails until a companion (shouting *Faito!*) passes him a phial of the stuff, enabling him to clamber over the top.

Graduation day in Hakone.

* * *

The company I went to work for was called Encyclopedia Britannica, Japan. It was probably not the worst initiation to office culture and work conditions in Japan, but it was plenty rough enough. Upon graduating from Sophia in 1969 I had been offered a job in the editorial department to work on the creation of English-language-learning programs for the Japanese market as a supplement to their main product, the encyclopedia. The EB office was on the second floor of a ten-story building in the commercial area of Minami-Shinjuku, a short walk from the southern exit of Shinjuku Station.

Most of the Japanese people who bought the leather-bound set of twenty-four volumes in English for $800 (about six-months salary for the average company worker) could not read them. Nevertheless, they were persuaded by skilled salesmen that just the fact of having these wondrous books in the house, full of all the knowledge in the world, would enable their children to grow up with enhanced IQs, pass the entrance examinations for Japan's top universities, and go on to work in an economy that depended increasingly on trade with the outside world, where English was the common language.

Thanks to its super-aggressive sales force, numbering in the thousands, Encyclopedia Britannica became one of the fastest growing companies in Japan. Their marketing was so aggressive, in fact, that some salesmen would visit prospective customers' houses at midnight after the man of the house had stumbled home and refuse to leave until a contract had been signed.

There was the famous case of an EB salesman who was arrested for late-night harassment of customers and whilst in a jail in Kobe, sold two sets of encyclopedias to the guards. He was made "Salesman of the Month."

It was not unusual to see a sales executive draped in a Savile Row suit, with gold cufflinks and a Rolex watch, a splendor not shared in the humbler editorial department where I worked with two other Americans to create English-learning texts and tapes to give away as premiums to encyclopedia purchasers. These products were hopefully something that customers could actually use, as opposed to the encyclopedias themselves.

EB Japan was a US-Japan joint venture, with 51 percent of the stock owned by local investors. Hence, most of my colleagues were Japanese, my immediate boss was Japanese, and there was definitely a Japanese Way of doing things. The workday started at nine and ended at five, according to the contract I signed. But as with the Mitsubishi employees and others I had known, no one wanted to be the one to leave first, even if the bosses were gone and there was no work to do. So we would sit there and play a game of *gaman kurabe*, as the Japanese put it, to see who could hold out the longest.

The Japanese Way also meant that there were daily meetings in which people from all sections of editorial—planning, production, and printing—as well as sales would attend. We would all have to listen to reports of work that did not concern us. Nothing was ever accomplished at these meetings and it was rare that someone actually expressed an opinion because that might conflict with someone else's opinion and disrupt the *wa*, or harmony, the nurturing of which was the point of the whole thing in the first place. I thought it was a waste of time given the work I had to do, but the building of team spirit had to take precedence.

* * *

The editorial office was an open bay, packed with file cabinets, desks cluttered with manuscripts, and stacks of books along the walls. It smelled of cigarette smoke and cleaning fluid. Our section chief, a stocky Japanese man in his forties named Chiaki, who was our immediate boss, sat in the far corner, chainsmoking Seven Star cigarettes through a cigarette holder.

He liked to say that that the highlight of his day was looking down at his shoes in the family *genkan* (entranceway) each morning as he set out to work. "I can't wait to put them on each day and get started," he would tell us.

Nineteen of the employees in editorial were Japanese. Besides myself, there were three Americans—two were graduates of the University of Michigan: Dwight, a bearded, disheveled ex-semi-pro hockey player with a BA in Psycholinguistics, and Mary Ann, a blonde from Croton-on-Hudson, New York, with a master's degree in French Language and Literature. Donald Boone, the third American, was our editor-in-chief. A graduate of Arizona State University, he was fluent in Japanese and directed his minions from a big office by the entrance.

We were all issued *meishi* (business cards) that announced our rank and status. Exchanging *meishi* was a mandatory ritual in Japan through which businesspeople determined tone, vocabulary, and body language appropriate to the respective positions and status of their counterparts. It showed where you stood in your organization's hierarchy (your "pigeon hole" as Dwight liked to say) and gave an approximation of how much decision-making authority you had so everybody would know how to behave toward you—obsequiously if their rank was far enough below you, dismissively if they stood far enough above you. The higher the rank, the deeper the bows and the more honorific the speech became on the part of those lower on the totem pole.

I would like to say that relations between the Japanese and American employees in our office were a model of cross-cultural understanding, but alas, that was not the case. The differences and the resulting strain were all too evident.

For one thing, the Americans made more money. We were paid on a wage scale that reflected US standards, while our Japanese counterparts had to settle for what the domestic labor market dictated. As a result, I made about twice what my Japanese boss earned. It was the cause for a good deal of grumbling, not all of it *sub rosa*.

"You make two times what I do so you should do the work of two people," Chiaki liked to say to me, dumping huge stacks of manuscripts on my desk for me to edit.

Then there was the deportment gap. Most Japanese sat quietly at their desks conversing only on work-related subjects and then in hushed tones. We Americans, on the other hand, were generally loud and gregarious, and we talked to our Japanese compatriots as we talked to each other—with an open, familiar, pat-on-the-back, tell-me-your-life-story attitude. It did not occur to us that Japanese might find this behavior invasive and rude.

Indeed, the reticence of our colleagues was for us the source of endless scoffing and disparagement. Dwight was particularly acerbic in his critique of the Japanese corporate way. They were too uptight, he said, to say what was really on their mind and incapable of making a decision until they had talked it to death and reassured themselves that everyone else was on board with whatever the idea was. Individually, Dwight said, they lacked spine.

Dwight loved to argue, to take a position on something and

hash it out according to the Socratic method, a skill he had polished as a Michigan PhD candidate—before dropping out to come to Japan. And he was quite good at it, as many of us, ears reddening over our beers, learned the hard way. One time, he took it into his head to instruct the governor of Tokyo, one Ryokichi Minobe, a socialist, on how to resolve the city's horrific pollution problem. In a carefully worded missive, in English, citing his full-fledged membership in the Sierra Club, he told the governor to ban all cars and trucks from the city limits and have everyone ride bicycles instead. Dwight was seriously offended when the governor's office did not reply.

Truth be told, we Americans were more than a little full of ourselves, the entitled and uninhibited products of the land of the free and the home of the brave, a nation whose influence now extended over the better part of the globe and, since July of 1969, to the moon as well. It was hard for us to imagine that anyone could presume to find fault with us—that is, until we went out drinking with our Japanese colleagues and their tongues loosened sufficiently to bring their own feelings out in the open.

They called us the *"gaijin butai,"* or foreign legion. The implication was that we were outliers, an auxiliary force with its own narrow uses, perhaps, but it was they, the Japanese staff, who were really carrying the load. They acknowledged—not without some envy—our superior knowledge of the English language, but that did not make us any less the ill-mannered and uncouth striplings that we were.

And worse yet, they said, we were mercenaries, only there for the money and ready to jump ship whenever it suited us. Whereas for them, joining the company was a lifetime commitment, like getting married.

All this was true enough, although I'm not sure listening to such criticisms did very much to change our American attitudes. We did, however, get a chance to prove our mettle when a subsequent well-publicized police investigation of the company's harassing sales techniques drove encyclopedia sales through the floor. Fortunately, a language course for children Dwight and I had created sold so well it helped keep the company solvent until the scandal died down. In some ways, we were like the *gaijin* baseball player in Japan who led the team in home runs but was left out of the team photo because the organization was resentful of his success. It made the Japanese look bad. In our case, we were not only left out of the photo but also did not receive a penny in royalties.

Ten Minutes to Kabuki-cho

In the meantime, I had moved into a box-like apartment on the second floor of the Kawamura Building in front of Higashi-Nakano Station, two stops from Shinjuku on the Chuo-sen, a commuter line that ran through the city all the way to Tokyo Station. I was moving up in the world because the Kawamura Building was what the Japanese called a *manshon* (taken from the completely misunderstood word "mansion"), a structure built from reinforced concrete. It was a more solid construction (and more expensive) than the *apaato* (a foreshortening of "apartment," the term denoting smaller box-like dwellings in wooden buildings) I had lived in in Komagome. For one's address to contain the word "mansion" gave one a certain status in Japan.

It was one of three similarly sized apartments on the second floor of a four-story building, named after my landlady, Mrs. Kawamura, a very proper Japanese widow who had the bottom floor all to herself. Mrs. Kawamura rented only to foreigners, not because she particularly liked *gaijin* but because the constant turnover meant a steady stream of key-money payments and deposits, which were quite substantial. Japanese tenants tended to move in and stay forever and were protected under Japanese law at the time, so there was no way to evict a tenant who did not want to leave.

I paid a monthly rent of ¥30,000, about $90 at the time, for a long rectangular space about 30 feet in length and 10 feet in width (about the size of a city bus), which was divided into a micro kitchen, a bathroom, a living room, and a bedroom. One window, by the bed, looked out at Shinjuku in the distance, while the other, a few feet away in the so-called "salon," looked out on the railroad tracks and the station *koban*, or police box, in front of it. There was a tiny Western-style flush toilet and a shower barely big enough to squeeze into and shut the door. Trains rumbled by every few minutes causing the entire structure to vibrate. I had a telephone, a gas space heater, a black-and-white Toshiba TV with rabbit ears, and a steady stream of neighborly cockroaches. It was better than my last apartment, where using my TV and stereo at the same time would cause the electrical circuits to blow. But it wasn't *that* much better. With no central heating, getting out of bed in the winter still required an act of courage.

As you may imagine, after a full day on the job, it was depressing going home to this. I preferred to stay in Shinjuku, an entertainment hub that had everything to dazzle the eye: huge department stores, fortune-telling sidewalk tables, assorted eating places, *pachinko* parlors, all-night movie theaters, avant-garde art houses, jazz *kissaten*, and the famous Koma Gekijo in Kabuki-cho where Japan's top musical stars performed.

There were also about 10,000 bars all within walking distance from my office—from large *conpa*, seating hundreds of people around circular bars, to the exclusive Skybar Polestar, a cocktail lounge on the forty-fifth floor of the ultramodern Keio Plaza Hotel, which had just gone up in Nishi-Shinjuku. At forty-seven stories the Keio Plaza was Japan's first skyscraper hotel and, at the time, the tallest building in the country. (However, it was deemed so ugly and antiseptic that the architect who designed it committed suicide.) The streets were filled with "scouts" offering attractive young female pedestrians high-paying jobs as nightclub hostesses.

A Shinjuku back street.

* * *

A favorite hangout for me was Saru no Koshikake, a popular, multilevel, upscale *izakaya* in the Shinjuku 3-chome area. There were tables made of polished Kyushu oak and sawed-off logs for seats. Mushrooms in fishnets were hung from the ceiling on the basement floor. The name translated to "The Monkey's Seat," but *saru no koshikake* mushrooms were also the main ingredient in a special tea praised for its supposedly miraculous therapeutic properties.

It was filled with people in their twenties and thirties, a mix of company workers, secretaries, and people in the entertainment business. Most of the latter worked on the other side of the camera—assistant directors, script girls, etc., but occasionally I would run into a big name like Shintaro Katsu, who played the blind swordsman Zatoichi, or Hiroshi Teshigahara, the avant-garde director of *Face of Another* and *Summer Soldier*, the latter a film about Beiheiren, the organization in Japan that opposed the Vietnam War and helped American soldiers desert.

It was a great place to make new friends. Among the friendliest were the "office ladies," or OL, as they were called in the vernacular, dressed to the teeth in the latest mini-skirted fashions, in search of adventure and romance. A list of the *tomodachi* I made there would include a twenty-two-year-old employee of the Chemical Bank, a Mitsubishi Bank teller, a receptionist at the Indonesian Embassy, an All Nippon Airways stewardess (soon to be renamed flight attendant), and a Kanebo saleswoman. They were all out for a good time. The Mitsubishi Bank teller, an attractive twenty-four-year-old, told me that she had been hired by the bank along with dozens of other young women as future wives for the male staff. She said that she wanted to enjoy herself before moving on to the next inevitable phase of her Mitsubishi career.

There was also a Toho casting director who wore sunglasses all the time—even when asleep because, as she put it, "That's what movie people do." She was out scouting for young Americans to play bit parts in a movie set in the 1950s about GIs raping innocent Japanese schoolgirls. She declined to offer me a part: "You don't look nasty enough," she said. Last but not least was a fashion model and winner of the Japan Miss World Contest. She was secretly transgender and the only human being I had ever met up to that time who was incapable of having conventional sex. She wanted to marry an American, she told me, because she figured Americans would be more open-minded about her situation.

I had dated an American girl at Sophia. She was the daughter of an Army colonel. Quiet. Sincere. I also had a Swedish girlfriend who was teaching in Japan. Statuesque and opinionated. But both of them left Japan, fed up with the sexism that was so characteristic of the culture—the gropers on crowded trains, off-color remarks about the size of their breasts from passersby.

"I feel like a piece of meat, living in this country," said the Swedish girl.

I also had a couple of other relationships with Japanese women, which lasted longer than the proverbial nine-and-a-half weeks, but they ultimately ended when the subject of a more-permanent arrangement came up—something I was not eager to pursue at that stage of my life.

Shinjuku also had a seamy side, which made you wonder about claims you often heard that the Japanese were close-minded and inhibited. There were, in fact, so many ways for a libidinous male to indulge himself in Kabuki-cho that it would take a book to tabulate them: hand job parlors, blow job parlors, massage parlors, peephole parlors, strip joints, private nude model joints, Turkish baths, anal bars, S/M clubs, cabarets with a hundred different beautiful women to pick from and take home, smaller intimate clubs catering to "sister boys," clubs with hostesses dressed like high school girls (in school uniforms and rolled down socks) as well as nurses, police women, or volleyball players. Anything you could imagine, Shinjuku had it all, including luxurious "host clubs" where smooth-mannered handsome young men ministered to wealthy lady customers into the wee hours of the morning. Shinjuku 2-chome was the city's gay center, with its multifarious cluster of bars and clubs that catered to every LGBT taste. In Golden Gai up the street, a warren of tiny ramshackle bars patronized by artists and musicians, every establishment had a private attic where the bar maid would entertain customers for a fee. Shinjuku was a wonderland of people who did not fit into the rigidity of the proper society and white-collar values.

There was a place called Camera Land, for example. You were ushered into a room with a chair and table on top of which sat a bottle of beer and a small Nikon camera. A girl would enter the room wearing nothing but a casual silk kimono and disrobe. She would instruct you to take photos of her in various poses and to use up the entire roll of Fuji film in the camera, which you could keep. When you had finished taking your pictures, you would get a hand job. Cost: ¥2,000 (at the time roughly $6).

Libidos aside, I could never understand those American businessmen and diplomats posted in the city, and their wives, who

You could get anything you wanted in Kabuki-cho, including emergency nursing care and a bottle of beer.

spent all their time at the Tokyo American Club communing with each other in English. There was an executive from Chicago at Encyclopedia Britannica whose only trip to Kabuki-cho in his two years in Japan was in a group tour. He came to work each day in a limousine and went home the same way, his route punctuated only by stopovers at TAC. What a total waste, it seemed to me, to come halfway around the world only to surround yourself with your fellow countrymen and pretend you were back home. (And how could you then complain that "Japan is closed" to your products and services?)

* * *

After an evening in Shinjuku, rather than go straight back to my cubbyhole, I would often stop off at a place across the street from my apartment for a nightcap and a bowl of *ochazuke*. By this time,

I understood exactly how single Japanese *salarymen* must have felt on their way home to their rabbit-hutch dormitory dwellings.

The "snack," as such late-night purveyors of potables and light foods were called, was patronized by members of the local Higashi-Nakano branch of Tokyo's largest criminal organization, the Sumiyoshi Rengo-kai. On the scene were assorted *chinpira* (young, low-ranking gangsters), with punch perms, bruised knuckles, and pouty, arrogant expressions, along with gang members moonlighting in construction at local sites, men with weatherbeaten faces, bandanas around their foreheads, and two-toed workers shoes on their feet. They all chain-smoked and drank cheap Torys whisky, as *enka* songs, the rough Japanese equivalent of blues, played in the background.

The proprietors tolerated my presence because I ran up a nice bar bill and because I could also be relied upon to contribute a couple of thousand yen each night to the electronic slot machines.

The name of the place, which as far as I could determine had no meaning, was Bokido, written in *katakana* (ボーキド) on the purple neon sign standing out among the usual assortment of station-front noodle shops, coffee shops, bars, *pachinko* parlors, and newspaper and cigarette kiosks. It had imitation leather booths, a counter with stools, and two slot machines.

I would come in around 11 p.m. and watch the sports news on the TV set above the bar. It was also at Bokido that I first saw the NTV late show in which Dr. Ikasemasu (literally, "Dr. Make Them Come"), a famous masseur, would invite young ladies to come to the Nippon Television studios in central Tokyo where, lying down on a cot on camera, they would give themselves over to his manipulations until they reached orgasm. Seriously. It was the most bizarre show I had ever seen on late-night Japanese television, or television anywhere for that matter, and it was also one of the most popular.

You could bet on baseball at Bokido. Small stuff. Gambling was illegal in Japan, except for certain types of state-sponsored forms:

boat racing, horse racing, bicycle racing, and motorcycle racing. But everybody gambled anyway, especially on mahjong. And the police looked the other way as long as you kept it within reason and people did not wind up losing their houses. At Bokido you could participate in a pool organized by the Sumiyoshi at ¥1,000 a pop on all the evening's games.

You filled in your selections on a chart and came in the next night after the game to take your winnings or settle your losses. A payout of ¥900 on a flat ¥1,000 bet was standard, the house—or rather the gangster, a frequent patron who ran the operation— taking a 10 percent *terasen*, or banker's cut. In the Bronx they would call it the "vig," short for the vigorish, the cut taken by the game runners. You could also make side bets, *kachi-make* (win or lose), with odds and point spreads, if you wanted.

Yakuza: Into the Abyss

I remember one particular side bet in October 1970 that involved a pitcher named Yutaka Enatsu.

I'd made bets on Enatsu, a strikeout sensation, and won many times. But by far the most important bet was one I lost. I don't remember the exact details except for the fact that he had blown an important game down the final stretch of the season, one that everyone had expected him to win, and I wound up ¥30,000 in the hole. I'd forgotten to go to the bank so I could pay it off at Bokido that evening and had gone straight home instead, intending to square accounts the following day.

Around midnight, there was a knock on my door. I opened it to find standing before me in the dim light of the *genkan* a young man in his late twenties, short, squat, muscular, built like a fireplug, buzz cut, assorted scars on his eyebrows and cheeks. He didn't bow when I opened the door as people ordinarily did. He just stood there staring at me, unsmiling, and said, "Whiting-san, *shukin desu*" (I'm here for the money). Then he pulled open his lapel to show the badge of the Sumiyoshi pinned to it.

In the 1980s it became illegal to show a badge or a *meishi* of a yakuza group, as it could be taken as a direct threat, an attempt at intimidation or extortion. In fact, a well-known actor named Kenichi Hagiwara would be arrested just for mentioning the name of his yakuza backer over the phone.

But at that time there was no such law and just about everybody knew what a Sumiyoshi badge looked like. The Sumiyoshi was the largest gang in Tokyo, and they operated almost like a local government. In lieu of local taxes, they collected tribute from all the eating and drinking establishments, sold drugs (methamphetamines from North Korea, China, and Taiwan), and ran hostess nightclubs, brothels, and gambling dens. They also helped retrieve unpaid loans, operated your neighborhood real estate and securities agencies, and kept psychopaths off the street. Just your friendly local thugs at work.

The Higashi-Nakano Sumiyoshi group belonged to the Sumiyoshi Kohei Ikka faction of the gang, which controlled the dense thicket of bars on the Odakyu Department Store side of Shinjuku Station and all points west on the commuter lines out of the city.

* * *

The gangster at my door was named Miyagi. I had seen him before. He was a collector and looked the part, but he was always dressed respectably in a suit and tie, or a suede jacket and twill slacks. He was a fixture around the watering holes and other nighttime enterprises that dominated both sides of the northern end of Higashi-Nakano Station.

I'd be sitting at the counter at Bokido when Miyagi would come in and stand by the cash register. Within minutes, the bartender or the proprietor would walk over, slide a *mizuwari* in front of him, and lay down an envelope. Something told me it did not contain love letters. Sometimes, without waiting for the bartender or saying a word to anyone, he would simply punch the cash register and take out what he wanted.

I wasn't surprised that he knew where I lived. The Sumiyoshi knew how to find things out. And I wasn't exactly invisible as a foreigner in Higashi-Nakano. There weren't that many of us in the neighborhood, and I assumed the local residents were as well informed as the ones in Komagome, where everybody seemed to know who I was, what I did each day, and what brand of toothpaste I used.

I told him I didn't have the money and he would have to wait until the banks opened the next day. He stared at me, eyes narrowed, for what seemed like a long time. I half expected him to launch an assault. Instead, he simply nodded and said I was to bring the money to him the following evening at Bokido, and that it would not be a good thing for either of us if I did not have it.

The next morning I went to the Mitsubishi Bank in Shinjuku and withdrew the funds from my account, a laborious process since cash cards had not yet been invented. I put the ¥30,000 in an envelope, as custom dictated, and took it to Bokido at around nine that evening. My friendly account adjuster was waiting, sitting in a back booth, drinking a beer and smoking a Hi-Lite cigarette. I handed him the envelope, he took out the three crisp ¥10,000 bills and pocketed them. Then he motioned for me to have a seat and ordered the bartender to bring me a glass.

"Call me Jiro," he said, pouring me a beer. Then he began peppering me with questions—the usual rote queries Japanese asked foreigners.

His interest picked up, oddly enough, when we got around to the fact that my graduation thesis had been on the factions of the Liberal Democratic Party. He said he and his gang were big fans of the LDP because the Sumiyoshi enjoyed a special relationship with the powerful political party, supporting its candidates at election time, donating money, and helping to get out the vote. In return, Sumiyoshi-related construction companies got those government contracts and other money-making opportunities accompanying them.

When I told Jiro that, through the auspices of a friend at the *Yomiuri Shimbun* and a professor at Sophia, I had met the rising LDP star Yasuhiro Nakasone, I shot up another several notches in his estimation. Nakasone, a future prime minister, was an ultra-nationalist who wanted a stronger military and a more assertive Japan. This made him a hero to the right wing, including the yakuza, who considered themselves patriots. Moreover, Nakasone's LDP was staunchly pro-business, and the yakuza, say what you will, were nothing if not capitalistic. (I opted not to mention that my Nakasone interview had lasted about ten minutes and consisted of stupid questions followed by nondescript answers. A model for how not to conduct an in-depth interview.)

After a few drinks, I asked Jiro what he did for the Sumiyoshi.

"This and that," he said. "I collect dues. I collect debts. Among other things. I also help protect the neighborhood from bad people."

He told me about his upbringing in Okinawa, Japan's southernmost most island chain, where 75 percent of the US military bases were located. His mother had been a bar girl; his father he never knew. He gravitated to the gangs in high school. He was good with his fists. The Sumiyoshi had recruited him, and he migrated to Tokyo.

At this juncture, he reached into his pocket and took out a small silver case that contained his business cards. Handing one to me with an air of solemnity, he uttered the formal greeting that centuries past might have been translated, "Your servant, sir," and gave a little bow. On the card below the Sumiyoshi crest, a circle of spikes with the *kanji* for *sumi* (live) inside, was printed his name and title, *wakagashira*, denoting a sort of junior capo.

I followed suit with my own card, which identified me as

Robert Whiting, Editor, Encyclopedia Britannica. It was, for me, an incongruous moment, but his next remark made it odder still. "You and I are alike," he declared.

I looked at him and I didn't see any similarities at all. He was a scarred, buzz-cut Japanese yakuza who collected dues and debts and supposedly kept psychopaths off the streets of the neighborhood. I was a long-haired Californian, a semi-hippie, if one who eschewed the pony tails, love beads, jewels, bandanas, and psychedelic drugs (strictly illegal in Japan in any event) of the time and disguised his counter-cultural proclivities in the dark suit and tie he wore to work as he puzzled over the linguistic keys to language learning. I did sport a dark mustache back then, prompting my Japanese colleagues to dub me "Bronson" after the film actor whose commercials for a men's cologne called "Mandom" filled the airwaves at that time. I would have found it hard, however, to manufacture the menace of Bronson's character in such films as *Death Wish*.

I was still pondering the source of our mutual affinity when Jiro spoke up again.

"We're both outsiders," he said. "I am from Okinawa and you are from America. Japanese don't like Okinawans—they think we are inferior—and they don't like *gaijin*. We're in the same boat, so let's be friends." He stood up and signaled me to follow him.

Disembarking from a taxi after a ten-minute ride, we went up to the ninth floor of a building in Koenji, a major stop on the Chuo commuter line, and found ourselves at the entrance to an expensive-looking nightclub. Beautiful young women in evening gowns lined up on either side to greet us, bowing deeply as we entered, along with a tuxedoed gentleman who appeared to be the manager.

"This is ours," Jiro said. "It belongs to the Sumiyoshi."

The manager was visibly tense in Jiro's presence, eyeing him as if he were a bomb that was that about to explode.

We went into the darkened interior, past a huge, brightly lit fish tank, and sat down in a booth. A band played Latin music as colored glitter balls sparkled overhead. A bottle of XO Reserve appeared with a bucket of ice, a platter of oysters, and assorted *tsumami* (nibbles to accompany drinks). Hostesses offered hot *oshibori* towels, poured our drinks, and lit our cigarettes.

One of them, a young woman named Emiko, was particularly stunning. She looked like something out of a Toho movie poster. Long dark tresses, lithe figure, shapely legs, gleaming white teeth, porcelain skin, and pearl necklace. She was perfect. Not a hair out of place.

"You want to screw her?" Jiro said, sticking his thumb between his index and middle fingers, a universal sign in Japan for the sex act. "Take her in the back to an empty booth."

My jaw fell.

"Don't worry," he said, "it doesn't bother her. She will do what I tell her to do. We own this place." He barked something in Japanese to her that was unintelligible to me but clearly understood by her, as she bowed obediently in response and grabbed my hand. Still flustered, embarrassed actually, I managed to conjure up a meaningless smile and stayed where I was.

"Maybe later," I mumbled awkwardly. "I'd like to get to know her a little bit first."

He shrugged and had the hostess beside him refill his glass. A couple of drinks later Jiro suddenly stood up and said, "Time to go." He laid several ¥10,000 bills on the table and bolted for the door, pulling me behind him. He had just remembered an assignment he had to carry out and sent me on my way.

The next morning at 8 a.m. there came another knock at my front door and there he was, not entirely sober, his eyes little black balls. With him were Emiko and a second hostess from the Koenji nightclub, still dressed to kill in their evening gowns.

"Let us in Bobu-san," he said. "We've come to say hello."

* * *

Thus, the bizarre friendship between the two of us began. Jiro appeared periodically, out of the blue sometimes. He stopped making the walk up the flight of stairs to my second-floor apartment. Instead he just stood on the street and yelled up at me to come out: "Bobu-san . . . BOBU-SAN!!! *Dete koi!*" (Come down!) He would then take me around to Sumiyoshi-run establishments, nightclubs, *pachinko* shops, and gambling dens.

I had never met anyone quite like him. What he really wanted out of me—if anything—was not clear. He was, however, the first Japanese friend I ever had who never wanted to speak English with me, which was somehow flattering.

I had gained access to a world few Japanese got to see, let alone foreigners. I guess that was part of the attraction in the beginning—a hidden aspect of Japanese culture, and one that accepted me to boot. It was a world in which the adrenalin was always pumping. There was some new adventure every night. A nightclub opening. Back room gambling with *hanafuda* (Japanese flower cards). A reception for a new *pachinko* shop. It was certainly more exciting than sitting behind a desk, even if it wasn't quite the same as what you would see in the Ken Takakura/Toei films, which romanticized the hell out the yakuza life. What I saw was not quite so idyllic.

Most members of the gang looked rather unhealthy, with sallow skin and pasty complexions, not at all like the robust faces of the film actors. They smoked nonstop, drank from early in the morning, read comic books, and opted for fashions that announced unmistakably who they were: dark double-breasted suits, the suit coat worn loose on the shoulders, loud print shirts, gold necklaces, and white shoes. Many of them were ethnic Koreans, I discovered, individuals on the lower rungs of society, looking for something to belong to and finding acceptance in the Japanese underworld.

The author Yasuharu Honda, who wrote the masterpiece *Kizu* about the life of a postwar Shibuya gangster, was famous for saying that there was no such thing as a "good yakuza." "It is a fallacy," he wrote. "I have seen the Toei yakuza movies where the yakuza hero is on the side of justice, but I don't know if such a figure actually exists. I don't know anyone who I can say is a 'good' yakuza."

It was a lesson I would also learn.

I knew the sayings about "moth to the flame" and "lying down with dogs." I had even learned the Japanese equivalent in language school, "If you immerse yourself in cinnabar, you're going to turn red," which did not exactly sing in translation. At the time, however, curiosity outweighed caution.

* * *

In time, Jiro introduced me to his boss, another big fan of the LDP who was suitably impressed to hear that I had actually met that great man, Yasuhiro Nakasone. The sit-down took place at the local Sumiyoshi headquarters a block from the Higashi-Nakano Station police box. The boss's office was furnished with a gigantic desk of polished oak, two matching leather sofas with a big glass coffee table in between, and assorted chairs on the other side of the room where the gang members sat. There was a large safe in one corner. Photos of the Sumiyoshi hierarchy adorned the walls, including one of Jiro's boss in formal *hakama*, a divided skirt with pleats, holding a fan. The *oyabun* himself was a stocky man of medium height, with a considerable paunch and slick-backed hair that exuded a flowery fragrance. I had seen him on the streets of Higashi-Nakano, riding around in a big Lincoln with dainty lace curtains on the windows, way too big for Tokyo's narrow roads.

The *oyabun* looked thoroughly dissipated from alcohol and, no doubt, other types of pharmaceutical aids. But he greeted me in a loud voice, motioned for me to sit down on the sofa, and had coffee served. He entertained me with stories of his rise through

the ranks, the memorable fights he had had, the business operations in Higashi-Nakano, minus the incriminating details, and his
stints in prison. He also made brief reference to fighting in the Pacific War,
working in the postwar black markets, and battling leftist dem-
onstrators in 1960, fighting alongside the police. He was, he said,
a lifelong supporter of conservative government and a staunch
friend of the United States.

He invited me to a reception they were about to hold in the
sake house they maintained downstairs. The occasion was some
anniversary in the gang, the explanation for which I could not
understand. Jiro led me down to a private room in the back, where
a long, low buffet table was laid out with sashimi, sushi, roast beef,
smoked salmon, beer, whisky, wine, Japanese sake, and a stronger
vodka-like concoction known as *shochu*.

I sat at the end of the table and listened as the boss, who had
changed into a silvery white kimono, gave a long flowery speech,
toasted his men, and then started in on serious drinking. About
half an hour later, thoroughly lubricated, he walked over to my
end of the table and plopped his rear end on a chair.

"Let's arm wrestle," he said, grinning.

That he would do that was not exactly a surprise. I had been
challenged before in drinking establishments by young men, evidently weightlifters, looking to score points with the crowd (and
themselves) by vanquishing a foreigner. After a couple of embarrassments I acquired a set of barbells so that I might preserve the
honor of my tribe, and I did not suffer many defeats after that.

But arm wrestling the gang boss of Higashi-Nakano was
another proposition. There was the delicate matter of face to be
considered here, and face lost on either side was not a desired out-
come. After a time, with a suitable amount of huffing and puffing,
he decided to call it a draw. He shook my hand vigorously. Then
he stood up, lowered his kimono top, and showed me his tattoo—
his arms and back covered in an ornately designed fire-breathing

dragon. It was quite remarkable. It had taken, I was certain, weeks of painful sessions with a tattoo artist.

The *oyabun* told me he was an admirer of the United States, but he couldn't understand why the country wasn't making more headway against the North Vietnamese.

"I absolutely hate communists!" he said, his face turning a shade redder as he pounded the table. "Nixon should go in there and take over the whole country. America has the power. They should use it. Why hold back?"

I thought of the protest marches of my days at Sophia. As though reading my mind, he then launched into a diatribe against the leftist students who were disrupting the social order. "Students hijacking universities," he spat, "it's a disgrace!" He thought they should all be rounded up and put in special education camps. Or better yet, Abashiri Prison in northern Hokkaido, where prisoners had to endure subzero temperatures with no heating.

Then, as the beer and sake continued to flow freely, the *oyabun* started to sing. He belted out an old Japanese war song and then another. Then he urged me to take a turn. So I got up on my knees and sang "God Bless America," a song I had added to my repertoire for such occasions. Abruptly, he grabbed me in a playful headlock, pulling my head into his lap and holding it there, applying more and more pressure until I began to feel uncomfortable. I remember looking at his feet, which were clad in expensive white silk socks, and noticing the odor. Then, just as abruptly, he released me, laughing. He patted me on the back and complimented me on my strength to everyone.

Tsuyoi desu ne, kono gaijin-san. What a strong foreigner.

Then he got down to business. Handguns. It was a personal hobby. Was there any way I could help him in expanding his collection? Perhaps I knew someone at one of the bases?

"A .44 Magnum would be nice," he said. "Like *Dirty Harry*." He said he would be very grateful.

Guns? I had never bought a handgun in my life. In fact, I had only held one once, during a security drill at the ELINT Center. The only time I had ever actually fired a weapon was during basic training at Lackland Air Force Base where I was required to learn to shoot an M-1 rifle. More importantly, there was something called the Sword and Firearms Law in Japan, and it demanded strict penalties for those who violated it. Mere possession of a handgun could get you thrown in jail for months, even years. I was stupid, but not that stupid. I left, thanking him for the hospitality and saying I'd give his request my sincerest consideration, hoping to delay long enough so that he would eventually forget about it.

As I soon learned, Jiro and his boss had another motive for their display of hospitality. The Sumiyoshi was going to open up a new nightclub in Shinjuku on the Nishiguchi side. It was to be staffed by hostesses brought in from Manila and Bangkok. The problem was that no one in the gang could speak English and none of the girls could speak Japanese, so Jiro had the bright idea of hiring me to manage them. He offered me the job, six nights a week, from seven until midnight for ¥300,000 a month, roughly $1,000 at the time.

I wasn't sure about that. For one thing, I already had a job and was making decent money. For another, I'd be working fifteen-hour days and would wear myself out. And beyond that, what the hell did I know about managing a nightclub? At the same time, however, the idea was intriguing—a new experience I never could have imagined would come my way. I said I would think about it and left it at that for the time being.

* * *

The more I got to know about the gang, the more I began to understand the myriad ways it carried on its affairs. Two men entering the restroom together in a local pub meant that a drug exchange was going on. The fliers bearing photos and telephone numbers of scantily clad young ladies, which one found plastered all over

I became an "unofficial advisor" to the Shinjuku Sumiyoshi Ikka family, members of which are pictured here.

telephone booths, were put there by *chinpira*. The *fudosan,* or real estate agency, near Higashi-Nakano Station was run by a man in a flashy double-breasted suit, pomaded hair, and high-heel boots who took his orders directly from the Sumiyoshi.

The connective tissue the underworld shared with the LDP was, first and foremost, through construction. (Later, during the bubble era of the 1980s, it would be banking.) Japan had the largest public works program in the world. From 1970 to 1990, Japan's GDP would roughly double, but construction investment would grow 5.5 times, reaching a peak in 1990 of more than 15 percent of the GDP. It was an astonishing figure, the highest in the world. It was a time when Japan, an island chain slightly smaller in area than the state of California, would pour thirty-two times as much concrete as the entire United States, a country with more than twice the population, but one without a Ministry of Construction.

This was one very important way for the LDP to retain power.

The government would use taxpayer funds to finance regional construction projects—dams, highways, bridges, concert halls, etc.—and the construction companies would kickback a percentage of the funds to LDP politicians for use at campaign time, as a way of saying thanks. Since the gangs were tied to the construction firms, with organized crime in Japan taking in some 15 percent of the total construction revenue through their various services and scams, it was no wonder the mob liked the LDP so much and worked for them at election time.

The Sumiyoshi gang was involved in a number of construction projects in the Shinjuku area, including several high-rises near the Keio Plaza Hotel. In addition to brothels and *bento* lunches, Jiro told me that they also provided hiring halls, cheap labor, dirt removal, and waste disposal—all at a handsome profit. Many lower-ranking gang members were also earning extra cash as construction workers.

One time as we were passing one of these sites together Jiro stopped and pointed to a knot of vociferous protestors shouting environmental slogans and demanding compensation for the supposed noise and air pollution the work was causing. "Members of one of our rival gangs, the Yamaguchi-gumi," he explained. "They were shut out of the project, so they come around posing as 'environmentalists' and cause as much trouble as they can. It's very common. We do the same thing."

* * *

In the meantime, I waited a decent interval before sending word through Jiro that my exhaustive search of on-base sources failed to come up with the desired Magnum. I made sure he would convey my profuse apologies as well. I also turned down the nightclub offer, for reasons already cited. But to demonstrate my sincerity, I offered to help out on the side, sending notes and so forth. They would ask me to write messages they could show the girls to ensure smooth club operations: "Don't drink so much," "Don't sleep with the customers," or "Please sleep with the customers." Sometimes, if they were having a problem with a particular hostess, I would go and have a talk with her. In this way I became an informal advisor, which is what they started calling me: *gaijin komon.*

At the time, there was a lot of reporting about human trafficking involving *yakuza* and young women from Southeast Asia. The latter were recruited under the pretense that they would work as entertainers, but when they got to Japan their passports were seized and they were forced to work in truck-stop brothels. But I didn't see any of that with the hostesses at the Sumiyoshi club. They were all in Japan because they wanted to make money, and they were clear-eyed about what they were doing. The problems they had were mostly with abusive customers. Abusive boyfriends. Health issues. A couple of unwanted pregnancies. So I would translate the complaint and relay it to Jiro.

By then, however, the combined workings of conscience and common sense began to give me pause about the whole business. The *oyabun's* headlock, while of little physical consequence, began to loom larger in a symbolic sense. The luster was wearing off. Then, a little further on, a couple of events would prove decisive.

* * *

My friends in the Higashi-Nakano gang liked to tell me that the yakuza were different from the mafia. The latter just worked for money, they said, but yakuza had a tradition of helping people out in times of trouble. They viewed themselves as an asset to the community. They collected debts for people, settled disputes, lent a hand in times of community crisis, and tracked down serial killers in cooperation with the police. The Mafia didn't do those things, they sniffed. They just sucked money out of the community.

But from what I could see, ordinary people in the neighborhood were scared shitless of the yakuza, and for good reason. They could be nice one moment, as polite as can be, then suddenly fly into a fit of anger and slam the table or hurl a glass against the wall. Everyone in the gang drank copiously and seemed to be taking some form of methamphetamine. The combination did slow damage to the central nervous system and caused a perpetual chemical imbalance that put them on edge, ready to fight at the first perceived insult. A psychologically stable yakuza was an oxymoron.

I remember a time in Bokido, one of the weatherbeaten gang members who moonlighted as a construction worker decided we should formally become friends and do the "friendship ceremony." Drunk (or stoned) out of his mind, he took a set of wooden chopsticks from one of the snack bar tables, split it in two, bit off the end of one stick, and then, with great flair, stabbed himself in the chest.

"That's how you do it," he said, after his scream died out. "Now you."

I declined the proffered second chopstick, my eyes fixed on the blood seeping from his wound, begging off on the pretext that I could not consider myself worthy of the friendship of so courageous a man, and got the hell out of there as soon as it seemed diplomatically appropriate. I didn't want him to complete my half of the ritual for me.

My friend Jiro was no different from the others. Jiro drank beer for breakfast, sipped *shochu* throughout the day, and smoked a hundred cigarettes daily. He took speed in the evening so he could stay awake until the wee hours making his rounds, then took sleeping pills with double shots of whisky to get to sleep. He was a bundle of nerves, perpetually on edge.

The more I got to know him, the more I saw of his dark side. After several drinks he was apt to fly into a sudden, uncontrollable rage over the smallest thing—running out of cigarettes, poor service—and overturn his table, sending beer bottles and glasses flying.

Having an explosive temper was of course helpful in Jiro's job, which was essentially scaring the hell out of people for money. But he could not seem to control it very well off duty. If there was no one around to fight, well, then he turned on himself. That's what happened one night at Bokido when he went on a maudlin tear about having no friends or family. In the midst of it he pulled a jackknife out of his pocket and slashed his cheek. "I'm human trash," he moaned. "*Ningen no kuzu.*"

At one point, Jiro disappeared from the neighborhood for several months. I heard he had been arrested. When he returned, he told me he had been serving a term in Fuchu Prison, but refused to say what for. He was minus the tip of his left pinkie, which he had had to slice off and give to his boss as penance for getting arrested in the first place. Otherwise he seemed to have no difficulty resuming his daily round.

One memorable, besotted evening around midnight, we stood together in the street as he tried in vain to flag down a cab. Midnight was the witching hour for Tokyo taxis in that era. It was when the last trains had taken off and cab drivers began refusing passengers and demanding multiples of the normal fare, long distance only.

The drivers would cruise past looking straight ahead, ignoring people waiting on the curb, until someone held up three or four fingers, signaling a willingness to pay three or four times the normal fare.

Jiro waved his hand at a cab coming up the road at about 5 miles an hour and the driver sailed by without even turning his head. This sent Jiro into paroxysms of anger.

He kicked the back end of the car where the fuel tank was, a karate-style kick that left a huge dent in the chassis. The driver slammed on the brakes and got out of the car. He looked at the dent, then started pointing his finger and yelling obscenities at Jiro. "*Kono yaro! Baka yaro!*" (You fucking idiot! Asshole! to loosely translate.)

This proved unwise. Jiro balled his fist and punched the driver in the face, three times in succession, knocking him to the asphalt. Jiro kicked him, then leapt on top of him, continuing to hit him in the face with a series of lefts and rights. Blood spurted from the driver's nose and he screamed in pain. Pedestrians stopped to watch, appalled by what they were seeing, but dared not intervene.

I felt sick.

I grabbed Jiro and pulled him away from the hapless driver, lying on the ground semiconscious.

"Jesus Christ," I said. "Stop it. You're going to kill the guy. You're going to get us arrested. Let's get out of here."

"It's his own fault," Jiro said, as we stumbled up the street in search of another cab. "The guy should have stopped and picked us up."

It was then that I decided to distance myself from the yakuza milieu once and for all.

* * *

The last time I ever saw Jiro was the night he showed up at my front door out of breath, looking nervous. He was in trouble of some sort, he said, and he desperately needed cash. For what, he did not elaborate.

"*Onegai da. Kane wo kashite kure.*" (I need a favor. Lend me some money.)

I had withdrawn some cash earlier that day and it was sitting there in full view on my rickety kitchen table. I got it and handed it to him. He stuffed the bills into his pocket, muttered thanks, and bolted away down the stairs.

And with that, he just disappeared from the neighborhood, and from my life.

Gaijin Complex

By my tenth year in Japan, I had reached a turning point. I had a good job making a good salary. I could have stayed and moved up the ranks, but I was getting tired of being a *gaijin* in Tokyo, with everything that the word implied. I was tired of having the same conversations with people I'd meet. Can you use chopsticks? Did you know Japan had four seasons? Why are you here?

I could answer the first two of those questions with no difficulty, but I was having increasing trouble with the last one.

Dwight, my coworker at EB, couldn't wait to get out of Japan. "Japan is a place to come when you are old, after you have lived your real life somewhere else," he liked to say. "You need to get back home to the Real World."

Dwight was one of those who never bothered to learn the language, arguing that you got a clearer view of the society without it. This perspective convinced him that Japan was no place "for young Americans like us, full of ideas and energy." I thought the first part of his argument absurd but found myself agreeing with the conclusion.

I recalled the words of Father Arthur Beaulieu: "Go back to your own country and make a life. Japan is no place for a young foreign man. Don't stay. You will lose yourself."

I knew I had missed ten years of American life and times, reduced to observing a huge chunk of it unfold from afar. I had seen the landmark film *Easy Rider* on a trip back to the United States to visit my parents, taking it in at a Waikiki Roadshow Theater during a Honolulu stopover, but I was so stoned from the huge cloud of marijuana produced by the SRO audience that it took me a while to understand that the point of the film was to extend a huge middle finger to Nixon's Silent Majority as well as a salutary nod to Oedipal anger.

I had watched the first moon landing in the show window

With my EB co-author Dwight in Roppongi.

of the Sony Building in Ginza, along with a group of awestruck pedestrians on July 21, 1969. I had followed the other events of the era—the Vietnam War, the Martin Luther King Jr. and Bobby Kennedy assassinations, Chappaquiddick, Women's Lib, the first Earth Day, the first Led Zeppelin album, the growth of the counter culture, the sit-ins, the marches, People Power, Flower Power, Black Power, psychedelic music, "Turn On, Tune In, and Drop Out," Woodstock, the Grateful Dead, the Charles Manson murders, the deaths of Janis Joplin and Jimmy Hendrix, and the NY Jets Super Bowl upset of the Baltimore Colts—all from 5,000 miles away.

The usual international news medium was film, which took twenty-four hours to be flown from the US to Japan and shown on television. Satellite TV was used sparely in those days. There was no cable TV, no internet, no email, no fax—only the clunky and expensive Teletype systems used by the AP and UPI wire services. Magazines like *Time* and *Newsweek* were available only at the major hotels and Western bookstores like Jena in the Ginza and Kinokuniya in Shinjuku. International telephone calls were expensive and often time consuming. Cell phones were non-existent. People still sent telegrams.

In compensation, I did have a front row seat for the Yukio Mishima ritual suicide on the balcony of the Japan Self-Defense Forces Headquarters in front of a lunchtime crowd and for the crackdown on the radical-leftist movement of the 1960s by the National Police. The latter culminated in a dramatic shootout between police and the Japanese revolutionary group, the United Red Army, in February 1972 at a mountain resort in Karuizawa, telecast live on nationwide TV. It garnered some of the highest ratings seen since the Women's Volleyball finals in the 1964 Olympics when Japan won the gold medal versus a larger, stronger Soviet squad, and it marked the end of the radical left in Japan.

* * *

But where did all that leave me? Ten years earlier, I had embarked on a voyage of self-discovery, but somewhere along the line I switched to autopilot. Life here had slowly changed me without my realizing it. I started to take notice and I didn't like what I saw.

I had developed bizarre social skills, to use the term loosely. I knew how to talk to my fellow Tokyoites but found I was becoming less conversant with Americans. I peppered my speech with Japanese words used all the time in daily conversation—*sugoi, shoganai, maitta* (wow, can't be helped, I give up)—without realizing what I was doing. Moreover, I had unconsciously adopted Japanese mannerisms: bowing when talking on the phone, sucking wind as Japanese do when trying to think of something to say, pouring beer for dinner partners.

This proved disconcerting to visiting Americans, including executives from EB headquarters in Chicago. So did my choice of dinner conversation topics: My enthusiastic comments on the Japanese pennant race or the latest doings of the LDP consistently drew blank stares.

I knew what Americans thought about their fellow countrymen who lived in Japan a long time. Gone native, they would say, shaking their heads. A lifer. Couldn't make it back in the Real World. Pity. What a waste.

I had reached my limit in other ways as well. I had become increasingly dissolute, tottering home drunk every night after midnight, eyes bleary, suit rumpled, some Shinjuku *zubeko* in tow, often as not. I knew every bar in Kabuki-cho, as well as everyone in Higashi-Nakano. I smoked sixty cigarettes a day. Whereas before I had prided myself on my health and physical fitness, I was grossly out of shape. Sometimes in the morning my hands shook so badly I could not hold a cup of coffee. My breakfast was a bottle of Lipovitan D, purchased at the train station kiosk as I stumbled up the stairs on my way to the office in Shinjuku.

I would wake up in the middle of the night, half-blotto, to hear people yelling my name on the street outside. In the days before I "washed my feet" (an underworld term for going straight), Jiro, or one of his yakuza friends, would insist that I come down and have a drink with them at 2 a.m. Sometimes I would actually crawl out of bed and comply. On more than one occasion, the late-night screamers were women.

One very hot and muggy summer's night, I was awakened by a duet of dulcet voices. Dragging myself to the window I saw a pair of provocatively dressed and heavily made-up young women—nurses at the local hospital who moonlighted at a small bar run by the Sumiyoshi down the street. Earlier, I had forgotten something at the place—a book, a lighter—I don't remember what it was, but they took it into their heads that now would be a good time to return it to me.

Encouraged by the sight of me at the window, they came bounding up the stairs to throw open the door—of my next-door neighbor's apartment, where a late-night poker game involving Swiss-German securities traders was going on. That did not go down well. The traders didn't mind, but their girlfriends, who were also present, did mind and an unpleasant shouting match ensued, which moved out into the hallway, waking other tenants.

I was mortified. And so was my landlady, who stopped me at the base of the stairwell the next morning and said, in her not so inscrutable way, "Whiting-san, *yoru ni yoku katsuyaku shite irrashaimasu ne*" (You have an active nightlife, I see). She had already grown tired of the late-night noise and I think that was the last straw. It was her way of asking me to move.

I attempted to repair the damage by giving her a set of encyclopedias, which I had bought at a really low discount from the company. However, Japan being the reciprocity-based society that it is, my gift elicited an enormous basket of fruit from her in return, furiously delivered within twelve hours of the receipt of the EB set. It was fruit in amounts that I could never hope to consume before it began to spoil. So I smuggled it out under cover of dark and gave it to the nurses. I sent two copies of the encyclopedia to the nurses as well. That made three sets of all the world's knowledge to people who couldn't read them.

It really was time to make a change.

EB wanted Dwight and me to stick around and do another program, this one for older children. The course we did was selling like hotcakes, but none of the revenue was going into our pockets. The company promised us salary raises and offered to pay for expensive expat-style apartments as well. However, they refused to pay royalties.

We turned them down and, mercenaries that we were, hopped in a cab down to Akasaka and the Tokyo headquarters of Grolier, Inc., publisher of the Encyclopedia Americana, and offered to produce a children's language course to compete with the *First Steps in English* package, which we had created for EB. Grolier accepted our proposal, agreeing to pay royalties.

It took a year to finish the project and within two months after that, I was gone.

I was thirty years old. I had enough savings to pay for a trip around the world and then live for a couple of years on the Grolier money. So I decided to move to New York and see what life had in store for me. Maybe the identity I had been looking for was waiting for me there.

The Penitent

New York Hegira

New York City turned out to be the polar opposite of Tokyo in many glaring respects. Less *Breakfast at Tiffany's* and more *Midnight Cowboy*, less *On the Town* and more *Taxi Driver*; a violent, decaying metropolis. There was garbage everywhere, dog shit on the streets. The subways were dark and dirty, the stations announced over the public address system were indecipherable. City cabs were like mobile trashcans. There was a beggar on every streetcorner, many not begging but demanding money, intercepting you as walked down the street, hand out, glaring with menace.

It was the era of Travis Bickle, Robert De Niro's depressed and angry lead character in *Taxi Driver*, when Times Square was an unrivalled cesspool, a gritty and desperate place where streetwalkers and drug dealers openly plied their trades. In all, there were 2,000 murders a year in New York according to police statistics. More than 90,000 robberies. Delivery boys were afraid to leave their bikes alone for five minutes. They had to padlock them, remove a wheel, and carry it with them as far as the doorway they were delivering to. At night, pedestrians walked on the outside edge of the sidewalk for fear that muggers were lurking inside darkened portals.

Determined to see it through, I rented an apartment on West 82nd Street, near Central Park West, just around the corner from the Museum of Natural History. It was a fourth-floor studio walkup with central heating and air conditioning, a fake brick fireplace, a four-burner stove, and a refrigerator. The rent was $240 a month. Nice neighborhood too.

One day shortly after I had moved in, I was standing under an awning in front of my local bodega on the corner of 81st and Central Park West, waiting for the rain to clear, holding my groceries. I watched a man in front of me, a young Hispanic male, pull a switchblade from his pocket, click it open, and stick it in the back of the person in front of him, another young Hispanic, then take off running. There had apparently been a dispute over a girl, or so the store clerk said later. The following week, the butcher shop up the street from Zabar's, the West Side's food emporium par excellence and a mecca for locals and tourists alike, was robbed by two men with shotguns in broad daylight. During my first year in New York, thieves used a sledgehammer to break through the wall of a friend's apartment to steal a purse.

An enduring memory was going to see the Charles Bronson movie *Death Wish*, about a self-appointed NYC West Side vigilante who takes his revenge on the city's muggers after three of them killed his wife and raped his daughter. The audience stood and cheered wildly every time Bronson blew someone away with his .39 Smith and Wesson.

Welcome to New York.

I did have friends in the city, people I knew from my EB Japan days who lived in the same Upper West Side neighborhood, principally Dwight and Mary Ann with their respective spouses, Mary and Dale. We would often assemble at Teacher's, located in between Zabar's and the robbed butcher shop on Broadway, or Marvin Gardens up the street on the corner of 81st, both popular watering holes frequented by young artists and writers. Everyone wore bell-bottomed trousers and listened to songs like Paul Simon's "Kodachrome" and Carly Simon's "You're So Vain" playing in the background, while holding forth on topics like Ram Dass's *Be Here Now*. The faint smell of marijuana invariably filled the air.

I spent a lot of time telling people what Tokyo was like. I told them about the high literacy rate, the low crime, the weapons law that made it almost impossible to own a handgun or a sword, and the consideration for others—for example, how people who had caught a cold would wear facemasks to prevent their germs from spreading to others. I praised the work ethic and the relentless perfectionism, such as when a train arriving twenty seconds late would elicit an apology by the stationmaster over the PA system.

If my interlocutor's eyes did not glaze over, I also went into the political system, the factions of the LDP, the labor unions, the *salaryman,* the yakuza, and the Tokyo bars. Oddly enough, what people seemed most interested in was baseball, how Japanese turned a wholly American game into something completely their own.

I would tell them about Sadaharu Oh taking "batting practice" with a sword, spring training that began in the freezing cold of midwinter, the 1,000-fungo drill, endless pre- and post-game meetings, the *ketsu batto,* and the anti-foreignism. That always seemed to get their interest.

The more I talked the clearer it became that the Japanese approach to baseball, with its focus on harmony and effort and the corollary distrust of foreign players, even when they wore the same uniform, was a metaphor for the society as a whole. Baseball provided a window into the culture, the national character— if there is such a thing—and on the values and assumptions that divide the Japanese version of the game from ours.

It was Dwight who suggested I write a book on the subject. He had heard all my stories multiple times and thought them interesting despite the fact that, as a former ice hockey player from Detroit, he found baseball boring, incomprehensible, and a waste of time. "Why do you watch that shit?" he would say. But now that he had become fixated on the book idea, he became its number-one advocate.

He persuaded our circle of friends that writing the book should, in fact, be my number-one priority as long as I was in New York, that it was in fact my duty to explain to American readers how the psyche of the world's #2 economy was put together and their duty as friends to see that I kept at it until it was done.

Did I find the idea of writing a book daunting? All I knew was how to read them. I didn't know anyone who had written one and I hadn't a clue how to go about it. I procrastinated despite the constant urging, nagging actually, of the West Side group. They kept at me. I kept procrastinating. Then they switched tactics:

"Well, Whiting, I guess you just don't have what it takes to write a book. Too bad. Maybe you should find something else to do, like driving a cab."

That did it. My juvenile pride kicked into gear and I made Dwight a bet of $500 that I would indeed do the book, and have it done in a year. I went to the Barnes and Noble store at 5th Avenue and 46th Street, across from Saks, bought a book on how to write nonfiction, and studied it.

Rule Number One, as I recall, was that an author should be able to express the thesis of his book in one sentence. Everything else should flow from that algorithm. I hammered out mine— "The Japanese national character as seen through baseball"—and the book's basic structure with Dale, Dwight, and other West Side friends in a skull session at Marvin Gardens. I clearly remember Marvin Gaye singing "Let's Get It On" in the background. Appropriate.

There was a clear narrative here. Japan's high schools and universities had learned baseball from American professors in the late 19th century, after centuries of feudal isolation, and had turned it into their own game, one with an intense focus on the essentials of the martial arts—endless training, discipline, and development of spirit—combined with group harmony or *wa*. With this model, they were able to defeat, on occasion, American amateur and professional teams in international competition.

Japanese professional leagues began in 1935 and took on touring MLB teams. Baseball became a symbol of Japan's determination to catch up with the more industrially advanced West, using the same model of dedication, or *magokoro* as they called it, and discipline. And after defeat in World War 2, success in baseball became a way for Japan to regain national pride on a global stage, with the home-run-hitting Oh becoming famous in the United States and other baseball-playing countries—so famous in the US that he made the cover of *Sports Illustrated*.

I spent the next few weeks at the New York Public Library poring over Japanese newspapers from the late 19th century on. A friend, a bodybuilding Tokyo stockbroker at Yamaichi Securities named Dyke Nakamura, sent me copies of the *Nikkan Sports* and *Chunichi Sports* a couple of times a week.

Then I started writing. It took me six months to finish the first draft, 75,000 words, living on pizza and beer.

Then, I gathered up my nerve and looked up Daryl Spencer, the baseball villain of *Kyojin no Hoshi* fame. The former Major Leaguer had just retired after seven years with the Hankyu Braves and was living in Wichita, Kansas, coaching the Coors baseball team, the Wichita Dreamliners, of the National Baseball Congress.

* * *

Spencer couldn't have been friendlier, especially when I told him I was writing a book and he was a big part of it. So I sent him a copy of my draft and then a couple of weeks later flew out to see him and talk about it. He picked me up at the Wichita Airport. He was still big and brawny in his mid-forties, the same 6'2", but about 50 pounds heavier than he had been in Japan. He took me to the cafeteria at the Coors factory and led me to a table in the corner.

He ordered a huge pitcher of beer and pulled out his copy of the manuscript, which he had marked up with a pencil. He put on a pair of spectacles and said with a laugh:

"Actually, I want you to know, this is the first book I have ever read from beginning to end."

Spencer went through the manuscript, endorsed the basic thesis, and pointed out the mistakes.

"The key to understanding Japan," he told me, "is to think backwards. Just think the opposite of what you did in the States and you will be ok. Don't argue with anybody because the Japanese don't like confrontation. And don't slide hard into base because you might hurt the fielder. I was always getting into trouble for that in Japan. They said I had bad deportment. They called me *kai-butsu*, a monster."

"Also," he continued, "don't tease your teammates. Don't play practical jokes on anybody. Show up for team meetings early. Work as hard in practice as you do in the game. Don't make too much noise in the dugout. Don't damage team harmony. And let the Japanese win the titles and take the credit."

It was a familiar mantra, a version of which I had learned myself. It actually made me feel a bit nostalgic.

"Baseball in Japan is all about losing face," he said. "Batters sacrifice bunt because they are afraid to swing away and possibly suffer the embarrassment of striking out. Also, in doing so, they can demonstrate that they are thinking of the team. Pitchers are fined if they gave up a hit while ahead in the count, so they nibble at the corners after two strikes. Coaches have to show they are doing their jobs, so they are constantly coming out to offer advice. That drags out the time and games go on much longer than in the United States. In the majors, it is just the opposite. Sacrifice bunts are considered a waste of an out. Three-pitch strikeouts are very common. Coaches leave you alone. Japanese and American baseball are like two different sports. In Japan, you need a chair to sit down in the infield because it takes so long to play an inning."

Daryl Spencer: "You have to learn to think backwards in Japan."

"Just how good are the Japanese?" I asked, as I prepared to leave. A tertiary but nevertheless necessary question.

"When I was in the Major Leagues," he replied, "I could hit most pitchers every now and then, but hardly ever the greats like Koufax or Drysdale. Yet I was a star in Japan. That's the difference. But I would pay to watch Oh and Nagashima. That's how good they are."

* * *

I flew back to New York and started on the second draft. You need a routine to write a book and I had mine. I would get up in the morning and head out to have breakfast at Ray's Pizza over on Broadway, stepping over the ubiquitous dog shit on the sidewalks. If I wanted an excuse to procrastinate, I might take in an early movie at Loew's 83rd or the New Yorker at 89th and Broadway (where I saw *The Getaway* and the *Eiger Sanction* on one glorious double bill). Another option was the Thalia, a tiny art theater on Broadway between 94th and 95th. That's where I saw *The Sorrow and the Pity*. Then I would come back and work from 3 p.m. to 9 p.m. After that I would often take my manuscript and head down to McClade's, a low-rent neighborhood Irish Pub around the corner on 82nd and Columbus. Elbowing through the clientele of neighborhood residents, assorted drunks, and welfare recipients, I'd find a quiet corner and review the day's work.

Once, while sitting at a back table, working on a chapter draft in the dim light, nursing a beer and smoking a Marlboro cigarette, I saw a rather heavyset woman of indeterminate age, face ravaged by alcohol, put a dime in the pay phone in front of the rest room, then spread her legs and urinate on the floor as she dialed.

Shortly after that I moved my secondary base of operations to the less sordid, if slightly more expensive, Tap a Keg, a watering hole down the street on 79th, which had a pool table, a Space Invaders game, and a younger crowd occupying the tables.

In pursuit of my goal I turned down all invitations to dinner, trips to the country, and other social activities. My friends made periodic visits to see if I was still alive. They seemed to think that the verdict on that was still out. They complained that I lived like a hermit, which in fact I did. There was never any food in the refrigerator, save for salami, mustard, and a loaf of Wonder bread. I wore the same pair of jeans and a shabby sport coat. But I was focused. I had something to prove to my friends, to my old professor at Sophia who had said I needed to learn how to write, and, most of all, to myself. Plus, I had a bet to win. I barely paid attention to the Watergate Senate hearings on my black-and-white Motorola TV.

* * *

Machiko was a regular visitor, in from Case Western Reserve in Cleveland. I'd met her at a private dinner in Tokyo in the spring of 1972 when we were both making plans to leave Japan, she on a Rotary Club scholarship to the States. Romance had blossomed and we kept it going despite the geographic complications. What a find she was. She was educated, cultured, and intelligent, all the things I wasn't. Among the many things I liked about

April 4, 1972: The date I met my future wife, Machiko Kondo.

Machiko was that she always had her nose in a book, as opposed to most of the young women whose company I had kept, who spent their time gazing in the mirror, as though it contained all the secrets of beauty, truth, and happiness. She also studied French, preparing for a possible career in the United Nations. She had a life. Equally important, she could also type and help out producing clean drafts of my manuscript.

Dwight asked, "What the hell is she doing with you?"

I finally finished the book in the fall of 1974, 100,000 words in all. After xeroxing copies, page by page, at a stationery store on Broadway, I started shopping it around with the help of friends of friends who worked in publishing as associate editors and administrative assistants. Twelve publishers in a row turned it down.

But then, finally, a stroke of luck. I took my opus over to *Sports Illustrated*, to see if I could at least sell an excerpt. A young woman working there read it and said that the magazine would indeed like to publish one of the chapters.

Then she said something completely out of the blue:

"It seems you are having a hard time getting your book published. So here is what I will do. We will hold this until you find a publisher. You can tell the next book editor you show *The Chrysanthemum and the Bat* to that *SI* is taking first serialization rights. That ought to grab their interest."

Then she gave me the name of a man to call at Dodd-Mead. That was on a Friday. By Monday I had an offer of a $2,000 advance, solely on the strength of the *SI* excerpt. It wasn't exactly in the same league as winning the $64,000 question. But it wasn't zero either and it ended my oh-for-thirteen schneid.

"That's quite a coup you pulled off with *SI*," said the editor there, a man named Peter Weed.

It was certainly not a coup of my doing. It was simply an act of kindness on the part of that young woman, whose name was Patricia Ryan. I have never forgotten it. Patricia went on to become the first woman managing editor of *People* magazine. No one was happier to hear of her success than I was. For my part, the experience taught me to have a little faith in people, and to keep swinging, even when you keep striking out.

* * *

I used the advance money to fly back to Tokyo the following February, when spring camp started, to do some follow-up research. Through introductions I was able to attend training camps for the

Chunichi Dragons in Hamamatsu, the Taiyo Whales in Shizuoka, and the Yomiuri Giants in Tamagawa.

Camp was an eye-opener, seeing Japanese-style training up close in person for the first time. Fending off the freezing cold as best I could, I watched from the stands as Japanese coaches put their teams through a series of brutal drills from dawn until dark, yelling (mock) insults all the while.

Former Yankee star Clete Boyer, who was playing for the Whales at that time, invited me to a gathering at his Tokyo apartment several days later and introduced me to all the *gaijin* players in town. Included in the group were many who had made names for themselves in the US Major Leagues, like Roger Repoz, Jim Lefebvre, Charlie Manuel, and John Sipin.

The theme of the evening was familiar: "Nice people, crazy baseball." Too many practices, they complained. Too many meetings. Too many sacrifice bunts. Boyer himself regarded the game in Japan with a mixture of respect and dismay. He admired the work ethic of the players and the astonishing skill of pitchers like Yutaka Enatsu and others who he thought could be stars if only they had a chance to play in the US Major Leagues. He was particularly impressed with the batting prowess of Sadaharu Oh.

"People in America just don't know how great an athlete Oh is," Boyer would say. "I think he's super. If he played in the MLB, he would be a Hall of Famer. He is like Hank Aaron and Ted Williams. In his own way, he is that good. Too bad Americans will never see him play." His expressed dismay was over the brutal abuse of players in training camp, where coaches would kick and slap those who displeased them, and the way teams overworked their pitchers' arms, which often caused premature retirement.

But, above all, Boyer had a special respect for Japan itself and for the organization he played for. He was the only foreign player I would ever know who signed a contract without discussing salary, leaving it up to the team owner to decide later what figure to put in. Tadahiro Ushigome, a Whales official who served as his interpreter,

It was good to be back in Tokyo. Ginza, December 1975.

told me, "The man had *character*. He understood how Japanese felt."

It seemed to me, however, that Boyer was in the midst of a mild depression. He had been one of the most famous players in North America. He had batted cleanup behind Hank Aaron. He had won the National League Gold Glove in 1969. Yet here he was, living alone in far-off Japan. Thirty-eight years old, he was coming off a successful season in which he had hit a solid .282 with 19 home runs and 65 RBIs in 118 games, winning his second straight Diamond Glove. But nobody back in his home country was paying attention. "Playing in Japan," he drawled in his Missouri accent, "I might as well be on Mars."

That was the way I was beginning to feel about being in New York and away from Tokyo.

Riki Mansion and Giant Baba

Being back in Tokyo had proved to be a huge emotional lift, much to my surprise. The streets were full of brand-new Toyota and Nissan automobiles. State-of-the-art Sony Trinitron color

TV sets were flying off the shelves. Everywhere you looked there were vending machines, selling everything from cigarettes and beer to flowers and underwear (and many of these machines even said "thank you" by automatically playing a recorded message of "*domo arigato gozaimashita*" with each purchase). Not one of them was ever vandalized. The city was on the go. The economy was booming. Black limousines clogged the streets of Marunouchi and Kasumigaseki, where the vast majority of large companies, financial institutions, and government agencies were headquartered. The Statehouse in Akasaka was being renovated to host the fifth G7 meeting, with British PM Margaret Thatcher and other luminaries attending, giving the city an enormous boost in prestige.

The west side of Shinjuku now had half a dozen skyscrapers, made possible by new anti-earthquake technology and led by the fifty-five-floor Shinjuku Mitsui building (although from the rooftop observatory Mt. Fuji was barely visible through the auto pollution). The debut of the revolutionary Sony Walkman was just around the corner. The positive energy of the place was infectious. Shibuya's Yoyogi Park was filled with young men in black leather and Elvis-inspired pompadours dancing with their girlfriends in poodle skirts to rockabilly music on their battery-operated stereo cassette players. White-gloved attendants greeted you at department stores with smiles and bows. Everyone seemed happy. Moreover, I was welcomed at old haunts in Shinjuku like the Saru no Koshikake with friendliness like I had never experienced back in the States. I didn't realize how much I missed Tokyo. It was, in fact, depressing to have to go back to New York.

I arrived back in Manhattan in March with a tote bag full of notes and started a rewrite. It took me five months. I ran out of savings in mid-April and had to do temp work as a Kelly-Girl typist, typing business correspondence for Manhattan corporations to make ends meet. By the time I had finished the book and turned it in to Dodd-Mead at the end of July 1975 I had $150 in my bank account, and my rent, which was due on August 1, was $240. I was

In 1968 the Kasumigaseki Building went up. At thirty-eight stories it was the tallest building in Asia. A wave of skyscrapers followed, transforming the city yet again.

beginning to channel my inner Travis Bickle, as I contemplated the depressing possibility of driving a taxi in Manhattan, when the phone rang.

It was someone at Time Life responding to a proposal Dwight and I had cooked up months earlier for a language-learning course for Japanese children, much like the ones we had done at EB, *First Steps in English*, and Grolier, *English Grab Bag*. I had completely forgotten about it.

"How would you like to go to our Tokyo office and do this project for us?" the man said. Of course, they would pay all expenses plus a handsome advance on royalties—so I could feel free to keep my apartment in New York if I so desired.

After I hung up, I sat staring at the phone as though it might ring again and inform me that it was all a joke. I'm not a believer in miracles, and this was the kind of thing that only happened in storybooks. If there were some kind of invisible force at work, however, it was all right with me.

Time Life put us up for two months at the luxury Hotel New Otani, of James Bond fame, while sorting out the particulars of the deal with their Tokyo-based executives. Dwight, for all his "real life" talk, was just as willing as I was to go back. Funny how a couple of years in New York could change your perspective on life

I eventually found a place at Riki Apartments, an eight-story 1963 building, which was part of a Western-style apartment complex in the Akasaka quarter that included the Riki Mansion, the first structures of their kind erected in Tokyo after the war. (The buildings, albeit renovated, still stand today.) I had a seventh-floor one-bedroom flat with a panoramic view of Tokyo Tower and environs. I moved in the fall of 1975 and soon after Machiko joined me.

Riki Apartments and Riki Mansion had been constructed by Rikidozan, the iconic professional wrestler who became a real estate baron at the peak of his fame and earning power before his premature demise at the tip of a gangster's knife.

Rikidozan's widow, a pleasant, attractive, moon-faced former-JAL stewardess and ex-policeman's daughter, was my landlady. She ran what was perhaps the most colorful apartment complex in Tokyo.

Future Prime Minister Yasuhiro Nakasone had a small

sub-office there, in addition to a larger one down the street near the old TBS Building. Tokyo restaurant impresario and underworld denizen Nick Zappetti kept an apartment there. A couple of small trading companies and a talent agency used it as a base of operations. There were nightclub hostesses from the top nightclubs, like the Copacabana, El Morocco, and New Latin Quarter, living there, as well as foreign models—tall, long-legged blondes from Australia, New Zealand, Canada, and America.

Assorted drifters, con artists, hustlers, smugglers, and other ne'er-do-wells also called it home. A famous songstress named Ayumi Ishida, who had recorded "Blue Light Yokohama" and other number-one hits, lived two doors down from me on the seventh floor. I occasionally ran into her in the elevator in the morning on her way down to the vending machine area, often looking somewhat drawn, as though she had been immersing herself in that blue light for longer than the recommended dosage.

Frequently milling around the lobby and parking lot area were men in dark suits and sunglasses. They were from the Tosei-kai, I was told, the ethnic-Korean yakuza group that had run the Ginza and other parts of Tokyo. In fact, bloodstains from a famous yakuza knife fight were faintly visible on the pavement of the driveway. The Tosei-kai had handled promotions for Rikidozan's professional wrestling group, Japan Wrestling Association. Their boss Ginza Machii was the auditor of the JWA. Rikidozan himself was from prewar North Korea, although—like my one-time friend from Happy Valley days—he had had to hide his identity and pretend to be a pureblooded Japanese given the prejudices against Koreans that existed during those days. The Tosei-kai and the Sumiyoshi were archrivals in the battle for control of Tokyo.

One of the more noticeable individuals in this rogues' gallery was a big, brawny, loud, and abusive character named Yamamoto, who tended to get drunk and cause a disruption in neighborhood bars. He was my landlady's protector, the man who ran Riki Enterprises. He claimed he wasn't a yakuza, but you could have fooled me. He wore his kimono open at the chest, even on chilly evenings, so you could see his tattoos as well as a scar from a sword wound. He was the walking definition of bellicosity, and he was there in the lobby office every day. The only time I ever saw him smile was when he was laughing at somebody. With such a character in charge, you naturally didn't want to get too far behind on your rent.

I later learned that the parking area had been the site of a famous sword-and-knife encounter in December 1963 involving foot soldiers from the Tosei-kai and the Sumiyoshi gangster who had stabbed Rikidozan at the New Latin Quarter. It was that yakuza contretemps that accounted for the aforementioned bloodstains.

Living directly above me, in the 8th-floor penthouse, was Giant Baba, a 6'8", 275-pound wrestling behemoth who had moved in after Rikidozan died. At night sometimes I could hear him practicing his falls, which sometimes caused tiny pieces of plaster to fall from my ceiling.

At the time, professional wrestling was a huge sport in Japan. The Friday night matches on live nationwide television drew top ratings, and Baba was a national hero. He was also one of the tallest people in the country, the result of a condition known as *kyojin byo* (gigantism), the result of an excess of growth hormone. Baba had a long, distinctive head, unusually narrow shoulders, and long, thin arms that were surprisingly powerful when he swung them. Getting hit by Baba, it was said, was like getting struck by a derrick boom moving at 60 miles per hour.

I would run into Baba from time to time at the *tonkatsu* (pork cutlet) restaurant Hyotantei next door, with his wife, the daughter of a long-time supporter, who was about half his size—which was nothing unusual because everybody was about half Baba's size. Later, there was a Space Invaders game installed there that we both enjoyed playing, providing occasion for the exchange of pleasantries.

"I can hear you practicing at night sometimes," I told him the first time we met, using the very politest forms of Japanese. "You are very diligent about training."

"*Domo sumimasen.* I am terribly sorry if I disturbed you," he replied in equally polite language, but in a deep, booming voice. "Please forgive my selfishness."

"It's no disturbance at all," I said. "I am proud that such a great wrestling hero is practicing his moves directly above my apartment. It is an honor. I cherish each piece of plaster that falls from the ceiling. Good luck in your coming matches."

"Thank you for your support."

Baba was a nice man, nothing like the ferocious beast he appeared to be in the ring. He was quite intelligent, too. It seemed he always had a book with him. Not some cheap novel, but a serious nonfiction book about a current topic of interest.

In a 2006 Nippon Television survey of the population's "most-liked" one hundred people in history, a list not restricted to Japan. Baba, who had died in 1999, would finish in the #92 slot, ahead of Abraham Lincoln at #93, Frederic Chopin at #95, and Isaac Newton, who came in at #98. Feudal lord Oda Nobunaga was #1, followed by Meiji-period revolutionary Ryoma Sakamoto at #2, and Thomas Edison at #3. Others on the list included Princess Diana at #12, Albert Einstein at #13, John Lennon at #27, Miyamoto Musashi at #29, Audrey Hepburn at #31, JFK at #39, Madame Curie at #64, and Cleopatra at #68.

Baba rose on my personal list after he rescued me from a dicey situation. I was sitting at the counter of the Hyotanei one winter night in 1975, a few months after I moved in, when Yamamoto walked in, blind, stinking drunk, and plopped down next to me. He ordered a jug of sake and wrapped his arm around me as if I were an old friend.

"Whiting-san, my favorite *gaijin*," he said loudly. "So nice to have you in my building." He started slapping my back, a little bit too hard, and hugging me, his rancid breath in my face. I was beginning to feel uncomfortable. Things like this happened occasionally during that era if you were a Westerner out drinking in the city. It was an occupational hazard. Yamamoto was yelling in

"Giant" Baba, my upstairs neighbor at Riki Apartments, inflicting pain in the ring.

my ear now, spittle flying, slurring his words, babbling on about how much he liked me and that he was cherishing our time together. "Whiting-san, *honto ni kawaii. Dai suki.*" (You're really cute. I like you a lot.) He reeked of alcohol. It seemed that he was intentionally trying to be annoying. I tried shoving him away but to no avail.

Giant Baba, who had been sitting at a table on the other side of the room, walked over and grabbed Yamamoto by the arm. "*Kaeri-masho*" (Let's go home), he said. Then he lightly lifted Yamamoto to his feet and pulled him out the door, inclining his head to me slightly as he left.

Grateful, I bowed right back, the movement causing a few beads of cold sweat to drop onto my pork cutlet.

The Chrysanthemum and the Bat

There were actually six seasons in Tokyo, starting with winter, from mid-December to the first half of March. It was cold to the bone, with the temperature often dropping below zero and occasional snow. There was not nearly as much snow in the city as there was in the northern island of Hokkaido or the Japan Alps and the western coast of Honshu, where record snowfalls buried towns and villages, but there was enough to slow traffic to a crawl and stop the trains. The highlight of winter was New Year, when Tokyoites dressed up in their finest kimono and went to the shrines and temples to say their prayers for the coming year, creating massive crowds. The most popular spot was the magnificent Meiji Jingu in Shibuya, a stately, serene complex of trees and Shinto structures. The first few days of the New Year was time for family gatherings, company receptions, and drinking hot sake.

Spring was heralded by the arrival of the cherry blossoms in late March accompanied by numerous cherry-blossom-viewing events. At Ueno park and other such venues people showed up with large blue tarpaulins and giant bottles of cold *shochu,* among other stimulants. They spread out the tarpaulins under the cherry tree branches and drank the *shochu* while oohing and aahing about the beauty of the little pink flowers and singing drinking songs. Consisting of three national holidays (later expanded to four), the so-called Golden Week followed at the end of April.

The rainy season arrived in mid-May and lasted until mid-July. The temperature and humidity shot up, and mold made its presence known. But it was arguably Tokyo's most beautiful season with the wet, glistening streets, the abundant hydrangeas in bloom, and the glow of the multicolored *kanji* neon signs in the evening mist. The period was called *tsuyu,* literally "plum rain," because it coincided with plum season and the production of plum wine.

Summer with its white-hot days and muggy nights was the draft-beer-drinking season as rooftop bars opened up all over the city. They were a great way to beat the heat, which grew increasingly unbearable. Tokyo emptied out in the middle of August for the Obon holidays, as people returned to their ancestral homes to pay respects at family graves, then lounged on the tatami, drink in hand, in front of the TV to watch the National High School Baseball Championship tournament at Koshien Stadium. The typhoon season kicked in late

The Chrysanthemum and The Bat. Dodd-Mead hardcover edition, 1977.

in the month to offer some relief from the high temperatures and humidity. Typhoon winds were fierce enough at times to knock down the city's ubiquitous telephone wires and other overhead cables and blow parked bicycles out into the streets. Despite heavy winds and torrential rains, however, Tokyo's watering holes usually managed to remain open in honor of the populace's favorite pastime.

Autumn was the best of all seasons, with three months of cool, crisp, clear weather. A time for malt beer. Autumn was also known as the "reading season" in Japan, conducive to passing contemplative hours in the company of a good book. As chance, and this non sequitur, would have it, that is when the Japanese translation of *The Chrysanthemum and the Bat*, known as *Kiku to Batto*, was published in 1977. This was three months after the book had come out in New York and been featured in *Time* magazine, and long after I had finished the Time Life project. The translation hit the bestseller list, much to my surprise, given how huge the publishing business was in Japan. I found myself invited to many media-sponsored end-of-the-year parties—*bonenkai* or "forget-the-year" parties as they are called—in major Tokyo hotels, such affairs being yet another excuse to drink.

At the time, when there was no internet and no digital media to speak of, Japan boasted one of the most highly developed media systems in the world. It had the three largest circulated newspapers in existence, in addition to other well-read dailies in fields ranging from finance to sports, two evening tabloids, and a raft of weekly and monthly magazines on every subject under the sun. There were roughly 4,000 publishing houses in Japan, two-thirds of which were based in Tokyo, and over 20,000 bookstores. The publishing industry cranked out a hundred thousand or so new books a year, and the aisles of said bookstores were clogged with patrons who stood leafing through shelf selections that had caught their fancy. The national and local TV networks boasted huge viewership.

The success of *C&B* in Japan was thanks in part to Tsuneo Watanabe. He had returned to Japan to take over as political editor of the *Yomiuri Shimbun* and had published an article about me in his newspaper read by thirteen million people. It vied for attention with the Lockheed bribery-scandal hearings in the Japanese Diet, which dominated the airwaves. Lockheed, the American aircraft manufacturer, had paid millions of dollars under the table to political and business leaders in Tokyo to secure aircraft sales contracts in Japan. Implicated in the scandal were the former PM and LDP kingmaker Kakuei Tanaka, who would spend years fighting the charges in court, and the aforementioned Yoshio Kodama, who turned out to be Lockheed's bagman.

The publication of *C&B* and its appearance in the top-ten rankings gave me an opportunity to work with the Japanese media for the first time. It was an eye-opening experience starting with

Playboy Japan, which had purchased first serialization rights to the Japanese-language version and wanted to publish an excerpt. *Playboy Japan* was the sister publication of the US magazine published by Hugh Hefner. It had a circulation of over one million, but it differed from the stateside version by virtue of the fact that pubic hair in nude photos was airbrushed out in accordance with Japanese law. (Uncensored copies of *Playboy* and *Penthouse* brought into Japan by overseas travelers were seized at the airport.)

The magazine asked me to choose a likely chapter for them to run. They rejected "Baseball Samurai Style," an overall analysis of the Japanese way of playing the game and how it was reflected in business, education, and other areas of Japanese life, as lacking in "drama." My next suggestion, "The Gaijin's Complaint," about the various difficulties foreign ballplayers experienced in Japan, including discrimination, was also turned down, presumably because it painted a picture unflattering to the Japanese side.

The magazine settled instead on "The Ugly American," chronicling the problems foreign athletes caused with their bad attitude and inability to adjust. The artwork was of a blond-haired, blue-eyed overweight ballplayer with flies buzzing around his head. It was voted the most popular article in the magazine issue in a survey of all *Playboy Japan* employees.

It was my first inkling about what it took to pass muster in the Tokyo media world.

The Chrysanthemum and the Bat was hailed as a revelation by many Japanese. An editor at *Bungei Shunju*, a respected monthly magazine, wrote in an essay about the work, "We never thought of foreign players as real people. We just thought, 'They are paid a lot of money to play baseball and that's that.' This book, however, really made us take a closer look."

I had long suspected that Japanese put *gaijin* in a category outside that of "real people," but to hear someone actually come out and say it was to me the revelation.

A flood of work offers from the media in Japan came in. Now

everyone wanted me to tell them what these foreign athletes were really like and how they really felt about living and playing in Japan.

There were, of course, Japanese interpreters who helped to overcome the language barrier as far as baseball was concerned, but most of them had never lived outside Japan and they were not necessarily adept at understanding and explaining the vast cultural and linguistic differences that separated the two worlds. Indeed, Japanese often had difficulty telling the difference between "normal" and "abnormal"—or eccentric and plain stupid—where a *gaijin* was concerned. They simply lacked the reference points. Thus, if you were a foreigner with mental health issues, Tokyo was a relatively comfortable place to hole up in.

Crazy Wright

One of my first and more memorable assignments was interviewing Clyde Wright, a former California Angels left-handed pitcher who joined the Yomiuri Giants in 1976. He was one of the most recognizable people in the city if not the entire nation. Wright was only the second Caucasian on a team that had traditionally taken pride in its pureblooded makeup—Oh's Chinese ancestry and the few closet Koreans on the roster notwithstanding. He was a brawny, hirsute six-footer—a self-described Tennessee farm boy, who spoke with a thick southern accent (e.g., *Ahm tard* for "I'm tired"). He helped the Giants win Central League pennants in 1976 and 1977 but was given to temper tantrums, a personality trait not well received in Japan. He set a record for fines in his nearly three years with the team for his outbursts of anger, more than anything else over his manager's quick hook. On one occasion, he tore up his uniform; on another, he trashed the clubhouse, throwing a coke bottle through the window of the manager's office. He also

Clyde "Crazy" Wright.

demolished the dugout water cooler, destroyed a photographer's camera, and urinated in the hat of a reporter who had written a negative story about him. He was nicknamed "Crazy Wright" by the Tokyo sports press. What was going on with him? An editor at the weekly magazine *Shukan Bunshun* wanted me to find out.

I spent an evening with Wright in the summer of 1978 at the lobby bar in the Hotel New Japan. He plopped down at my table and showed me a drawing of a T-shirt with "Crazy Wright" printed on it. He said he was going to have thousands of Crazy Wright T-Shirts made up and sell them to Giant fans.

"They think I'm crazy," he drawled. "Hell, this place would drive anyone out of his mind. I might as well make some money at it."

Wright complained he could not understand Japan. He hated the long practices, the endless meetings, and the constant control, which made him feel as though he was in the military. He spoke incredulously about a coach who had pulled him aside after a string of good outings and suggested that he was winning too much and that the other members of the starting rotation were getting "jealous." He further complained that a Giants front-office executive called him in after a series of bad outings and suggested that he might want to send his blond-haired, blue-eyed wife back to Los Angeles, because sex was obviously interfering with his pitching. He provided other intimate details of life on the Giants—players pulling on his chest hair for luck during a game, even yanking his genitals in the shower as a show of "affection." He also gave me the particulars of a drunken fistfight he had had with Yakult Swallows outfielder Charlie Manuel.

We were in the world's largest city, one of the most ostensibly cosmopolitan places on the planet, the host of the most successful Olympics in history, yet, said Wright, "I am treated like a creature from outer space."

At one point, a young man from a nearby table approached with a request for an autograph and asked permission to touch the thick black hair on Wright's forearms. Wright charitably consented, muttering to me under his breath, "I get this all the time. I must be the only person in Japan with body hair."

So we sat there for four hours, downing bottle after bottle of Kirin beer, while he talked and I took furious notes on a thick pocket notepad. By the end of the evening, I was completely plastered, and Wright was still going strong. In fact, I never met anyone who could drink like Clyde Wright (until I met screenwriter/ film director Paul Schrader years later). Neither had the bartenders, who stared at our table in amazement. I barely had enough yen in my Levis pocket to cover the bill. But I had one of the most interesting interviews a writer could hope for, although the effects of the alcohol had turned the latter part of my notes into a barely decipherable scrawl. There seemed to be nothing Wright would not say.

Wright abruptly departed the team shortly after our meeting in peevish opposition to some injustice, and I published the interview. It was a big sensation, especially the part about Wright smashing grapes from a buffet table on coach Yukinobu Kuroe's chest in angry retaliation for Kuroe having grabbed Wright's testicles a bit too hard.

The story greatly upset the control freaks in the Giants front office, whose job it was to sift through every article published about the Giants in the print media and see that the authors of the negative ones were made to understand that such would not be tolerated. Under the Giants restrictive system, players were not allowed to do sit-down interviews with reporters without explicit permission from the front office, or without a substantial fee paid to the team for the privilege. It was a notable departure from the way things were done in the United States.

"Whiting-san," said a Giants PR official, collaring me on the field at Korakuen Stadium before one game as I waited to interview one of the players. He held up a copy of the weekly *Shukan Bunshun* in which the sordid details of the Giants shower room and other subjects were revealed. "We simply can't allow this sort of thing."

"Raito-san is not a member of the Giants anymore," I protested. "He should have the right to say what he wants to whom he wants. Don't you believe in free speech?"

"Yes. He is not a member of the Giants anymore, so he can say what he wants. He is gone now. But you, on the other hand, are not gone. We can make life difficult for writers like you. A word to the wise."

The Destroyer

With the publication of *C&B*, the phone starting ringing with job offers and requests to write for various magazines, both in the United States and Japan. I found it liberating. I could write what I wanted and support myself from the income. I was beholden to no one but myself.

Living in the house that Rikidozan built, and right below his successor as the icon of the sport, it was only natural that I next turn my attention to the subject of professional wrestling. I did a series of articles for *Number* magazine, then the Tokyo-based fledgling sister publication of *Sports Illustrated*.

One thing that piqued my interest was the degree to which *puro-resu*, as it was called, was taken seriously in Japan. It was given a place of honor in the pantheon of sport.

Like baseball in Japan, *puro-resu* was layered with symbolism. If, on the surface, matches were just a way to capitalize on the public's desire to see foreigners vanquished, regardless of whether or not a thumb on the scales was required to do it, there was a good deal more to the sport than that.

For one thing, the Japanese had come to appreciate professional wrestling in a way that was fundamentally different from the way Americans viewed it. In most places in the United States, *anybody* could become a pro-wrestler. There were no prerequisites. You didn't have to go to a wrestling school. You didn't have to pass a test. All you had to do was apply. You went to the relevant commission and obtained a license. Then you went to a promoter who got you a booking.

The Japanese, on the other hand, had instituted an apprentice system similar to that found in sumo. Stars like Baba and his archrival Antonio Inoki developed their own cadres of *kobun* and demanded perfection. They would take a youth of fifteen or sixteen into the stable and train him intensely before ever allowing him to appear in a match. I remember visiting the Baba gym in the city, and it was like a military training camp. It fell to the novice to do all the menial work—set up the ring every day, put out the body-building equipment, and attend to the other wrestlers' needs, all while sedulously learning the various holds and techniques. It was a system designed to inculcate obedience and fighting spirit as well as skill. When young wrestlers were dispatched to the US for an obligatory stint of training there, it was the old-time masters of the sport, like the Belgian-German Carl Gotch and American Vern Gagne, to whom they were sent.

"The Japanese are the most dedicated wrestlers I've ever seen," Gotch would tell me when I interviewed him later on. "They treat their sport as a martial art. By the time they are ready to debut, they really know their technique."

Baba, my upstairs neighbor, came to wrestling circuitously and, with his relatively limited repertoire, could not wholly be considered an exemplar of the sport. With his narrow shoulders and long, thin arms, he did not look the part. But he had tremendous lower-body strength and more breath control than anyone in the business. It was said he could take a breath test and blow into the tube forever. Most wrestlers were tired by the time they completed a sixty-minute match, but not Baba. He could wrestle three bouts in a row and still not be winded.

His real name was Shohei Baba, and before entering professional wrestling he had been a pitcher for the Yomiuri Giants, a former high school star who was signed at the age of sixteen. Baba's pitching career ended, however, when he slipped in the team bath, smashing a glass door and slicing open his arm, an injury that required seventeen stitches. He left professional baseball in 1962 and became a novice professional wrestler under Rikidozan, the sport's reigning kingpin, in the latter's Nippon Wrestling Association.

Sent on a tour of the US in January 1962, he became a surprising hit. He strolled the streets of Manhattan in a red kimono and high *geta* (wooden sandals) and drew huge crowds at Madison Square Garden. The New York press dubbed Baba the "Frankenstein Monster." He was so successful that he was offered a shot at the NWA world title, the crown jewel of professional wrestling, then held by Buddy Rogers. Although Baba lost that match, he acquitted himself admirably, adding to his appeal.

Baba's popularity earned him the ire of Rikidozan, who didn't want anyone stealing his own thunder and who contrived thereafter to make Baba's life miserable, both in practice, where he would have opponents pile on endlessly until his disciple wilted to the floor, and in the ring, where he would surreptitiously instruct the foreign opponents to "beat the hell out of him."

"It was awful to watch," a Japanese reporter who covered the scene told me.

Baba's partner in misery was one Antonio Inoki, who later fought Muhammed Ali. Inoki was beaten so badly that at one point he vowed to kill Rikidozan.

Rikidozan's untimely death liberated Baba from the vise he had been put in, and he went on to form his own stable. There he would make professional wrestling history by taking the unheard of step of bringing a foreigner, quixotically named "the Destroyer," into his group. The Destroyer, whose real name was Richard Beyer, had been the last wrestler to defeat Rikidozan in an epic 1963 match and was already quite well known—if not yet loved—in Japan. Baba had to have taken some satisfaction in promoting him as the only foreigner to have bested his former mentor and nemesis.

The invitation to Beyer came when Baba's wrestling troupe had fallen on hard times. Baba no longer had any big-gate attractions besides himself. When he signed on the American, many Japanese observers dismissed it as a desperation move.

It was considered a big gamble because the American Beyer would have to wrestle as a kind of surrogate pure-hearted Japanese, so to speak, against foreign villains, something Japanese fans had never seen. Heretofore, the lines had always been clearly drawn: the villain inevitably a *gaijin*, the hero invariably home-grown. No one quite knew how the viewing public would react to such a drastic change in script.

To demonstrate his purity of heart, Beyer was compelled to hold aloft a small Japanese flag as he entered the ring. He also had to modify his wrestling style to suit the sensibilities of the Japanese fan. In the Destroyer's previous appearances there, playing the role of malefactor, he had obligingly pulled hair, kicked, and elbowed with impunity, while his Japanese opponent fought with the fairest of hearts, because that, of course, is what the fans wanted to see. Now, however, wrestling on the Japanese side, he could no longer be that bad guy. He had to purge himself of all evil, so to speak, and fight with the cleanliness that Japanese fans were accustomed to in their heroes.

Beyer and Baba together, the 5'10", 200-pound American technician and the 6'10", 275-pound Japanese behemoth, began to pack auditoriums wherever they appeared. As the crowds became accustomed to seeing the white-masked, white-skinned American in their corner, some fans even began to cheer when on occasion he would revert to previous tactics and throw an illegal elbow at a particularly odious opponent. Before anyone realized what had happened, the Destroyer became that rarity in Japanese sports—a bona fide *gaijin* star.

What turned the Destroyer into a national celebrity was not just wrestling, however, but talents hitherto masked behind his fearsome ring presence. In July 1973 he appeared in a five-minute skit on the musical television program *Besuto Ten*, wearing his mask, of course, and fighting off eight stunt men dressed as ninja assaulting a popular songstress. The Destroyer leapt onto the stage, grabbed the ninja one by one, twirled them in airplane spins, and sent them flying through fake brick walls.

The station received so many enthusiastic letters about the Destroyer's performance that the program's producers invited him back for a second time. In the fall of 1973 he was a guest on a new weekly comedy-variety program *Uwasa no Channeru* (The Rumor Channel). He appeared in polka dot shorts, a *happi* coat, a Destroyer mask, and a German Army helmet, clutching, naturally, his little Japanese flag. He performed an obligatory wrestling exhibition, and then he did a skit with an actress named Akiko Wada in which he tried, unsuccessfully, to mimic the words and phrases she spoke rapidly in Japanese.

"I like to put the Figure Four Leglock on skeptical reporters like you to show them just how painful professional wrestling can be. I've had broken ribs, arms, legs, noses. If it's fixed, nobody has told me."

The audience broke into hysterics at the resulting gobbledygook. And he became a regular.

Before Beyer's first year was out, he recorded a Christmas album entitled *Destroyer's Christmas*; he authored a best-selling exercise book; he appeared in TV commercials pitching everything from shaving cream to toilet cleanser; and he guest-starred in numerous celebrity golf tourneys and charity functions.

"He was everywhere," editor Atsushi Imamura of the *Shukan Bunshun* told me. "It reached the point where you could ask any Japanese if he or she knew who the Destroyer was, and you would always get a 'yes' no matter the gender or the age group."

Beyer could be driving his car, mask on, through the dense, traffic-filled Roppongi strip and other drivers would stop and, with a friendly wave, let him go first. Even gang bosses, riding in the back seats of their Lincoln convertibles, would have their chauffeurs stop just so they could get a close-up look.

But unlike Rikidozan, Beyer had no gangland connections. His deportment and lifestyle were helping to erase wrestling's negative image and turn it into "family entertainment."

Also unlike Rikidozan, who had a habit of getting drunk and starting fights almost on a daily basis, Beyer was always cheerful, always willing to sign autographs, always willing to visit an old folks home or play Santa Claus at an orphanage. Unlike, say, many American baseball players in Japan—those over-the-hill ex-major-leaguers who took their money and went home each fall—he chose to live in Japan year round, despite the fact that he was a wrestler of some stature in the United States. Many Japanese viewed this as a compliment of some significance.

"They accepted me, I think," said Beyer, "because I tried to become one of them. I was probably the first American to do that."

In a survey taken in 1977, the Destroyer had an amazing recognition factor in Japan of 96 percent, a mark exceeded only by Lockheed Corporation, and far above that of Steve McQueen and Alain Delon, then regarded as the two most popular male Western movie stars among the Japanese public. (Forty years later, he would be honored by the emperor, who awarded him the Order of the Rising Sun, for a "lifetime spent promoting goodwill and bicultural exchanges between Japan and the United States.")

* * *

I visited Beyer in 1979, at his home in Buffalo, New York, where he had just returned for a time, and became one of the few residents of Japan to see him without his mask. (He looked not unlike French actor Jean Gabin at a similar age.)

A photographer and I spent the weekend with him, watching him train high school athletes in wrestling and conducting a series of interviews. At one point, I asked him how much of professional wrestling was fake and how much wasn't.

He bristled at the question.

"If professional wrestling is a show," he said, "nobody has told me yet. And nobody ever said my matches were shows. Mike Wallace and Tom Snyder both did pieces on me over the course of my career and neither one saw fit to question the legality or the honesty of my matches.

"I have had my nose broken eight times, my collarbone broken twice, and my leg once," he went on. "I also suffered torn knee cartilage and assorted other bruises, sprains, and cuts—more than one of which I had to have stitched up at ringside. I have never taken a dive, and I have never lost a fall on purpose."

If need be, Beyer said, he might carry a weaker opponent because he knew that winning quickly would disappoint the fans. He also drew the line at seriously injuring anyone. After all, he said, professional wrestling was a business and the participants all had families to support. But he never ever resorted to the cheap, gory sensationalism of a wrestler like the Butcher, who intentionally cut his bald scalp to bleed for the fans. He took pride in the fact that he could fill an auditorium on talent and technique alone.

"I have a way of dealing with skeptical reporters impugning my profession," he said. "I demonstrate the figure four leg-lock, locking onto their legs and squeezing hard until they scream out in pain. Then I let them up and ask, 'So what do you think now? You still think it's a show? Now, maybe you'd like to let somebody pick you up and slam you down or throw you into the turnbuckle.

Then you'll see. It hurts, no matter how well you know how to fall or to roll with the punches.'"

He challenged me to submit to the figure four.

Well, what do you do in a situation like that? If you're really a professional journalist, you would have to say yes, wouldn't you? Especially after you had asked the type of questions I had just finished asking.

We went to his house the next morning. Beyer went into his bedroom and put on his wrestling trunks and mask for the benefit of the photographer. He motioned for me to lie down on his living room carpet in my coat and Levis and then wrapped his legs around mine.

"Are you ready?" he said.

"Yes, of course," I replied, feigning bravado, "show me what you got."

At 5'11", 170 pounds, and 37 years of age, I may have been his weakest opponent ever.

He tightened his legs and the pain shot through my lower back and down through my knees into the balls of my feet. It was indescribable. I screamed. He relaxed his hold for a couple of seconds, so I could breathe, then reapplied it, this time harder.

I screamed again. I thought he was going break my leg. I thought maybe I was going to die of a heart attack.

Thanks to my editor at *Number* magazine, there was a two-page full-color spread of my capitulation in the magazine.

It was a bizarre experience to say the least. But it paled in comparison to what would come later back in Tokyo.

Reggie: On Racism in Japan

Not every foreign player was a malcontent like Clyde Wright or saw himself as an alien from another planet. Roy White, the ex-Yankee, who played for Yomiuri for three years, did everything the Giants asked him to, and he did it with a smile on his face. That included the extra drills and the sacrifice bunts. He also learned to speak Japanese. "I love this place," he would say. The Japanese loved him back. "I wish Howaito-san were Japanese so he could stay in Japan forever," wrote one reporter. Then there were the Lee brothers, Leron and Leon, both models of propriety and well respected by their Japanese peers.

As Leon used to say, "You get invited to someone's house, you don't complain about the drapes, the decor, the food—you act like a guest and just put up quietly with whatever you don't like. It's not your house." They were among the most popular foreign players in the country.

But more often than not, there was friction. There were more than enough dissidents who were unhappy with the Japanese style of play and their maltreatment by a hostile media—"salary thief" was a common insult for foreign players off to a slow start, as was "giant human fan" for any *gaijin* slugger who struck out too much—not to mention the frequent calls by the powers-that-be in Japanese baseball, including the commissioner, to ban further *gaijin* participation.

Among the more memorable dissenters that Japanese fans and reporters had difficulty fully appreciating was the brilliant Reggie Smith, a former all-star outfielder for the Boston Red Sox, St. Louis Cardinals, and LA Dodgers, who had come to Japan after a long career for one last big payday with the Yomiuri Giants in 1983. He was thirty-eight at the time, with bad knees and a bad shoulder, but he was still good enough to get the Giants to pay him $1 million for one more year of baseball. At the time, it was the highest salary ever paid to anyone in the Japanese game and not that far behind the top MLB salary roof of $1,657,000 paid at the time to Mike Schmidt of the Philadelphia Phillies. Smith's contract dominated the sports news headlines and so did his afro hair style and mustache.

Never in the proud history of the super clean-cut Yomiuri

Giants had any player been allowed to wear facial hair or indeed anything but a short military-style buzz cut. Even the august NHK, Japan's version of the BBC, took up the subject in its iconic nationwide evening newscast. *"Masaka!"* the announcer had said, an expression that literally means "It can't be!" But Reggie had insisted. If the Giants didn't like it, they could keep their million dollars, he told them, and in the end, the Giants relented. However, Giants fans and pro-Giants reporters complained about yet another crack in the temple of team purity.

Japanese baseball is like Japanese society. People are afraid of confrontation.

Smith was an intelligent man who had many interests outside baseball. He could play several musical instruments. He had a pilot's license. He went to museums in his free time.

"I don't go to bars with the guys, get drunk, and chew my glass up," he told me. "I have other interests."

He also had a history of involvement in political issues. During the height of the busing turmoil in Boston, when Smith was playing for the Red Sox, he incurred the wrath of mayor Kevin White when, in a newspaper interview, he declared, "Boston is a racist city." He was proud, willful, and outspoken, and he had a very quick temper. Once, while in Boston, he became so angered at a sportswriter that he picked the man up and stuffed him upside down into a clubhouse trashcan. In San Francisco he had gone into the stands after a heckling fan who had called him the N-word. In Japanese parlance, he was the "nail that sticks up" and "must be hammered down."

The first time I interviewed Smith it was at the Yomiuri Giants training camp in Miyazaki, Kyushu, in the habitual freezing cold of February. Like Clyde Wright, Smith, at 6'1", 190 pounds, was physically imposing and, to tell the truth, with his mustache and afro, and his hard look, a little unnerving. The two of us, along with a photographer from *Number* magazine, sat down in a room at Miyazaki Stadium and talked. He was polite and engaging, but also brutally frank. When I asked him about his stormy relations with the press, he gave me a little stare that lasted just long enough to make me feel uncomfortable, and then replied:

"The problem with some reporters is that they put themselves above us baseball players simply because they have more education and won spelling bees when they were kids, or something. I won't be looked down on that way. You're a writer, yes, with a college degree. I'm a professional athlete without a college degree. But I can do what you do but you can't do what I do. I've done TV and radio for the Dodgers in LA. I have written for newspapers. But have you ever hit a Major League fastball, Bob?"

"It's the off-speed stuff that gives me fits," I replied, straight-faced. It took a couple of seconds, but the corners of his mouth lifted into a kind of sardonic smile. The interview went smoothly after that.

From the start, Smith had all sorts of problems with Japanese baseball. He had arguments with coaches over his refusal to do the 100-fly-ball drill and other grueling exercises. He had arguments with umpires who gave him what he termed an expanded strike zone after he hit three big home runs in his opening weekend, and he had arguments with pitchers who intentionally walked him, even with the bases loaded, a practice he termed "gutless."

"Japanese baseball is just like Japanese society," he said. "People are afraid of confrontation. But baseball *is* confrontation. Why the hell else would you play the game?"

There may have been truth in what he said, but it was hardly the most diplomatic way to start off his tenure in Japanese baseball, and it did not win him any friends when those remarks were published.

In April, he injured his knee sliding into base and spent most of his first two months on the bench, reduced to a pinch-hitting role, with stretches on the disabled list. That was when the Japanese press started in on him in earnest. The *Nikkan Gendai*, a sort of Japanese *New York Post*, was especially vitriolic in its criticism.

> Smith must be thinking there is no other job as good as this, sitting on the bench and occasionally walking out to pinch-hit. . . . The coaches smile at him and say, "thank you," and Smith goes around with a big, self-important 'I'm a major-leaguer' look on his face? Isn't this all because of the *gaijin* complex that the Japanese have, letting an old, broken-down wreck like Smith act as importantly as he does? It is not too late. Fire him and send him back to America. This is not just a problem of the Giants and Reggie Smith. This is not just a problem of pro baseball. This is a problem of Japan.

I had occasion to interview Smith extensively during this period, despite the fact that the Giants had stopped giving anyone, including me, permission to conduct such interviews because of the incendiary comments he was making to the press. Smith told me to pay no attention to the new restrictions. He said that prior to coming to Japan, he had heard of the Giants' excessive control of their players and had had a clause written into his contract that allowed him to talk to anyone in the press he wanted to, when he wanted to.

During the multiple interviews with Reggie I managed, thankfully, to stay out of the clubhouse trashcan. Just to be sure, however, we varied the venues. I met with him in Roppongi restaurants, in his Tokyo apartment in the Hiroo district of the city, and in his hotel room on the road.

"It gets to you, living here," he said at one point. "I ride the subway to the ballpark to mingle with Japanese and I feel hands slipping under my shirt, feeling my chest hair. Somebody poking me in the rear end with a stick, like I am a piece of meat on display at the department store. It's degrading. I know all Japanese aren't like that, but Jesus Christ.

"I have heard the world 'nigger' more often in Japan, especially from the Hanshin Tigers outfield crowd, than I have during my entire career in the Major Leagues—except that it comes out as *nee-gah* or *nee-gah-roh*, which actually made me laugh because it sounded so absurd."

I could attest to this. At one point in the season I had sat in the outfield seats at the Tigers' Koshien Stadium, right next to the home team's rooting section (*oendan*), with Reggie manning right field just below us. The stream of epithets was continuous— Japanese equivalents for "moron," "shithead," and the standard "Yankee go home"—in addition to the racial slurs (not to mention the batteries, sake bottles, and other paraphernalia hurled onto the outfield grass). I wondered whether the mostly blue-collar fans yelling *nee-gah* really understood what they were saying and concluded probably not. Reggie went 1-4, with a single and three called strikeouts. I think the umpires bothered him more that night than the fans.

I went on to publish several stories about Reggie Smith in the Japanese media, not exactly endearing myself to the Yomiuri front office. But there was more to come.

* * *

In midseason, famed American journalist David Halberstam suddenly contacted me for help. He had been living in Japan for several months researching *The Reckoning*, a book on the Japanese auto industry. While there, he had also been asked to write a piece for *Playboy* about Reggie Smith, so he contacted the Giants' front office shortly before the season started and requested an interview with Smith. But the Giants stonewalled him.

"It is easier to deal with the White House than it is to deal with the Yomiuri Giants," Halberstam said. "My deadline is fast approaching. Can you get me an introduction to Reggie Smith? And tickets to a game?"

The former was easy, but the latter less so. The Giants were always sold out and the front office, predictably, refused my request for complimentary tickets and special press passes.

So as a last resort, I went to see the commissioner of Japanese baseball, Takezo Shimoda, to ask for his help. This was totally out of the blue, to give you an idea of how desperate I was. I had never even met the man. But he agreed, nonetheless, to give me an audience. Shimoda was a former Japanese ambassador to the United States, a tall, elegant gentleman who was also a retired Supreme Court justice. He could not have been more gracious, despite a serious faux pas on my part.

I had taken him a bottle of Johnny Walker Red as a gift, a strict requirement in Japanese culture in such circumstances, only to discover later from an acquaintance that anything less than Johnny Walker Black was tantamount to an insult. JW Black was the most expensive whisky on the market at the time, JW Blue having not yet been invented. The Commissioner accepted the cheaper whisky with no trace of umbrage, however, and told me how much he had enjoyed reading *Kiku to Batto*, the Japanese translation of *The Chrysanthemum and the Bat*. Then he opened his desk and handed me tickets to his own personal box at

Japanese Baseball and American Pros

1

2

3

1. They were called the Babe Ruth and Lou Gehrig of Japan. The half-Chinese slugger Sadaharu Oh led all of baseball in home runs but he trailed in popularity to his pure-blooded teammate Shigeo Nagashima.

2. With baseball star Bob Horner in 1987.

3. Clyde Wright set an all-time record for fines while in Japan.

4. With Leon Lee: "You get invited to someone's house, you don't complain about the drapes, the decor, the food—you act like a guest and just put up quietly with whatever you don't like. It's not your house."

4

Korakuen for an afternoon game on Constitution Day, one of the three national Golden Week holidays that year—along with two special passes to restricted areas. Just like that.

So it was that I took David to the stadium. We sat in the box sipping beer and watched the game, his big athlete's frame squeezed into the small Korakuen box seat.

"They play baseball as if they're wearing blue suits," he said during the seventh-inning stretch. "The cheering section up in the stands is more dynamic than the players on the field."

That evening, Reggie, David, and I went to dinner at an Italian restaurant in Hiroo. After the espresso, I got up to leave and let David do his interview. The last thing I heard Reggie say was, "It's not baseball they play here. It's ping-pong."

* * *

The American *Playboy* piece came out after the midseason all-star game break. It was entitled "The Education of Reggie Smith," and, as expected, it was not very complimentary to the Giants. In it, among other things, Smith compared Japan's anti-foreign attitude to the former Confederate states of the South, "still fighting the last war."

But in time Smith's knee healed, and he started a phenomenal hot streak that almost singlehandedly carried the Giants to the pennant. He hit twenty homers in the last forty games, belting out three in the final game of the season. The papers that had earlier demanded he be sent home were now respectfully referring to him as "Dr. Baseball," a hero beyond compare. Giant owner Toru Shoriki declared that Smith had been a "bargain at a million dollars a year." It was amazing how quickly things could change.

* * *

The following season Reggie's injuries worsened, and it appeared his physical skills were in serious decline. He spent much of the season on the bench and made the headlines only once, when he got into a fistfight with a Hanshin Tigers fan outside Korakuen Stadium who had called Smith a "*nee-gah*" and shoved his sixteen-year-old son to the ground. Smith was detained by the police after the game and questioned at a nearby precinct. The authorities eventually cleared him of any charges and issued a public admonishment to Tigers fans to try to behave themselves in pubilc. Without Smith's hot bat, the Giants sank out of contention. A Tokyo resident, Katsumi Tanaka, was so upset over the team's poor play that year, according to Tokyo Police, that he set fire to fifteen of his neighbors' houses; this earned him extensive coverage in Japan's daily newspapers and in the *New York Times.*

The Professional

Tokyo Media

From the late seventies through the eighties I was deeply immersed in the Tokyo media, both consuming it and working for it. I wrote regularly for a number of publications and appeared often on TV. Malcolm Gladwell said that to be truly proficient in something you had to put in 10,000 hours working at it. I put in at least double that, I would estimate, during the 1980s. I went through the entire year of 1981 without a day's rest because of the constant stream of deadlines—*shimekiri*, as the Japanese put it—that I had to meet.

For all the time I was putting in, however, I discovered that I had nothing on my Japanese counterparts, who matched or exceeded me in hours logged. Japanese journalists, some of them among the best journalists in the world, worked harder than anyone else in the field, as a comparison between *Sports Graphic Number* in Tokyo and *Sports Illustrated* in New York, two organizations I worked for, will illustrate. *Sports Illustrated* had spacious offices high up in the forty-eight-story Time Life Building on West 51st and Avenue of the Americas. There were eighty or nintey individuals in the editorial department, all of them with their own private partitions. They worked four days a week: Monday,

Wednesday, Thursday, and Sunday. The hours were nine to five, with the exception of Sunday, which was closing day and required the staff to stay however long it took to put the magazine to bed, which was often past midnight.

At *Number* magazine offices in the Bungei Shunju Building in Kioi-cho, there were only a dozen people in editorial and they worked seven days a week, as best I could determine, from 9 a.m. to 11 p.m. or later every single night. The office was an open bay with rows of contiguous desks. Staffers would often sleep there overnight on couches or cots set up in adjoining rooms. It was, as one editor put it, *"henshu no jigoku"* (editorial hell). But he had a smile on his face when he said it. You couldn't help but admire the dedication.

The level of professionalism at *SI* and *Number*, at its best, was generally comparable; at its worst, not so much. But there was one significant difference. At *SI*, editorial workers joined the magazine and stayed there for years, decades, in fact. Editor Robert Creamer, author of *Babe*, worked there for more than thirty years. At Bungei Shunju, *Number* was just one out of a large family of popular magazines, including *Bungei Shunju* itself, *Shukan Bunshun*, *Crea*, and others. Staffers rotated from one publication department to another every three years or so—a system similar to that of large corporations and government ministries in Japan. The rationale was to nurture a workforce that understood the operations of the entire organization—a host of interchangeable human resources who could ideally excel at each post, as diverse as sales one year and supply chain the next. It was the same at the TV networks. One would see veteran news anchors, known to millions of viewers, suddenly disappear from the air because their time to rotate to the sales or advertising department had come. This approach engendered a versatile and loyal body of employees, but at times it meant sacrificing the sort of expertise found only in veteran teams with deep skills and experience. An older editor at *Number* magazine, with whom I had worked on several baseball and wrestling features over a span of four years, was unceremoniously transferred to accounting at one point in the 1980s. He knew nothing about that particular field, but he uncomplainingly set about learning everything he could.

* * *

Machiko and I had been living together ever since her return to Tokyo. She continued working for International Social Services in Japan, a quasi-governmental social welfare organization. In May 1983, we put the official seal on our decade-long relationship, trotting down to the United States Embassy in Akasaka, she in her best dress and pearl necklace, me in the only suit I had, filling out marriage application forms and paying a small fee to have the paperwork processed. Thirty minutes later, after standing at attention and swearing with right hands raised that everything we had written in the application was true (the closest thing there was to a ceremony), we were issued a document and instructed to take it to the Akasaka branch of the Minato Ward office to have our marriage registered with the city government. We paid a revenue stamp fee and were informed that we would receive a Certificate of Acceptance of Notification of Marriage in the mail within a few days. That was that. It all went off without a hitch, but there was something clinical and sterile about the whole affair. It was only when we went out for a celebratory dinner that evening at the posh Keyaki Grill in the Tokyo Hilton Hotel (where the Beatles had stayed during their 1964 visit)—Caesar salad prepared in front of us, sizzling Kobe steak, a bottle of Bordeaux wine, and congratulatory cake with a candle in the middle—that we actually felt we had done something to speak of that day.

Not every family in Japan was overjoyed at the idea of having a foreigner marry into their ranks. I know of one Tokyo family who had threatened to disown their daughter rather than accept an American into the family. The mother had crawled across the tatami and begged the prospective groom to call the whole thing off and go back to the United States. They even offered to pay his way. The couple got married all the same and the parents did eventually come around, although it took three years.

Fortunately, Machiko's family did not fall into that category. They were warm and open in their acceptance of me. Her father, a railway engineer, liked to discuss German philosophy—Hegel, no less—using his Taisho-period Japanese. I had no idea what he was saying half the time. I had enough difficulty understanding Hegel in English. When he got on the subject of Kant, it was even worse. My future father-in-law was, fortunately for him, too short to be drafted by the Imperial Army or Navy during the Pacific War, so he remained with the JNR throughout the war years. He was a kindly, cultured man, and he seemed to welcome me without any major reservations, as did Machiko's two brothers and two sisters, one of whom had married an American Southern Baptist minister and moved to a small town in Pennsylvania. Her mother had passed away from an illness years before. They were a modern, educated, open-minded, and close-knit family. I felt very fortunate to become a part of it.

We moved into a new apartment in Akasaka a short walk from the Riki Apartment complex, which was being torn down. It was a small sixth-floor two-bedroom unit in the Akasaka Village Building located at Akasaka 6-chome. Next door, in a perfectly ordinary-looking residential building, was the Tokyo headquarters of the Sumiyoshi-gumi, the gang's crest discreetly displayed above the mailbox in the lobby, just below the security cameras. Parked outside was a long, black Lincoln Continental, a pouty-faced, cigarette-smoking youth stationed behind the wheel, waiting to chauffeur the boss, a bald-headed man, habitually dressed in *haori* jacket and *hakama,* and his wife, whose hair was dyed blue, around the city.

We did our shopping at the neighborhood mom and pop fish, meat, vegetable, and sake stores, with occasional forays to the Western-style supermarket Kinokuniya in Aoyama for exotic imported fare like Cheerios. Some months after we got married, my wife was recruited by the United Nations High Commissioner for Refugees (UNCHR) and asked to relocate to Geneva, Switzerland, for orientation and training. It was a big break for her. The dream of a lifetime. But I also had my career in Tokyo to consider—the phone was constantly ringing with offers of work from assorted magazines and TV stations. So what do you do? You opt to make a bicontinental marriage work.

Machiko moved to Geneva, taking our cat, named Kitty, with her. We kept our place in Tokyo and I began a routine of going back and forth twice, sometimes three times, a year on round-the-world tickets from Pan Am. I started work on a book (which would become *You Gotta Have Wa*). I would spend the spring and fall in Japan doing research and interviews, and summer and winter in Geneva working on the draft, as well as various magazine assignments. She would spend her vacation time in Tokyo. Writing about Japanese baseball from Europe gave me a whole new perspective on my work. How could you possibly explain Japan through baseball to a French Swiss who knew nothing about either subject? You had to reduce the subject to its very basics.

The biggest negative about this lifestyle was Narita Airport, Tokyo's new international hub nearly 40 miles away in Chiba, perhaps the most inconvenient airport in the world. It had opened in 1978, and from the beginning operations were hampered by angry leftists demonstrating over the government's expropriation of land without consulting the farmers who lived there. It was surrounded by high opaque metal fences, with guard towers and armed guards on patrol. It was the only airport in the world I had ever visited where ID was required just to enter the premises. It was also the only airport in the world where the trip there, along a grimly soulless stretch of road flanked by warehouses and factories, could possibly take longer than the flight to your destination if you were going to, say, nearby Seoul, South Korea.

Kisha Club / Blacklist

The Japanese tendency to organize, a possible hangover from centuries of feudalism, manifested itself in many areas of life, from micromanaged corporations to a by-the-numbers healthcare system that leaves little time to get to know your doctor. My field, journalism, was no exception. The regulating mechanism was a Japanese invention called the *kisha* (reporter's) club, which oversaw news-source access and content control and did it with great zeal. It differed substantially from the system in the United States.

In the US, if you wanted to interview someone, you got the individual's phone number and called him or her directly to ask if they would talk to you. If you had any kind of respectable media credentials, you could get into most press conferences if there was room for you. It was an open and free system. In Japan, however, the open and free exchange of information was impeded by the aforementioned *kisha* club system. And it was a serious impediment.

Every organization of any size, from the prime minister's office to Mitsubishi Heavy Industries to the Yomiuri Giants, had a *kisha* club. Journalists who wanted to report on the activities of those organizations had to be accredited by the relevant club; access to representatives of the organization in question and their press conferences, as well as advance access to press dispatches and copies of other official statements, was limited to club members. The only individuals who could join a *kisha* club were reporters from the daily newspapers and TV/radio organizations. Magazine reporters and freelancers were not allowed. Each *kisha* club had a captain elected by the reporters who controlled access to *kisha* club Q&A sessions—and made sure the questions asked did not ruffle any feathers. It was a scandalously biased system. In return for being granted access, reporters were expected to write what they were told.

As Andrew Horvat, a former AP journalist familiar with both Western and Japanese press reporting customs, once explained to me: "In the West, we are taught to pursue the scoop, to get information other reporters don't have. That's how you build a reputation. In Japan, you are taught not to make waves. Publishing a scoop will make everyone else in the *kisha* club uncomfortable and ruin group harmony, so they avoid doing it." That analysis remains largely true today.

Reporters in Japan could get around these restrictions by selling their stories to the weekly and monthly magazines using pen names or by simply giving their research to fellow reporters operating outside the *kisha* club system, so there was always a way for important information to get out. But to do that was also to invite expulsion from the *kisha* club or other forms of retribution if the truth were discovered.

I learned my own painful lesson in this regard in 1985 when I was asked by the prestigious monthly magazine *Bungei Shunju* to write an article explaining the American view of the Japanese *kisha* club system. I accepted the assignment, researched, and wrote the article. I included several examples of how the reporters' clubs had prevented members of the Foreign Correspondents Club of Japan from doing their jobs.

One such example involved the South Korean political dissident Kim Dae-jung, who had been living in exile in the United States. Kim was an important political figure—charismatic, fearless, and determined to overturn the brutal authoritarian regime of Park Chung-hee in the Republic of Korea (ROK).

Kim had finished second in the South Korean presidential election of 1971, narrowly losing to Park, and he believed a subsequent automobile accident he was involved in to be an attempt on his life. He fled to Japan to start an exile movement for democracy, accusing the Park regime, which had turned into a military dictatorship, of corruption and ballot-box fixing.

On August 8, 1973, while attending a conference at the

Grand Palace Hotel in Tokyo, Kim was kidnapped by agents of South Korea's intelligence agency, the KCIA, working with local ethnic-Korean gangsters. He was drugged and taken to Osaka, where he was put aboard a boat, which then headed into the Sea of Japan in the direction of the Korean Peninsula. The agents bound and gagged him, attached weights to his feet, and made ready to cast him overboard. But then suddenly, a Japan Maritime Self-Defense Force (JMSDF) helicopter appeared overhead and fired at Kim's captors, warning them by loudspeaker to cease and desist. Informants had alerted the Japanese government, which then dispatched the JMSDF to pursue Kim's vessel. The boat Kim was on was subsequently escorted by the US military to Seoul, where US Ambassador Philip Habib was waiting to intervene on his behalf.

Kim remained alive. He was put under house arrest and banned from ROK politics. He elected to stay but continued to speak out to foreign reporters and was subsequently imprisoned for two years for criticizing the Seoul government. He was then arrested again in 1980 on charges of sedition and conspiracy and sentenced to death. Amnesty International, Pope John Paul II, and the US government interceded, and Kim was granted exile in America. He taught at Harvard University until 1985 when he suddenly announced he was returning to his homeland and would hold a press conference at Narita Airport during a stopover on his way to Seoul. It was a big story, one of the biggest of the year. *New York Times* Tokyo correspondent Clyde Haberman dashed out to Narita Airport to participate in the press conference, but he was not allowed to enter the pressroom because he was not a member of the Narita Airport *kisha* club. Haberman furiously protested. There was some pushing and shoving, but in the end he was still not allowed inside.

I wrote about Haberman's experience in the *Bungei* article and quoted him as saying that closed-door policies of the type that prevented him from attending the Kim presser would damage Japan's reputation around the world, especially in light of the nation's growing imbalance of payments and accusatory cries of unfair trade. The magazine containing my story came out on a Friday morning. At 10 a.m., I got a call from a Mr. Odano in the Foreign Ministry, demanding that I report to him immediately to explain the article. It was apparently the job of his office to examine all potential controversial stories in the media. More curious than concerned, I decided to go. Besides, it was only a short cab ride from my Akasaka apartment to the drab Gaimusho offices in Kasumigaseki, near the Imperial Palace moat and the Metropolitan Police Department.

Upon arriving I was escorted to a conference room for an "interview" with Mr. Odano, who, in person, looked the part of a bland government bureaucrat in a blue suit and dark tie.

We exchanged name cards, as ritual required, mine saying "Author, Journalist" and his "Foreign Ministry," and then he began to grill me in English.

"Who are you, Mr. Whiting?" he asked. "Why are you writing stories like this critical of Japan?"

"I am a freelance journalist living in Tokyo," I said, "and I am writing this story because it is a story that needs to be written. Japan has to stop being so insular and open itself up or it is going to incur the wrath of the world."

I was being overly dramatic, but what the hell; it was my first foray into the inner sanctum of Japanese bureaucracy and I figured a little bombast would suit the occasion. I also believed there to be more than a few grains of truth there.

"Yes, I understand that point," Odano replied. "But *who* are you and why are you writing stories like this?"

"Did I make any errors in my story? Is there something wrong with my analysis?"

"No, no. But I want to know who you are and why did you write this story?"

It went on like this for two or three hours. Other Foreign Ministry officials were brought in and they asked me essentially the same questions, forcing me to recount the details of my time in Japan to them.

I told them about the books I had written and the columns and magazine stories I had done, but every time they would come back to the same question.

"Yes, but who are you really and why are you writing stories like this?"

Franz Kafka could not have scripted it better. Finally, they let me go and I went home. As soon as I walked in the door the phone rang. It was my wife calling from Geneva. She sounded alarmed.

"Bob, what on earth have you done?"

"What do you mean what have I done?" I said.

"I just got a call a call from an official in the Japanese consulate here in Geneva. He asked me, 'Who is Robert Whiting and why is he writing stories criticizing Japan?'"

Amazing, I thought. Very impressive. I intentionally hadn't told Mr. Odano or any of his cohorts that I was married to a Japanese woman and that she had recently been hired by the UNCHR and dispatched to Switzerland. How they found out, I still don't know. The War Office?

I didn't hear from the Foreign Ministry again about this issue, but *Bungei Shunju* editors told me the government had complained to them. And it was their guess that the Foreign Ministry thought I was working for the CIA or some other intelligence agency and was trying to undermine the stability of the nation of Japan somehow. Perhaps it had something to do with bilateral trade friction, which was heating up at the time.

Wow. I thought. All this for an article on *kisha* clubs?

That wasn't quite the end of the story, however. That summer I headed off to Geneva, and when I came back through Narita in September, I was pulled out of line at immigration and taken into an office, where an immigration official sat me down and began the questioning. It was the only time that had ever happened to me entering or leaving Tokyo.

"Who are you and why are you coming in and out of Japan so often?"

Eventually they let me go and stamped my passport, but it was an unnerving experience. As veteran journalist Sam Jameson, then the *LA Times* Tokyo correspondent, explained to me one day at the Foreign Correspondents Press Club of Japan, high above Tokyo on the twentieth floor of the Yurakucho Denki Building: "You have to show your love for Japan. If you do, they will leave you alone. Criticize too much and you're asking for trouble."

Unfortunately, asking for trouble seemed to be a big part of my journalistic MO.

It came again after my 1986 interview with Warren Cromartie, who had joined the Yomiuri Giants in 1984. In it, he stated that executives in the Giants front office were "racist," noting that they showed far less respect to the then Giants manager Sadaharu Oh, half Japanese and half Chinese, than they did to the previous manager, Shigeo Nagashima, a pureblooded Japanese.

"I'm a black son-of-a-bitch," Cromartie said, "and I can spot a racist a mile away. They were just rude to Oh in general. But they kissed Nagashima's ass. Oh, in my opinion, is worth ten of Nagashima."

The interview was published in the December 1986 issue of the Japanese monthly *Penthouse,* nestled amidst nude photos of women with their vital areas airbrushed out, as required by Japan's obscenity laws. Two months later in a meeting of PR representatives from Central League teams, the Yomiuri Giants rep, a former reporter named Wakabayashi, announced that I was to be banned from entering the Giants' new park, the Tokyo Dome, as a reporter, beginning in 1987, for two years. I could buy a ticket, if there were any left that is, and go in; but I was not allowed on the field or in the press box.

"I'm here to guide the media," he was quoted as saying, "and we can't have *gaijin* ballplayers expressing their *honne* (true feelings) to *gaijin* reporters."

The team took no action against Cromartie, however. He had finished the season with a .363 batting average, 37 homeruns and 98 RBIs, leading Yomiuri to the Central League Championship. In fact, they gave him a new three-year contract with a huge raise.

Blacklisted along with me was my friend Masayuki Tamaki, one of Japan's leading sports journalists, who had also written articles critical of the Giants.

Tamaki, one of the smartest people I had met in my time in Japan, broke the mold. A big, bearded ex-rugby player with a deep infectious laugh and an iconoclastic bent, he had dropped out of Tokyo University, Japan's most ferociously competitive gateway to elite careers in business and government, to begin a career as a freelance journalist—at a time when freelancing was more-or-less unheard of in Japan. I particularly admired his penchant for asking direct, uncomfortable questions and setting things out the way he saw them. He once drew the ire of the High School Baseball Federation for writing that the ubiquitously shaven heads of the high school baseball players (a mass demonstration of pureheartedness) participating in the annual summer tournament at Koshien looked like those of inmates in a Japanese prison.

He criticized the Yomiuri Giants severe training methods in a magazine article and so upset the front office that the following year in spring training camp he was forced to wear a yellow hat while covering training on the Giants practice field—a symbol to Giants players that he was to be viewed as an adversary and to not respond to his questions.

From that time on, PR guru Wakabayashi made it Giants policy that any publication wanting to interview a Giants player had to submit a list of questions in advance for approval. In addition, the publication had to submit the finished article for approval as well. There was also a required fee of several hundred dollars to be divided between the team and the player.

This policy stayed in place for years. In 1991, for example, an NBC News crew wanted to interview former Major Leaguer

Phil Bradley about his experiences playing with the Giants. As requested, they submitted a list of five questions:

1. How do you like Japan?
2. How do you like playing Japanese baseball?
3. How do you like playing for the Yomiuri Giants?
4. How do you like playing for your manager?
5. How does your family like living in Japan?

The Giants front office ruled out questions 2, 3, and 4.

Wakabayashi, a former journalist who had pursued a scoop or two himself during his long career, insisted that his employer, the *Yomiuri Shimbun*, the world's largest newspaper, was indeed dedicated to the pursuit of truth and justice—just not all the time.

Bubble Era

Tokyo is the largest metropolitan economy in existence, as I write this, a center of insurance, banking, electronics, broadcasting, and publishing without peer. According to most surveys, it is the wealthiest city in the world, with a GDP of over $1.5 trillion, and it is also one of the most expensive cities in the world.

There was a time, however, when the city felt even richer, and more expensive, than it is today. That was back in the 1980s during a period known as the bubble era, when the top ten banks in the world were all based in Tokyo and it was said that the value of the Imperial Palace exceeded the value of all the real estate in California. BMWs filled the streets. Sushi sprinkled with flakes of gold was served at certain restaurants, along with the most exorbitantly priced imported French wines. Nearly half of all the cash in the world was in the hands of Tokyoites.

The bubble era was triggered in part by the Plaza Accord of

1985 in which the leading nations of the world banded together to limit Japan's skyrocketing exports of cameras, cars, TVs, and computer chips—products of superior quality manufactured by assembly line robotics that were creating havoc in global markets—and turn the country's energies inward to spur domestic growth. Within a span of eighteen months the yen doubled in value against the dollar. Combined with the subsequent slashing of interest and tax rates by the Bank of Japan and the Nakasone government, this sparked an explosion of real estate and securities transactions. The stock exchange index tripled, the Nikkei Average rising from ¥13,000 to ¥38,916. Many individuals became millionaires seemingly overnight by speculating in the stock and real estate markets. Companies started making more profit in the so-called Money Game, known as *zaitech*, than in their business proper.

Those same companies then went on overseas buying sprees. During the period from 1989 to 1990 Sony bought Columbia Pictures, Matsushita bought Universal Studios, Mitsubishi Estates bought Rockefeller Center, and a Japanese investor paid an estimated $850 million for the iconic Pebble Beach Golf Club. A Japanese insurance company purchased a Van Gogh masterpiece, *Still Life: Vase with Fifteen Sunflowers*, for a then-record $39.9 million, a version that was later claimed to be fake, while shortly thereafter, a paper-industry billionaire paid $82.4 million for another Van Gogh painting, *Dr. Gachet*. During this time, many high-rise "intelligent" buildings of glass and steel went up. Ark Hills, a high-gloss complex of red brick and marble, complete with outdoor pool, showcased the ANA Hotel with its polished-marble lobby and shimmering waterfall. It was the most glamorous spot in the city.

It was a crazy, frothy time. Wild. Mammonesque. The austerity that had characterized the country in an earlier time disappeared, giving way to a startling new extravagance. Louis Vuitton and Gucci handbags became de rigueur for many young Tokyo women, the former selling better in Japan than in the brand's home market, while men began wearing Savile Row and Giorgio Armani.

Overseas and domestic travel skyrocketed. Taking a flight from Tokyo to eat sushi in Sapporo and flying back on the same day was not rare. Neither was flying to Hawaii for the weekend. One in every four employed workers owned a set of golf clubs costing over a thousand dollars. Toyota began giving all of its new college-graduate hires a car as a signing bonus. Some people signed the contract, received the car, and then took another job at a different firm. Gold teeth disappeared in favor of more modern dental work.

Pricey nightclubs served drugs in back rooms—the drug of choice during the bubble was *shabu* (methamphetamines), popular, among other things, for sex, with marijuana the runner-up. Latin American gangs also introduced crack cocaine and powder to Japan during this time. One of the most popular spots in the early 1990s was Juliana's, famous for its dance platforms in which scantily clad office ladies—many wearing revealing bandage dresses—performed suggestive disco routines. Roughly 5,000 people came nightly to the three-story hall that had a capacity of only 1,500. Other clubs ramped up the competition by allowing women to dance in their underwear or letting women wearing G-strings in for free. *No-pan kissa* (no-panties cafés), where female waitresses wore short skirts with no undergarments, became a fad. There were shops and vending machines that sold the used panties of high school girls.

By the end of the decade, prices of Tokyo-area condominiums, hardly spacious by US standards, had risen so much that the only way most Japanese could afford to buy one was with a 50- to 100-year multi-generational-family loan. Average Tokyoites were unable to finance buying a small home with a small garden, unless they occupied a management-level position in a reputable firm with an attendant salary. This usually did not happen until

Juliana's: bubble-era symbol of excess.

around the age of forty, and then they would have to look in locations averaging well over an hour commute from their office or factory. This period was particularly hard on government workers, who did not see pay increases during the bubble but still had to bear the rising costs of living.

Many Americans in Tokyo on dollar-based incomes found they could no longer afford to live there and moved out. It was a dramatic turnaround from the city I had discovered only twenty-five years earlier, with its lack of plumbing and humble street carts.

I had a close-up view of bubble-era changes from the windows of my new Akasaka apartment.

Where once the only foreign car in the neighborhood was the Lincoln Continental owned by the Sumiyoshi boss next door, now expensive foreign cars—Audis, BMWs, Jaguars, and others—were becoming much more commonplace.

The family-run *izakaya* a few doors away, a rickety fixture in Akasaka since the postwar era and a place where I had whiled

With 1,200 hostesses at its peak, the Mikado was the world's largest cabaret.

away many an evening, quaffing beer and eating *yakitori*, suddenly closed its doors and gave way to groundwork for a modern high-rise office building. The owner, an affable, bespectacled gentleman in his fifties, whom I had never seen without his white chef's uniform, usually slaving over fried tempura, had sold the property and moved his family to an expensive new condominium in trendy Ebisu. He bought himself a foreign sports car, which he proudly displayed for everyone in a return visit to the neighborhood. Only now he was wearing a leather jacket with silver studs, designer parachute pants, sunglasses, and an earring in his left ear. He looked like Don Johnson in *Miami Vice*.

He wasn't the only one. There were a lot of small business owners like that all over Tokyo, lucky ones who became millionaires simply because they had a wood shack sitting on a land lease, which entitled them, under the old laws, to roughly 75 percent of the land value. I knew of a fourth-generation sushi chef, living above the restaurant with his wife, who sold out for ¥1.1 billion, around $9.1 million, to make way for the new Gap flagship building in Omotesando. The bubble triggered a huge diaspora from

Each hostess had a numbered electronic pager in her bra.

old neighborhoods all across the city. It changed the character of the town.

I was swept up in the insanity. Fees I received for appearing on TV, writing columns, and doing telephone interviews also began to climb. I was invited to a surprisingly lucrative lunch at a five-star restaurant by the mayor of Yokohama, who wanted to know my opinion on whether or not his city should build a domed base-ball stadium.

"I dislike domed stadiums," I said, as we sat down. "Baseball should be played outside in the fresh air, not inside some over-sized warehouse. Besides, a beautiful port-side city like Yokohama should have an outdoor ballpark for the citizens to enjoy."

"Domo arigato, Whiting-san," he said.

Thanking me for my advice, he said it was time to forget busi-ness and start enjoying our repast. He ordered several bottles of expensive wine to accompany the series of sumptuous steak and lobster dishes we were served. When it was over, one of the may-or's assistants handed me an envelope thick with cash, as a way of showing appreciation for the thirty-eight words of wisdom I had offered up at the start of the meal. Counting up the bills afterward, it came to about $26 dollars a word. Adding in the probable cost of the luncheon, it was a lot of money to spend for a little desultory conversation.

I lived in the beating heart of Tokyo and all around me were endless amusements. In the early evening, you could see geisha, the city's most elite entertainers, scurrying along Akasaka's streets in ornate kimono on their way to exclusive *ryotei* (high-end restaurants with private rooms) where they would cater to Japan's politicians and corporate executives, who arrived in sleek black limousines. The district also featured expensive hostess clubs, like the 1,200-hostess Mikado cabaret and the New Latin Quarter as well as two of Tokyo's most famous discos, Mugen and Byblos.

Up the street in Roppongi were even more entertainments: St. Julians, the trendy karaoke bar with one of the city's most powerful stereo systems; Mr. James, an authentic country and western hangout, complete with Japanese cowboys, right on Roppongi Crossing; the Hard Rock Café, with a paper-mache King Kong climbing up its side; Tony Roma's; Spago; and Maggie's Revenge, an Aussie-themed bar serving big, thick, juicy Australian steaks and live rock music. Maggie's attracted the new hip stockbroker set who were capitalizing on the remarkable run up in the value of the Nikkei Dow. Australian hostess Maggie had a ban on neckties and would take a pair of scissors and snip off any tie attached to a human neck, then hang the offending object on the "necktie trophy wall" on one side of the room. These were among the 2,000 bars and restaurants within walking distance from my front door, perhaps the densest collection of such establishments in the world.

The asset bubble came to my own home one day in late 1986 in the form of a foppish Japanese real estate agent named Konno. He was a slightly built male in his forties with a pencil-thin mustache, wearing an Armani power suit under a fur-collar coat draped around his shoulders and expensive leather boots with extremely pointed toes. He carried a diamond-encrusted cane in one hand and a briefcase in the other.

He was there to inform me, he said, that my apartment, which I had been renting for ¥200,000 (about $2,000) a month, had just been purchased by his company, which, from the looks of Mr. Konno, was in the same family of entrepreneurs as the Sumiyoshi crime group next door. Would I mind moving out in six months to make way for a new tenant?

This was the second time in six years I had been asked to move.

My exit from the Riki Apartments in 1980 had been caused by the collapse of the building's electrical system. The landlady, Rikidozan's widow, decided to tear down the building and put up a new one to take advantage of climbing real estate prices. She called me into her downstairs office to offer me a year's rent free and moving costs, including deposit and key money, to find another place to live. I was told it was the standard deal in Tokyo if your landlord—or landlady, as it was in this case—wanted you out. So I happily accepted, not knowing until later that other tenants had held out for much more. Japanese law at the time gave great power to the tenant. If you didn't want to move, you didn't have to. You could stay there forever—or until the building collapsed.

"I quite like living here," I told Mr. Konno, "and I certainly don't want to move."

"We're going to double the rent," he said, "and two years after that we are going to double it again."

"That seems a violation of my rights," I said.

Japanese tenant law, I had also discovered, prohibited landlords from raising the rent above market values, which was good. But market values were also, unfortunately, going through the roof.

Before long, I was visited by an associate of Mr. Konno, from the same firm, a man named Morita. He spoke English, having been educated in the United States. He took me out to a *yakitoriya* down the street, owned by an official in the Japan Communist Party, and offered me $10,000 cash to move out.

"That's $10,000 Mr. Whiting," he urged. "That's a lot of money."

So I went to see Kiyoshi Wakukawa, a lawyer introduced to me by people at the Foreign Correspondents Press Club. He was a man in his forties who had studied law at the University of Illinois. He laughed when I told him the story of the visit by Mr. Konno and the one by Mr. Morita.

"Let me take over now," he said. "It's clear they are taking you lightly. They think that because you are a *gaijin* that you are stupid. Don't talk to them again."

A few days later I had another visit from Mr. Morita.

"I thought we could be friends and settle this thing amicably," he said. "I'm very disappointed that you had to involve a lawyer. I will give you one last chance. I will up my offer to $20,000 on the condition that you sign an agreement to leave now."

I amicably declined and, to make a long story short, within a few weeks my lawyer had settled a deal for me to move out in return for ¥6 million, or roughly $60,000, when the lease expired, with him taking a 20 percent commission.

Then things got dicey. I had thought to find another apartment in the same neighborhood, which I quite liked. I had always felt accepted there. But apparently, I wasn't as accepted as I thought, because when I started visiting the local storefront real estate agents, known as *fudosan,* every single one—and there must have been half a dozen in the larger vicinity—had the same message for me: Sorry, no foreigners. My "foreignness" had not been a problem years earlier, when I moved into Riki Apartments. Now suddenly I was persona non grata. I widened my search but everywhere I went the response was the same: *Gaijin dame.* No foreigners. Japanese landlords didn't want to deal with them, I was told. Too noisy, too troublesome, too . . . *foreign.*

My lawyer said that in his opinion, this was part of a larger problem—a latent xenophobia in Japan, which periodically manifested itself and was coming out now because of Japan's economic

Prime Minister Yasuhiro Nakasone at the 1986 G7 in Tokyo.

power and the criticism it faced over its growing trade imbalances with the rest of the world.

"Most Japanese don't really like *gaijin*," he told me with a shrug. "A certain segment of the population, maybe. But most people don't. They just tolerate them. But now that the Japanese are rich and buying up so much of the world, they feel superior. They don't feel the need to have to deal with or accommodate foreigners, at least not here in Japan. And the trade dispute doesn't help."

Indeed, during that era of the bubble, more and more signs began to appear outside restaurants and nightclubs saying, "Japanese Only." It also became harder to get a cab.

Of course, if some Japanese were displaying attitudes that smacked of racism, they were more than matched by their counterparts on the other side of the ocean. In Detroit, where Japanese imports were cutting into Big Three sales and countless autoworkers were getting laid off, the anti-Japanese demonstrations were particularly ugly. At one memorable protest in 1982, autoworkers smashed a Japanese car to pieces to cheers from onlookers. In another famous incident, in 1987, Republican lawmakers destroyed a Toshiba boombox with sledgehammers, angry that Toshiba had exported vital submarine technology to the Soviet Union. Watching the news one night, I was appalled to learn of an incident where a Chinese American named Vincent Chin, a Detroit resident, was beaten to death with a baseball bat by a Chrysler plant superintendent and his stepson because the two men believed Chin to be Japanese.

"It's because of you little motherfuckers that we're out of work!" the older of the two attackers was reported to have said as he wielded his bat.

Japanese Prime Minister Yasuhiro Nakasone did not help matters in a speech he made to junior members of the ruling Liberal Democratic Party in 1986, suggesting that America's minority groups were dragging the country down and making it uncompetitive. "The level of Japanese society far surpasses that of the United States," he told his compatriots. "There are many blacks, Puerto Ricans, and Mexicans in the United States whose average level is extremely low." The speech was subsequently broadcast on Japanese national television.

Outrage predictably followed in the United States and was intensified when Nakasone tried to extricate himself from the mess by praising the "great achievements" of the United States, while adding that ". . . things are easier in Japan because we are a mono-racial society."

鎌倉 Kamakura

Unable to find a place in the neighborhood I loved and pressed for time, I wound up moving out of the city, to the seaside town of Kamakura, an hour's ride on the Yokosuka Line running south from Tokyo Station.

My close friend and business partner Greg Davis was giving up his house there in the Nikaido area, so I took it over. It was a one-bedroom affair surrounded by 300 *tsubo* (over 10,000 square feet) of bamboo groves, oak trees, and grass, located in a quiet neighborhood midway between Kamakura Shrine (a ten-minute bus ride from the station) and Kakuon-ji temple, with its beautiful statues of Buddha.

Kamakura was filled with majestic Buddhist temples and Shinto shrines dating back to the 12th century, including the statue of the Great Buddha, all lustrous reminders of its glorious past when the city was the capital of Japan and regarded as the center of the universe by the Japanese. The *Kamakura jidai* (Kamakura period) ran from 1185 to 1333. It marked the end of imperial rule based in Kyoto and the transfer of power to the emerging feudal political system under the control of the samurai class.

The watchwords of this new military class were simplicity, frugality, manliness, and physical and mental vigor, not to mention loyalty, duty, self-perfection, conquest of the fear of death, and compassion for the weak, if you believed the 19th-century author Inazo Nitobe. It replaced the perfumed embroidery of the court and intellectual elitism of the entrenched monasteries, as my gregarious new neighbor Mark Schumacher, a chunky Johns Hopkins graduate from Minnesota and an expert on Buddhist statues, explained to me after I had moved in.

But by the time I got to Kamakura, the samurai were long gone, of course, and the city's 170,000 residents were seriously aging. There were lots of empty houses, abandoned by people who could not afford to pay Japan's crippling inheritance taxes.

In the daytime the city was packed with tourists and school tours, so much so that there was a wait to buy tickets at the train station vending machines. At night, it was like a ghost town. Everything, with a few exceptions, shut down by 7:30. That was good, of course, if you wanted to avoid the temptations of Japanese nightlife and get some work done.

Unfortunately or otherwise, I found it necessary to go into the capital at least three times a week for editorial meetings, interviews, and dinners. So much for clean living. However, I could use the hour each way to and from Tokyo Station for working on manuscripts—unless, of course, I fell asleep on my way back at night and woke up at the last stop, Kurihama, all the way past Yokosuka at the southern tip of the Miura Peninsula. If the train I dozed off on happened to be the last of the evening, then it was a long and expensive taxi ride home after a protracted wait in line behind the other hapless commuters stuck there at the end of their own lengthy day.

You Gotta Have Wa

You Gotta Have Wa, published in June 1989 in New York, was essentially a book about the inability of Japanese and Americans to get along. It was issued at the very height of the trade war between the two countries, one that had caused US-Japan relations to drop to their lowest level since World War 2. Japan, having been vanquished militarily, seemed poised to conquer the world economically.

I did most of the writing in Mogadishu, Somalia, where my wife was assigned by the UNHCR. Mogadishu was actually a pleasant little town at that time, before civil war erupted in 1991 and tore the place apart. Somalia had once been an Italian colony and, as a result, there was a huge Italian cathedral and a seaside *fortezza* in the city to complement the mosques, the souk, and other Muslim architecture. There were also lots of fascinating, if primitive, shops and restaurants. Mogadishu was one of the poorest places in the world, but even so it was far cleaner than the New Delhi and Bombay slums I had visited. It was quite romantic, in fact, especially at dusk after the heat died down and the evening call to prayer began.

You Gotta Have Wa, trade paperback edition.

My wife and I lived in an Italian colonial home overlooking the sea. I arranged to have the *Nikkan Sports* sent to me there every day via the diplomatic pouch, which made me very popular with the Japanese NGOs in the city, who did not have such access. I wrote every day from nine to three on my Toshiba T1100PLUS laptop (electricity permitting), then drove down to the American Club pool for a swim. Sharks in the water prevented ocean swimming. The four-year-old daughter of a Swedish UN rep had been attacked and killed by sharks, in fact, while standing in shallow water. The only problems with driving in the city were the rocks thrown at the car by the street kids, and the corrupt Mogadishu motorcycle cops who would see the blue-and-white UN license plate and automatically stop you and charge you with a fine, payable on the spot, for some imagined violation or another. I was pulled over for speeding once when I was going 20 miles an hour in a 30-mile-per-hour zone.

When I had finished the final draft of *Wa*, I went out on the balcony and read it out loud into the wind that blew in from the Indian Ocean, the dhows plying the waters off the coast in the distance. The Somali UNCHR security guards watched bemusedly, as did our cat. It took me two full days. I am certain I am the only person in the world to have written a book about baseball in Japan while living on the continent of Africa.

You Gotta Have Wa came out in the US amidst several books and magazine articles that had capitalized on the intensifying trade disputes with Japan. Foremost among them were *MITI and the Japanese Miracle* by Chalmers Johnson, which explained how Japanese industrial policy created an economic and trade juggernaut; *Containing Japan*, a two-part series in *The Atlantic* by James Fallows, which cast the US-Japan relationship in Cold War terms; *The Enigma of Japanese Power* by Karel van Wolferen, a critical account of Japan's political, business, and social structure; and *Trading Places* by Clyde Prestowitz, a polemic that alleged the United States was abdicating its future to Japan. They were followed by *The Rising Sun* (1992) by Michael Crichton, an over-the-the-top, jingoistic novel about unscrupulous Japanese businessmen in the US who commit murder and other crimes in the interests of profit and market share. Characters therein were demeaning caricatures of real Japanese, almost as bad as the propaganda films produced by the US government during World War 2 that depicted enemy soldiers as fanatical, buck-toothed killing machines wearing thick spectacles that, unfortunately, never seemed to impair their aim. Among them was a nasty individual who liked to slice up women with a samurai sword during sex. The movie version, featuring Sean Connery as a Japan expert (who spoke badly fractured Japanese), was a big financial success.

To grossly overgeneralize, this was the group that viewed Japan as a single-minded entity, a troubled, overworked, quasi-feudal, racist, and sexist society that sacrificed individual rights to the goals of a megalomaniacal "Japan Inc." The above-mentioned nonfiction writers became known as "the revisionists" or, more colloquially, the Gang of Four.

On the other side, espousing equally simplified views, was the Chrysanthemum Club, led by a group of scholars who, in *New Yorker* correspondent Patrick Smith's words, were "uncritical apologists for Japan," writers who praised Japan's "contented conformity" and glossed over any perceived flaws. Edwin Reischauer was the unofficial leader of this group. Self-interest was often involved here, as many in the Chrysanthemum Club received favors from the Japanese government.

There was, to state the obvious, a vast chasm between the two sides.

* * *

Where did *Wa* stand in all this? The fundamental thesis of *You Gotta Have Wa* was the incompatibility of two different value systems, individualism (*kojinshugi*) versus groupism (*shudanshugi*). Americans in general tended to fall into the first category, while the Japanese were mostly grouped in the second. "Let it all hang out" and "Do your own thing" were mottoes of contemporary American society, while the Japanese had their own credo in the well-worn proverb "The nail that sticks up gets hammered down." It was practically a national slogan. These of course were sweeping generalities, but in the baseball world, where Japanese and new American recruits had to face each other across the cultural divide, year after year, the differences in values, customs, and approaches to the game yielded results that were as predictable as the typhoons that hit the country every September.

Simple case in point: MLB teams seldom held team meetings, operating on the theory the players were professionals and, therefore, knew their jobs and what they had to do. Meetings were regarded as a waste of time unless the subject was extremely important, like the first game of the playoffs. Japanese teams held pre-game team meetings everyday followed by post-game *hansei-kai,* or self-reflection conferences, where fines were handed out for poor play and special practices ordered for those who had really screwed up in the game. The thinking was that players were inherently dumb and lazy and had to be constantly reminded of their duties. There were frequent protests on this one issue from Americans on Japanese teams, with AWOL *gaijin* comparing the daily mandatory get-togethers as akin to "being in kindergarten." Restrictions on foreign-player participation remained in place. This naturally drew unavoidable parallels with Japan's foreign-trade policy, which protected its markets behind tariffs and non-tariff barriers to impede American exports such as autos and cell phones (the latter were, for many years, banned from sale in Tokyo and Osaka). An American could lead the league in home runs and still not be allowed to play in the midseason all-star games because of the limit of two foreigners per side. That happened more than once.

Randy Bass's story is particularly instructive. A huge hero in Kansai after winning the Triple Crown and leading the Hanshin Tigers to a Japan Series victory in 1985, he had established himself as perhaps the most valuable player in the professional game in Japan. In April 1988 he left the team to care for his hospitalized and seriously ill son. When his return was delayed, a team executive, who felt personally responsible for Bass's prolonged absence, committed suicide. As Hanshin Tiger manager Minoru Murayama put it, "A *gaijin* can never be the real leader of a Japanese team because his main interest is only himself. No Japanese would desert his team like Bass did." Many a corporate CEO in Japan has said something similar.

Shintaro Ishihara: "I Am Not the Devil"

You Gotta Have Wa was a bestseller in both America and Japan —as well as a nominee for several awards including the Pulitzer Prize—and opened up a new dimension in my *Alice in Wonderland* experience. The Japanese translation of *Wa* had come out amidst Japanese-language versions of the aforementioned books by Japan-bashing authors and other tomes by Japanese writers who argued that, since Japan was now the #2 economy in the world, and its executives ranked among the most dynamic, it could find its own way without slavish dependence on the United States. The subject dominated the public discourse. "Catching up with the West," the mantra of the Meiji-period leaders, it was argued, had already been achieved.

One no longer heard a joke often used in the early 1960s to express Japan's standing in the world: "When the United States sneezes, Japan catches a cold." The current joke went: "When Japan sneezes, America gets cancer." Some Japanese telling the joke broke up into laughter.

Moreover, to the charge that Japan's markets were closed, Japanese leaders now retorted more forcefully, insisting that in fact most of Japan's markets had been opened but that foreigners hadn't made a sufficient effort to penetrate them. In truth, the availability of foreign goods had skyrocketed—from Chinese-made underwear to Swedish furniture, from American photography film and cosmetics to French perfumes and clothes designed by foreign fashion leaders around the globe. But when it came to the bedrock necessities for prosperity and growth, as well as for daily living, a conviction that Japan made virtually everything it needed—and did it better and cheaper than anyone else—emerged among business leaders, bureaucrats, and the general public.

A particularly popular work at that time was the best-selling

1989 book *The Japan That Can Say No* by the ultra-rightist politician, Japan Diet member, and novelist Shintaro Ishihara. Ishihara never lacked for conviction about anything he took it into his head to proselytize about. Among other things, he insisted that Japan's prewar occupation of the Korean Peninsula had been justified and often referred to the Chinese in the most pejorative terms. Foreigners of any stripe, including people of mixed heritage, were not among his favorite people.

His polemic, in which he urged Japan to stand up to "American bullying" and forge its own path in the world, sold a million copies, an incredible number for a political work, and all the media were buzzing about Ishihara's strong stance vis-à-vis the USA. There were daily demonstrations in front of the FCCJ with protestors carrying huge signs railing against US oppression.

Among other things, Ishihara echoed the claim of former PM Nakasone that America suffered a trade deficit with Japan because the level of its workforce was so low, in contrast to that of Japanese workers, who benefited from a superior education and an innately superior character. He claimed that the pursuit of immediate profits by American business rather than the long-range economic planning Japan embraced was harming its competitiveness. He stated further that the US decision to drop the A-bomb on Japan was evidence of American racism.

Ishihara had teamed with Akio Morita, the silver-haired chairman of Sony, to do a series of joint interviews for *Bungei Shunju*, which then became the basis for the original Japanese-language version of the book. When the controversial work hit the bestseller lists in Japan, it was translated by the Pentagon and photocopies were circulated all over Washington. It was eventually entered into the Congressional Record.

Ishihara complained about the pirated English edition, citing certain inaccuracies in the translation as well as the important fact that he hadn't been paid any royalties. He arranged for a new, expanded edition with Simon and Schuster, which came out in 1991. However, Morita, an astute business leader who was famous worldwide and who had lived in New York for some time, refused to participate to avoid offending his American customer base, leaving Ishihara to publish the English version alone.

Morita's withdrawal from the debate was unfortunate, because he was the more thoughtful and less belligerent of the two, his positions more nuanced. He argued that American CEOs were overpaid and were too quick to fire employees to cut costs during hard times, unlike Japanese companies who viewed their employees as their most valuable asset. He said, accurately, that American companies did not try hard enough to develop products for the Japanese market, citing the refusal of US auto manufacturers to build vehicles suited to the left-side drive system used in Japan. At the same time, he was much more conciliatory than Ishihara. He refrained from attacking the American character and intelligence level, and he frequently cited Japan's insularity at home and the reluctance of its businesspeople abroad to socialize with locals as factors contributing to trade friction.

I wrote a column about the book for the *Shukan Asahi*. In it I called Morita the angel in the US-Japan relationship and Ishihara the devil for his inflammatory comments. The day after it came out, I received a phone call from Ishihara's office, inviting me for lunch. I immediately accepted of course—how could you miss a chance to meet Japan's most famous hawk? The following week I joined him and his aide-de-camp at the luxury Capital Tokyu Hotel (formerly known as the Tokyo Hilton), in its expensive basement restaurant, the Keyaki Grill. Fittingly, it was just down the hill from the Diet Building and government offices in Nagata-cho, including the posh Palais Royal with its million-dollar apartments where lawmakers and fixers met to hammer out multi-million-dollar deals and negotiate bribe amounts.

Ishihara was smooth, I will say that for him. He was tall, urbane, and charming (except for a habit of nervous blinking). Dressed in an expensive tailored suit, he quoted Balzac and

Dostoyevsky in our preliminary banter and ordered the most expensive wines on the menu.

It was easy to forget that in 1968 he had been a member of the notorious right-wing political association Seirankai, or "Blue Storm Group," members of which had to pledge loyalty in their own blood, and that, further, he had been a habitual denier of Japan's wartime atrocities, which was akin to someone in Germany saying the Holocaust had never happened.

He famously claimed in a 1990 interview with the American magazine *Playboy* that the 1937 Rape of Nanjing, in which Japanese Imperial Army soldiers massacred some 300,000 Chinese civilians by some accounts, was a fabrication, that it was purely Chinese propaganda. His statement angered many historians and made the Chinese apoplectic.

He also called for all US military forces to leave Japan and for Japan to strengthen its own military, including the development of a nuclear weapons capability—a position that was anathema to many people on both sides of the Pacific. In some quarters, Ishihara was called the Jean-Marie Le Pen of Japan.

My conversation with Ishihara was all in Japanese. Once, when his aide spoke to me in English, Ishihara snapped, *"Nihongo de hanase"* (Speak Japanese).

After we had finished lunch and started on our third bottle of wine, Ishihara got down to business. He had just come back from Detroit (this was June 1990), where he had spoken to a group of hostile blue-collar workers and survived the ordeal. He had even gained applause when he attacked US auto executives for their relentless pursuit of quarterly profits at the expense of worker security. That, I must admit, impressed me.

"Mr. Whiting," he began, "I am not an enemy of the United States. I am not the devil. I am one of the first to admit that Japan's system is rigged against imports. Our government kept high-quality Motorola phones out of the Tokyo market and forced Japanese to use lower-quality Japanese phones to give local manufacturers time to catch up. I just speak the truth. I feel sorry for the American work-ers who put in their time for low wages while the CEOs take in all the money, and then coldly fire those same workers when it suits them to increase profit share. So maybe it is bet-ter to have a devil in the US equation who tells the truth than an angel who will flatter just for market share."

He added that he meant no disrespect by impugning the intellectual level of the American worker. That was just the way it was.

Shintaro Ishihara. The man who could say "No" to America invited me to lunch. I said, "Yes."

I was starting to feel the buzz from all the wine we had gone through. Yet he did not seem to show any effects from the alcohol at all. He was flatter-ing, prepossessing. I must confess, I quite liked him, which I sup-pose was the idea. Who was it that said, "Keep your friends close, but your enemies closer"? We also had something in common, it turned out. He had a house in Zushi and sometimes rode the same Yokosuka Line as I did—on the rare occasion when his chauffeur had the day off, that is.

Toward the end of our conversation, he asked me what I was working on and if there was any way he could help me with it. I said I was starting a book about the Tokyo underworld and certain of its more colorful characters, like Nick Zappetti, a postwar black marketeer and ne'er-do-well.

"Oh yes, him," he said, slashing his cheek with his finger in the universal sign in Japan for a yakuza. "He's Mafia, I hear."

I mentioned that Zappetti was a close friend of Rikidozan, the pro-wrestling icon, who went on to make millions as a Tokyo entrepreneur and who would also be a big part of the book.

"I knew Rikidozan really well," said Ishihara. "He came out on my yacht many times. I know everything about him. Ask me anything."

So I asked.

"Was it true that Rikidozan was a secret member of the ethnic-Korean yakuza gang Tosei-kai in Tokyo? And if so, what was his role?" I had seen the police report on the Tosei-kai, which stated unequivocally that the famous wrestler was in fact a *saiko komon* (supreme advisor) for gang boss Hisayuki Machii. So I already knew the answer.

His eyes immediately narrowed. It was not a question he had expected me to ask. He turned to his aide and whispered, "Machii?" The aide muttered something in reply, with "yakuza" the only word that I could catch.

Ishihara turned to me and said, "I never heard of him."

I did not believe him.

I did not think it was possible that Ishihara did not know Machii given the latter's involvement in the LDP as "security chief" for the infamous right-wing fixer Yoshio Kodama, a key figure in the Lockheed scandal.

Ishihara suddenly looked at his watch and said he had to get back to the Diet but promised he would be in touch about the Rikidozan question.

The next day I got a call from his aide. "I am terribly sorry," he said, "but Mr. Ishihara is unable to help you. He doesn't know anything."

Doesn't he? I thought to myself. He couldn't have given me a more revealing answer.

By way of thanks, I paid tribute to him in *Tokyo Underworld*, calling him "Japan's leading American basher," among other things.

It was the least I could do.

Tokyo Dome

A gaudy, if sterile, symbol of the bubble era was the aforementioned Tokyo Dome that served as the new home of the Yomiuri Giants. It was erected in 1987, right next to the site of Korakuen Stadium, which had been torn down, in a new complex along with the roller coaster, boxing hall, pinball arcade, and other longtime amusements of the area. The atmosphere inside the Dome was several steps down from its predecessors, which had far more color and character. I found it suffocating. Stifling. As my friend Tamaki put it, "It's artificial and the air is bad. Attending a game there is like watching baseball played inside a jumbo jet."

The new stadium, owned by Korakuen KK, was purportedly a copy of Minnesota's Metro Dome. It advertised a capacity of 56,000, and during every single home game a stadium employee would flash an announcement on the scoreboard, seen by the 26 million people watching the nationwide live telecast, that the Kyojin had another full house of 56,000 people. The Yomiuri organization claimed the world record of most consecutive nights of capacity crowds (which helped them achieve putative attendance records of well over 3,000,000 a year). It fit right in with the Japan-As-Number-One theme of the times. The problem was, it wasn't true.

Tokyo Dome. The Yomiuri Giants inflated their attendance by 10,000 a game and claimed a
new record. They banned me when I revealed the true capacity of the ballpark.

Tokyo Dome was too small to hold that many people. It seemed to me to be about the size of Candlestick Park when it was first built, with a capacity of about 43,000. So when the editor at *Shukan Asahi* asked me to investigate rumors that the Giants were inflating their attendance figures, I counted the house. Twice. Both times I came up with a total of 42,716 seats, plus standing room for another 3,500. If you do the math, you will see that is considerably less than 56,000 people.

My arithmetical acumen did not put me in line for a Fields Medal, but my subsequent column in the *Shukan Asahi* revealing the Dome's true capacity and the reason for the deception—the team had already announced the 56,000 capacity figure before construction began, and when architects and engineers informed them that it was impossible to get that many people into that limited space, Yomiuri was too embarrassed to reveal the truth—did serve to earn me another ban from the Tokyo Dome. A Japanese reporter I knew who was friendly to the Giants called me up to deliver the news that the Giants were once again banning me from the stadium, this time, indefinitely.

Moreover, as I discovered later from Sam Jameson, my column destroyed whatever was left of my relationship with Tsuneo Watanabe, my former student, who had climbed to the top position in the Yomiuri empire, acquiring the official title of "owner" of the Yomiuri Giants along with his other posts of Representative Director and Editor-in-Chief of the Yomiuri Shimbun Holdings company, which publishes the gigantic *Yomiuri Shimbun* and essentially controls the largest Japanese commercial television network. He was one of the most powerful people in Japan, who had even helped elevate Yasuhiro Nakasone to the post of LDP president and prime minister during the 1980s.

Watanabe was angry at me not just for calling out the Big Lie his organization had perpetrated but for doing so in an *Asahi Shimbun* publication. As you may recall, Watanabe hated the archrival *Asahi* because of its leftist leanings—views which, ironically, the younger Watanabe might have agreed with—referring to it as the *Akai Shimbun* (the Red Newspaper).

"I'll never forgive Bob Whiting for writing that in the *Asahi*," he told Sam, who still belonged to the study group (*benkyo-kai*) with Watanabe and PM Nakasone, as well as Nakasone's secretary, among other individuals from the LDP.

On the bright side, however, I got a letter from the GM of the Seibu Lions, a Pacific League team owned by real estate baron Yoshiaki Tsutsumi, one of the richest men in the world, according to *Forbes* magazine. It went, "Mr. Whiting, you are more than welcome to come to our stadium anytime you desire." Joji Abe, a beefy yakuza turned novelist, who wrote a best-selling book about his life in prison, cornered me at a literary reception and said, "I will be happy to escort you to Tokyo Dome anytime you want. Let them try to kick you out."

Burst Bubble

Emperor Hirohito died on January 7, 1989 of intestinal cancer. The man once viewed as a "war criminal" and a symbol of brutal Japanese military aggression was honored in a state funeral in Tokyo seven weeks later, on February 24, attended by government heads and other representatives of the international community, including US President George H. W. Bush. Bush's presence was especially meaningful given that, as a navy pilot during World War 2, he had been shot down by the Japanese and rescued by an American submarine. The 163 representatives from foreign countries made it the largest state funeral in history, and their presence was seen as a sign of respect for Japan's global economic clout. Prime Minister Noboru Takeshita, happy for a respite from a corruption scandal that would force him to resign before the year was out, made sure to meet all of the important mourners.

Members of the FCCJ, some getting drunk, watched the marathon series of ceremonies unfold on a bank of twentieth-floor TV monitors. It took thirteen hours in all. Famous American news anchors Dan Rather, Peter Jennings, and Tom Brokaw were in Tokyo to report the event live. An estimated quarter of a million people lined the streets in the cold and steady rain as the funeral cortege—costumed Imperial Court attendants carrying Hirohito's 1,000-pound coffin on a black lacquer palanquin, followed on foot by the new emperor Akihito, his wife the Empress Michiko, and Crown Prince Naruhito—made the long trek from the Imperial Palace to the Shinjuku Gyoen park, where the main rites were conducted at a specially constructed funeral hall. The funeral procession then moved on to the final resting place at the Imperial Burial Ground in Hachioji, some 30 miles away. Black and white bunting was everywhere.

Although there were no military uniforms in sight, the Shinto trappings on display during the rituals and interment were reminiscent of Japan's wartime past, when the then state religion was used by Japan's military leaders to galvanize the public. There were minor protests by individuals and groups unhappy with the ruling LDP's policy of downplaying Japan's responsibility as a wartime aggressor. However, right-wing extremists were on hand to stifle the critics.

A threatening letter and a bullet were delivered to the home of Hitoshi Motoshima, the mayor of Nagasaki, who had declared in December 1988 that the emperor bore some responsibility for the war. Motoshima refused to retract his remarks as demanded by the local LDP Prefectural Committee. As a result, in January 1990, a member of the rightwing group Sekijuku shot him in the back on the streets of Nagasaki. Motoshima survived and continued to speak his mind, causing controversy when next he called the A-bomb attacks on Japan one of the two greatest crimes against humanity in the 20th century, along with the Holocaust, but added this striking qualifier: "It was a matter of course for atomic bombs to have been dropped on Japan, which had launched a war of aggression. Japan does not have the right to criticize the atomic bomb."

In all, the funeral cost an estimated $80 million and was, in its own way, symbolic of the excesses of the decade. (That was in addition to the $50 million and more spent annually on running the Imperial Palace, the sprawling park-like estate in the heart of Tokyo with its work force of 2,000 people, half of whom were police.) Hirohito's death at age eighty-seven meant that he would not be around to witness the painful fall that was just over the horizon, marking the beginning of the worst recession to hit the country since its defeat in World War 2 and the end of the Japanese miracle.

* * *

The Nikkei 225 stock index had reached its all-time high of 38,916 on December 29, 1989. Then, as the Bank of Japan began raising interest rates—to a peak of 6 percent in 1990—and the Ministry of Finance put restrictions on the total loan volume of real estate lending (*soryo-kisei*) and large-scale land transactions, prices started to fall.

From there, the Nikkei 225 embarked on a white-knuckle ride that would see it lose nearly 60 percent of its value by December 1992. A decade later it would reach a low of 8,579. Accordingly, land prices (residential, commercial, and industrial sites) in Tokyo also fell sharply. The yen, for its part, would continue to appreciate, hitting ¥83 to the US dollar in May 1995 and peaking at ¥76 in August 2011.

Neither Japanese stocks nor Tokyo property prices—nor the Japanese people, for that matter—ever fully recovered those previous giddy heights. Instead, years of torpor and stagnant growth ensued, in what came to be known as Japan's "Lost Decade." News reports during that time were filled with accounts of long-established businesses going bankrupt and leaving their employees stranded.

I have heard credible foreign analysts of Japan express the view that the Japanese were uncomfortable with success, that given their long history with typhoons, earthquakes, fire, and other disasters, they were more at home with anxiety. The country had yet another opportunity to test that thesis when the economic bubble burst.

People who had taken out million-dollar loans to buy Tokyo apartments now found themselves out of work and unable to pay off the debt. Selling the apartment they were living in and moving to a cheaper place was not an option because sales values had plummeted 80 percent from their peak. Banks continued their policy of easy mortgages, far beyond what family incomes should have allowed, to the bitter end. The fallout extended to family, friends, and business associates who signed as "guarantors."

I knew an individual who had taken out a hundred-year loan

from a bank to buy an apartment for his family. The idea was that his children and his grandchildren would continue to pay off the loan and live in the apartment. The publishing company he worked for, however, downsized in the sudden slump and he was out of a job. The value of his apartment dropped until it was worth a fraction of its former bubble-era value, but he—and his descendants—were still stuck with the loan. He wound up working two jobs in order to keep paying it off.

Vacation homes, pleasure boats, and new ski condos in high demand during the bubble, and purchased at peak prices by investors or vacationers, were now being sold at bargain-basement prices—some ski condos going for the rock-bottom price of ¥50,000. Nobody wanted them; the taxes and maintenance fees were too high.

Unscrupulous transactions involving underworld groups and political and business leaders also came to light. There was the arrest and indictment of LDP powerbroker Shin Kanemaru in a corruption scandal involving yakuza and a major transportation company, Sagawa Kyubin, as well as tax-evasion schemes. Police searched Kanemaru's home and found over $50 million worth of bearer bonds and gold. This was followed by the ouster (if only temporary) of the LDP from power in 1994.

It was discovered that Japan's banks held huge sums of bad debt, incurred during the bubble, by making interest-free loans to yakuza groups to buy land, persuading recalcitrant owners to sell and move, for resale to the banks, who would then repackage the real estate in development packages. Attempts to collect those bad loans as the market crashed proved to be very risky as well, in more than one instance. One morning in 1994, the manager of a Nagoya branch of the Sumitomo Bank, who had aggressively sought to collect on overdue loans, answered a knock on his door and was shot in the head. A year earlier, an executive at the Osaka Hanwa Bank engaged in bad-loan collection was also murdered.

The crisis caused larger banks to merge in order to deal with their mounting bad loans; it also put a damper on corporate investment and consumer spending. Yamaichi Securities, one of Japan's oldest and most important securities companies, was forced to close its doors because of hidden debt and the revelation that the company had made illegal payments of hush money to yakuza to keep quiet about the company's huge financial losses. This cost the job of a good man, Dyke Nakamura, my old friend who used to send me Japanese sports dailies when I was living in New York. He was out on the street, just like that.

In a separate scandal, there were revelations that Nomura Securities and other brokerages were secretly compensating their top clients for losses incurred. The Nomura president was arrested in 1997. The morning news in those years resembled a police report.

Nicola: "The Mafia Boss of Tokyo"

There are roughly half a million foreigners living in Tokyo as of this writing. Forty percent are Chinese. Twenty per cent are South Korean, not counting the stateless *zai-nichi*. Nearly 20,000 are Americans, although the US Embassy will tell you there are actually 100,000 Americans in the city at any one time if you count tourists and others without resident cards (or at least there were before the novel coronavirus pandemic hit). There are approximately 6,000 French nationals and 6,000 citizens of the UK.

Tokyo is not exactly a melting pot like New York where over two hundred languages are spoken and half of the denizens speak a language other than English at home.

But there is enough going on to make life interesting. There are neighborhoods like the Shin-Okubo district, known as Korean Town, in the ward of Shinjuku, which is three-quarters foreign and includes Muslim, Vietnamese, and Nepalese communities, among others.

There is a long-standing community of Westerners in the Tokyo–Yokohama area, a small but vibrant community, I should add, that dates back to the early Meiji period when the government opened its doors to foreign advisors—academics, engineers, and military specialists from the US and Europe—in its effort to modernize. Some of these people stayed on and planted roots and started businesses. Swiss immigrants started Sieber-Hegner, a trading company, in the 1860s, which went on to make trillions. A wave of Russians migrated to the safety of Japan during the Bolshevik Revolution of 1917 and stayed on, attending weekly mass at the Nikolai-do in Ochanomizu. Hundreds of Americans chose to remain in Tokyo after the Occupation. Many of these people became involved in businesses like real estate, shipping, and insurance. They occupied all levels of the social strata, from the high to the low.

Among the more notable characters were Helmut Ketel, who came to Japan in 1919 after being captured by Japanese forces in China, stayed, and married a Japanese girl, then opened up a pair of German restaurants, Rheingold and Ketel, that became a haunt for Nazi Germans based in Tokyo. Red-haired Frances Baker, a University of Washington graduate, first came to Tokyo in the 1920s, painting coffee house murals in the Ginza, as one of only five hundred English-speaking foreigners in the city. After the war she put together US State Department exhibits for the San Francisco peace conference and the peaceful use of nuclear energy. For years she ran the Frannell Art Gallery at the posh Hotel Okura. American lawyer Thomas Blakemore, who first studied at the Imperial University in 1939, represented the Rockefeller family in Tokyo for forty years in postwar Japan and was decorated by the emperor for having helped devise the Japanese constitution during his stint at the GHQ. (He wound up married to Frances Baker.) Another American lawyer, Raymond Bushell, the aforementioned "lefthanded groom," had one of the world's most valuable *netsuke* collections. Harbin-born White Russian Eugene Aksenoff, a multilingual stateless doctor, migrated to Tokyo in 1943 to attend medical school, treated world leaders and famous movie stars at his Roppongi clinic, and received one of Japan's most prestigious awards, the Eiji Yoshikawa Prize, for his lifework.

However, the "low end," for lack of a better term, was far more interesting. As I searched for a subject for a new book, I discovered characters who absolutely oozed color.

One of the most interesting was Wally Gayda, who had been a pilot in the Flying Tigers during the war and a pilot for Air America afterward, flying drugs and other contraband across the Himalayas. He had come to Japan during the Occupation and in 1949 became the first American to open a nightclub, the Golden Gate, a Far East version of Rick's Café, where the aforementioned Larry Allen was the star attraction. The place thrived until it was shut down on a morality charge seven years later. Another was Al Shattuck, the Club 88 proprietor and Canon Agency spy mentioned earlier, who had also partnered with the Mafia gambler Ted Lewin, a Manila casino baron and Bataan Death March survivor, in a variety of ventures.

Among later arrivals was a man named Craig Spence, a former ABC News correspondent who was kicked out of Saigon for black marketeering during the Vietnam War and moved to Tokyo, where he did public relations consulting for the government-supported Japan External Trade Organization and a number of Japanese corporations. I had gotten to know him doing publicity for my first book, appearing alongside him on a TV program. Spence also consorted with homosexual escorts and became a registered foreign agent for Japan in Washington, DC. He took close friends, including those from a DC callboy ring, on illicit midnight tours of the White House.

One might also mention Maggie, of Maggie's Revenge fame, whose Australian boyfriend was doing drug deals with the

Sumiyoshi in Akasaka, dispatching letters describing shipments of "fish" for Maggie's Japanese-speaking restaurant partners to translate, unwittingly, and send on to a certain Sumiyoshi captain. When Maggie's partners refused her demand for a bigger share of the take, they were visited by Sumiyoshi gang members who threatened to disrupt the restaurant operations.

I looked into the possibility of interviewing all of these people for a book. But Ketel had died. Blakemore, whom I visited in Seattle where he was living in an assisted-care facility with Frances, had Alzheimer's. He could barely remember his name (although he recalled his days in the GHQ with striking clarity). Frances was not much better off and Bushell's story turned out to have limited scope. Dr. Aksenoff was promising. The Russians from the nearby Soviet Embassy, who filled his waiting room, drew the attention of the US and Japanese authorities, who suspected him of being a Russian spy. Japanese intelligence agents arrested him for espionage because he'd been seen with a transmitter bearing markings that resembled Cyrillic. But he was released a week later when a Toshiba engineer explained that the symbols were Toshiba's markings for digital equipment and the transmitter wasn't a Soviet radio at all. Aksenoff had also treated John Wayne, Jacques Chirac, Angelina Jolie, Brad Pitt, Madonna, and Michael Jackson. (Madonna had perfect skin, he told me, while Michael Jackson had a skin disorder than made his skin tone uneven. Brad Pitt was extremely self-effacing, he added, while John Wayne, a he-man in the movies, had been deathly afraid of needles.) But I discovered Aksenoff was already doing his own book with a Japanese journalist.

Gayda, for his part, had been run over by a truck in San Diego in 1991, crossing the street from the flophouse where he lived to the liquor store he patronized daily. His nineteen-year-old Filipino mistress from Angeles City had absconded with his life savings, running off with a Las Vegas blackjack dealer, and leaving Gayda impoverished. Shattuck had long since stopped coming to

Japan. He had left the country in 1960 at the invitation of the Japanese government and was living, it was said, somewhere in Brazil, while his partner Lewin had died earlier of a heart attack in 1971. Spence, facing certain death from AIDS, committed suicide in the posh Boston Ritz-Carlton in 1989. Dressed in a tuxedo, he downed a bottle of sleeping pills with a fifth of expensive Scotch whisky while listening to Mozart. Maggie, I was told, had returned to Australia and was indisposed.

Then Nick Zappetti appeared on the scene. In terms of high drama, his story was off the charts. It just so happened that I was sitting in his famous restaurant, Nicola's, enjoying a medium pepperoni accompanied by a mug of draft beer, when the proprietor walked over to my table, a copy of *You Gotta Have Wa* in hand.

"Did you write this?" he asked. I told him I had.

"Not bad," he said. "I was thinking after reading it that maybe you'd be interested in listening to my story."

"What story is that?" I asked.

"Half a century in Tokyo. Gangsters. Crime. A dozen arrests. Deportations. Two fortunes made and lost. Ten lawsuits. A suicide attempt. Four marriages. Three divorces. I can't believe half the shit I did."

I knew about Nick Zappetti, of course. I was a frequent visitor to his restaurant and I had heard stories. I had also seen Bill Whitaker interview him on the *CBS Evening News*, during coverage of Emperor Hirohito's state funeral in 1989, as one of the very few early Occupationaires still living in Japan. "We were kings," I remembered him saying as he stood on the roof of the TBS Building in Akasaka and surveyed a cityscape that had improved considerably since his arrival in 1945, when half the capital was in ashes, "but it's all changed now."

Nicola's was strategically located near Roppongi Crossing and I continued to drop in even after I had moved to suburban Kamakura. The pizza was good, as was the pasta, and the kitchen stayed open until 4 a.m., which made it a convenient place to eat and wait for the trains to start running after a night of bar hopping in the area. Foreign visitors, including film stars and other celebrities, were regular customers. The restaurant had a history. Established in 1956, it was the shop that popularized pizza in Tokyo and helped make Roppongi a go-to destination, in addition to making Zappetti wildly rich.

In all the time I had been patroniz-

Nick Zappetti at age seventy-one in 1991. End of an era.

ing Nicola's, however, I had never had a conversation with Nick Zappetti other than perfunctory hellos. He was a little scary. Several rumors floating around connected him with the yakuza and the Mafia. Years earlier, a friend I'd known at Sophia named Larry Wallace, a Tokyo-based DEA agent who was shot and killed in Guam in 1975 during a controlled buy that went bad, told me that the Tokyo Embassy had had Zappetti on a watch list for dealing drugs and that the FBI was investigating him for arms dealing to the Japanese underworld. Another friend of mine, former *Stars and Stripes* editor Tom Scully, had been to his house, tagging along with acquaintances to a party there, where he saw a case filled with shotguns that Zappetti was selling to his gangster friends. Zappetti was quite often described as an "arrogant bastard," which the man himself readily admitted he was.

I told Nick I would conduct an interview session with him. Armed with the tools of my trade, a notepad and a tape recorder, I returned several days later. We sat down in a back booth and he started talking. Up close Zappetti, sixty-nine years old at the time, did not look very robust. His skin was pallid, his eyes sunken and tired, but he spoke with great energy and enthusiasm, sounding not a little like the actor Joe Pesci.

He told me in very candid detail about his early days in Tokyo just after the war, living in a military Quonset hut complex located near where the Supreme Court Building stands now, just in front of the Imperial Palace.

Everybody called it Palace Heights. It was a very nice place to live in because we had Quonset huts and all the cots. And girls were sleeping in the cots. You walked into your hut and picked anyone you want. And they never said no. You got in bed, you pulled the blanket over you, and you fucked. Nobody thought anything of it. That's the way it was. They weren't pan-pan girls. They were just ordinary girls who had lost their homes in the bombing. Drabby clothes, matted hair. You couldn't tell if they were beautiful or not. They just wanted someplace warm to sleep and something to eat. We'd give them eggs and coffee in the morning, chocolate bars. It was depressing. It was demeaning. And I don't imagine many guys wrote home to mother about it. But that was the reality.

Zappetti had been one of the very first Americans to marry a Japanese after the war.

She was an ex-naval officer. A dentist. No disco baby, but she spoke good English. Better than me. She was a step up from the others. I met her on the Yokosuka Line. I invited her to ride in the car reserved for Americans. Some punks in front of Yokosuka Station called her a whore—a *pansuke*. It didn't take me long to deck them all. We got married in 1947. We had two kids before we got divorced. But she never went to America. She was angry at the wheels who questioned her before we got permission to marry. They accused her of marrying me just so she could get a ticket to the States. That pissed her off so much she refused to go. Went all over the world in her life, but not the US. Can you imagine?

That session would become the first of forty hours of interviews, interviews filled with remarkable tales of the postwar black markets, the Tokyo underworld, and some of the biggest names in the news that I had read about in my early Japan days, told in Zappetti's uniquely colorful fractured English. I'd never met anyone quite like him. "Life is a funny situation," he liked to say. One time he asked me, "If your wife was a tough American broad, would you marry her?" He also advised never to "let sex get involved in your fucking." And there was this favorite gem: "A gun is a violent act." How could you argue?

He talked of selling beer from the BX to Japanese gangs on the black market (doubling his income as a civilian employee of the GHQ in the Civil Custodian Department), about getting caught and being deported, then making his way back on a fake passport he had made back in East Harlem, New York, with the help of a Mafia relative. A stint selling fake dollar checks followed, until his involvement in an infamous diamond robbery put him in a Tokyo jail. When he got out, he opened up his restaurant. Liz Taylor and Frank Sinatra, on tour in Tokyo, came to eat there. So did John Wayne, who was making *The Barbarian and the Geisha*. So did Crown Prince Akihito and his fiancée, the soon-to-be Princess Michiko. Other frequent guests were the gang boss Ginza Machii and his partner Rikidozan, the professional wrestler.

Riki and I used to go out quite often. As a matter of fact, there used to be three of us. The other guy was Mr. Machii. Mr. Crime Incorporated, you know. And we'd go out. And those two guys would make typhoons. They'd go in a club and just tear it up. Riki and Machii would fight with each other. The purpose would be to destroy the club. Either just for the hell of it, or for business reasons. They had a lot of their own interests in nightclubs and restaurants and what not. And that was one way of eliminating the competition. They did it for me, too.

Zappetti's eyes sparkled as he told this story. He seemed absolutely gleeful. You just turned on the tape and let him talk. He was subject to violet fits of coughing. He took glycerin pills from a small metal container he kept in his shirt pocket, sticking them under his tongue. But somehow he kept it up. He was a tremendously entertaining storyteller and I was hooked, despite all the violence and profanity, or perhaps because of it. His story was a one-man history of the postwar era, populated with some of the key figures that helped shape that epoch in Japan.

He also had an entirely American sense of entitlement, power, and superiority. "Whipped dogs" was his term for Japanese men in the early postwar period. He believed it was wholly proper for the Americans to be on top, to take the real estate, money, and women of the losers. Later on, as Japan recovered, he complained frequently of suspicion, deceit, and masked hatred on the part of the Japanese, as if they had no grounds whatever for resenting the predations of the victors, his own conspicuously included. Not once did I ever hear him express sympathy for the Hiroshima and Nagasaki victims or the horrific Tokyo fire bombings.

* * *

Much of the Zappetti tale was a kind of swaggering triumphalism followed by the gall and angst of "getting his comeuppance." How he went from a cocky, arrogant American in Japan who had it all and acted like he owned the streets of Roppongi to a white-haired old man, nearly bankrupt, broken in body and spirit—a naturalized Japanese with a Japanese name filled with hatred for his hosts—became the backbone of *Tokyo Underworld.*

He symbolized so much: the story of the economic, political, and social progression of Japan from defeated country to superpower, the rise of women's rights, the growth of the crime organizations, and the ineluctable ties to the American agenda on all levels of the corrupt side of the US-Japan relationship, from high (CIA) to low (black markets). He was a walking history of the city, from the ashes of August 1945 to the dizzying heights of the bubble era and the misery of the subsequent economic collapse.

Moreover, I'd never met anyone so willing to talk about the most intimate details of his life. He would say anything. For example, he confessed that decades of booze and debauchery and four marriages and heart attacks had rendered him impotent by the age of sixty-four.

Then there was this: "Did I ever tell you about the time I committed suicide?" he said during one session. He then proceeded to tell me one of the most extraordinary stories I would ever hear.

He had a girlfriend, a nineteen-year-old Korean model named Yoshiko. They were living together. He was madly in love. Then one day after he had started a fight with a couple of yakuza *chinpira* who had peed in their front yard, resulting in Nick's spending the night in jail, she told him she was going to leave. He behaved like an animal, she said. It was mortifying to someone of her refined taste. He threatened to commit suicide if she left. She said go ahead. In her presence, he downed a fifth of Johnny Walker whisky and a bottle of sleeping pills. When he awoke the next morning with a terrible hangover, she was gone. He went to her father's house in Meguro where Yoshiko was hiding. It was located above a *pachinko* shop. Nick started a fight with the *pachinko*-shop employees. The police came and arrested him again. He got the idea that he could win her back by participating in a robbery of the Imperial Hotel diamond shop, which would make him rich. This landed him in jail a third time. When he got out, he tracked Yoshiko down at a ski lodge where she was vacationing with her new boyfriend. Another fight ensued, another arrest. Finally, he came to his senses. After reading up on the art of pizza making in his cell, he borrowed money and opened his first restaurant. He grew that into an empire, marrying his cash register girl, until a wild love affair with a terminally unfaithful Hokkaido beauty queen nearly destroyed it all, costing him half of his assets in a divorce settlement.

It was a fantastic tale. I have interviewed a lot of people and heard a lot of wild stories, but for strangeness this one broke the meter. I thought maybe Nick Zappetti was crazy or that he was suffering from the early onset of dementia. I didn't know what to believe. But I later talked to the Metropolitan Police Department official, a Mr. Mogami, who had investigated the Yoshiko case and the other episodes Nick was involved in, and he verified that they were all true.

Zappetti passed away in 1991 shortly after our last interview. Along the way, we developed our own sort of friendship and I never regretted the time I spent with him. But there was still a lot of legwork left to do.

It took me six years of research to finish. By then, I had interviewed nearly two hundred people and read an equal number of nonfiction books, mostly in Japanese.

The Reckoning

NYC vs. Tokyo: "It's Time to Come Home."

During the 1990s, I circumnavigated the globe two or three times every year, usually using the Star Alliance Round-the-World Business Class Tickets program, starting from Tokyo for wherever it was that my wife had been posted by the UNHCR. That meant Tanjung, Pinang, Indonesia, or Geneva, in that particular era, with obligatory stopovers in New York and San Francisco—the latter to visit my family who were now all living in the Monterey/Carmel/Salinas area of California.

I spent a lot of time in New York seeing my agent and my publisher and visiting friends. In 1991, I stayed several weeks at the Regency Hotel, 63rd and Park Avenue, doing research on the Occupation era at the NY Public Library at 42nd Street and the Museum of TV and Radio on West 52nd.

I seriously contemplated the idea of moving back to NYC, encouraged by David Halberstam and his wife Jean. "It's still a great city," he would say. They introduced me to an apartment building on the corner of West 67th and Central Park West, a few doors down from their own apartment across the street from ABC TV headquarters.

With Machiko in Kenya's Great Rift Valley. 1987.

"It's $250,000 for a two bedroom," big Dave said. "You've got money. It's time to spend it. Come back where you belong. I'll introduce you to Graydon Carter at *Vanity Fair* and the editor at *Entertainment Weekly*. We'll set you up."

I had always thought that someday I would eventually move back to the United States and that New York would be the place I would settle down. It had been in the back of my mind for a while, but David's urging brought it to the front. I almost went through with it. But in the end, I didn't.

For one thing my wife Machiko, a dyed-in-the-wool Tokyo gal, was dead set against it. She'd spent more time with me in the city during the nineties at the Regency and she had mixed feelings about the place—the crime, the panhandling, the people who menaced you as you walked down the street. She didn't like the idea of buying an apartment there and leaving it empty for half a year, which is probably what would have happened, given the way we both traveled.

There were other compelling reasons why I was reluctant to make that move. In Tokyo, I already had a vibrant, interesting life. My phone was constantly ringing with requests to write for some magazine or go on some TV program. I didn't want to have to give up what I had in Tokyo.

Beyond the work, I also enjoyed the red-lanterned *izakaya* where I habitually unwound after the day's exertions. I relished the excitement of the Koshien high school tournament finals, the deciding day of the Grand Sumo tournament, the history-rich matchups between the Yomiuri Giants and the Hanshin Tigers, and other sporting events, lingering into conversations with my sports-writing friends Abe and Tamaki. Beyond the glitter of a great city whose entertainment hubs dwarfed Times Square, and whose myriad temples and shrines, so rich in culture and tradition, invited impromptu visits whenever I was out and about—beyond all of that was the simple and, I now saw, incontrovertible fact that Tokyo was home. It was a startling realization.

I had long come to terms with being a *gaijin*, a state of existence that had once caused me to pack up and return to the US believing I would never again live in Japan. Having lived and worked in New York City (and remaining relatively sober during that time) helped me see things in a different light. Japan was a place where it simply wasn't necessary to win every argument—or even argue at all, for that matter.

Furthermore, I had an extended family that was more than interesting. I counted two PhDs, one in chemical engineering, the other in astronomy, and a government-certified calligraphy expert among my in-laws. I also had a niece who was a handball champion and a nephew who was a black belt in taekwondo. He was the nicest, gentlest twenty-one-year-old kid you would ever want to meet except for rare occasions, like the time he stopped two thugs who were molesting a young woman at Yokohama Station and put them in the hospital. So, in the end, I took the money earmarked for the Central Park West apartment and bought a house for my parents, now in Salinas, California, together with the rest of the family—my brother and sister—and continued on as before.

Lost Decade

The burst bubble changed Tokyo in many ways. Although the end to that insane period of growth had officially come in 1989 when the Nikkei 225 hit its peak, there was an effective lag in the actual behavior and spending habits of Japanese consumers. As a McKinsey consultant I knew named Jun Sasaki pointed out, "If you carefully analyzed just who exactly may have been flush with riches during the real estate bubble, it was a smaller minority than one might think." The rest, he argued, were caught up in the expectation and belief that things were going great and loosened their purse strings accordingly.

Thus, even though there was the acknowledgment that this thing called the bubble had imploded, it took a while for many to realize it wasn't coming back, because the aforementioned revisionist books about Superpower Japan had reinforced the already prevailing belief that Japan's inherent strength would win out and that it was just a matter of time until the recovery kicked in.

However, the reality of the recession slowly manifested itself in a number of ways. It became harder and harder for new university graduates to find jobs. *Salaryman* bonuses were cut drastically, from a high of around twenty months of base pay at the peak of the bubble down to two months in some cases. Suicides spiked because the lower income would not allow people to pay their mortgage bills or money due on their previous years' residence tax bills. Then there were the many Japanese *salarymen* who were "restructured out" (*restora*, as it was popularly known during that era), ending the myth of lifetime employment. Among them were men who, out of shame, would hide the fact of their predicament and leave the house every morning wearing suits and neckties and carrying their briefcases as if on their way to work. They would spend the day hiding in public parks or libraries until it was time to go home.

The loan-sharking business took off rapidly during this period, as banks stopped lending and many newly minted landlords suddenly found that their obligations were far greater than their incomes. They were forced to borrow from loan sharks to pay their bills to banks or other creditors. The loan sharks' collection efforts grew correspondingly harsher, causing a further uptick in suicides.

Japan's used-car dealerships were swamped with people trying to sell their BMWs or Porsches. This gave rise to a burgeoning used-car export business to Australia, New Zealand, Pakistan, and other right-hand drive nations such as former British colonies in Africa or Southeast Asia. Pawnshops found themselves awash in Rolexes, high-end jewelry, and fashion goods being dumped by people desperate for cash.

The Siberian Husky, a breed that became a status symbol during the bubble, lost its popularity and many of the unfortunate animals ended up being gassed to death as people discarded their pets. Sales of puppies declined, leading many pet dealers to summarily dispose of their excess inventory. The Siberian Husky soon became a rarity again.

The Inagawa-kai, the nation's third-largest yakuza gang, once valued at $1.5 billion, went bankrupt. One of their top captains committed suicide.

Some sectors of the economy managed to survive the carnage. Remarkably enough, the bars and restaurants I patronized were still packed at night, my books continued to sell, and work rolled in as before. And through it all, the city of Tokyo kept rejuvenating itself, barely skipping a beat, thanks in part to government stimulus measures and long-term municipal planning. Out of its massive sea of red ink rose one building colossus after another. There was the soaring fifty-two-floor Shinjuku Park Tower, which opened in 1994. Designed by famed Olympic architect Kenzo Tange, the structure housed the luxury Park Hyatt Hotel (which would be the setting for the award-winning 2003 Sofia Coppola film *Lost in Translation*). The forty-four-floor Shinjuku I Land Tower followed in 1995. The fifty-four-floor Tokyo Opera City Tower, which housed the new National Theater on lower floors, with Microsoft, Apple, and NTT occupying the higher ones, opened in 1996. That same year came the Tokyo International Forum, a multipurpose exhibition center in Yurakucho in the heart of Tokyo, designed by famed Uruguayan architect Rafael Vinol.

The star attraction in Shinjuku, indeed, in the entire city, was the new forty-eight-story Tokyo Metropolitan Government Building, opened in 1991, which many said resembled a cross between Batman's headquarters and a giant computer chip. The new "Tocho," as it was known, had the great distinction of being destroyed by Godzilla in the 1991 Toho film *Godzilla vs. King Ghidorah*. This inspired many cities across Japan to lobby for the honor of being annihilated by the monster in his next film, assuring them instant fame and a boost in tourism.

During this time, the Tokyo Government was also busy overseeing the construction of a brand-new commercial and leisure center on an artificial island in the middle of Tokyo Bay—directly across from the only place in Tokyo where access to the sea is not blocked by warehouses and ports—that would eclipse past landfill constructions. Called Odaiba, it was designed as a leading commercial, residential, and entertainment area, much like Canary Wharf in London. It became a second city center. Among its attractions were the futuristic Fuji Television Studios; Tokyo Leisure Land, with its Ferris wheel and game arcades; Legoland Discovery Center, a theme park constructed from three million Lego bricks; assorted shopping malls; the Museum of Maritime Science; and the Miraikan, Japan's Science and Technology Agency Museum. It was connected to central Tokyo by the new suspension Rainbow Bridge, opened in 1993, which offered stunning views of the cityscape on one side and Mt. Fuji on the other, and was illuminated at night by a spectacular gradation of rainbow colors. An overhead, fully automated, driverless transit system known as the

Rainbow Bridge, opened in 1993, offered stunning views of Tokyo Tower and the surrounding cityscape.

Yurikamome (whose name is taken from the official bird of the prefecture, the black-headed gull, found in the Tokyo Bay environs) went into operation to provide transportation around the area. With its stunning harbor views, the Yurikamome became an attraction in itself.

I visited every single one of these places as they opened up, amazed at the ability of the city of Tokyo to keep growing and to keep building, in a way that New York or Paris or other major capitals did not. I rode the Ferris wheel, learned about local sea life, and mastered Lego skills I never imagined I was capable of.

I also made the half-hour trek across the Rainbow Bridge, which was on the way to becoming a suicide spot of note. People were finding creative ways to climb over the 10-foot-high restraining fences on both sides to make the 161-foot leap to the water below. The first one came in 1997. A twenty-eight-year-old company worker removed his shoes, placed them together (as per Japanese suicide custom to indicate the descent into the hereafter was voluntary), and jumped the equivalent of seventeen stories into the bay. I personally saw another jumper fished out of the water on one of my early morning walks—a young man in a suit and tie, his eyeglasses, lens shattered, still affixed to his head. All in all, it was less traumatic for bystanders than the standard go-to method of jumping in front of a commuter train from a crowded station platform, which tended to be quite messy and cause troublesome train delays.

Tokyo Underworld 1999: "We Hope This Finds You in Good Health"

Tokyo Underworld was published in 1999. To promote it, I went on a speaking tour of Japan Society gatherings in a number of American cities. In Los Angeles, hours before I was scheduled to speak, two FBI agents came to my hotel room and informed me that there had been an anonymous death threat against me. They escorted me to my talk that evening and stood guard at the doors. Then they took me to the airport the following morning and saw me through security. That was something that, fortunately, didn't happen every day. They would not give me any details, but I assumed it was probably from West Coast representatives of the Tosei-kai, whose suspected illicit activities in California and Hawaii I had delineated in *Tokyo Underworld*.

Tokyo Underworld, in Japanese translation, had hit the #1 spot in Tokyo book sales, but not everyone was singing its praises. Katsushi Murata, the Sumiyoshi gangster who had stabbed Riki-dozan in the men's room of the New Latin Quarter, an injury that led to the wrestler's premature death, was so incensed over *Tokyo Underworld* that he stormed into the glass and steel offices of my publisher Kadokawa, just down the street from the Yasukuni Shrine, the place of worship for yakuza and crazy right-wingers, and demanded retribution. Murata was in his sixties and (according to news reports) suffering from diabetes, but he was still an active gangster and a scary individual. His nickname was "Kami-sori Murata" (Razor Murata) for his sharp punches in street fights.

He was upset because I had put photos of him and his wife, who was nearly forty years younger, in the book. The photos were mugshots provided by the Tokyo Metropolitan Police, taken after the couple had been arrested. Mr. and Mrs. Murata, the police report said, had burst into the apartment of a hostess who worked for one of their nightclubs and seized her belongings, including a TV, a stereo, and other appliances. They were partial repayment, Murata claimed, for a loan the young woman had failed to pay back. Much screaming and shouting had ensued, causing the neighbors to call the police, who arrived on the scene to take the felonious pair into custody. The mugshots were published on the back page of the *Yukan Fuji* the next day, which is where I came upon them and later, with permission from police authorities, put them in the photo section of the Japanese version of *Tokyo Underworld*.

Murata, wearing a brown-striped, double-breasted suit, unbuttoned in accordance with yakuza fashion, approached the Kadokawa receptionist and demanded to talk to the editor of the book, Satoshi Gunji. Gunji was a superb editor. He was fluent in English and spoke Urdu as well, having lived in Pakistan for a time. He had done a superlative job on *TU*, as he had on *Wa*. But on that particular day, he was out of the office, so it was left to the assistant editor, Tetsuya Sugahara, to deal with the aggrieved mobster.

Murata handed the very nervous Sugahara a name card of extremely thick paper, framed in gold, with his name rendered in flowing calligraphy. It read:

Murata Katsushi	村田勝志
Kumi-*cho*	組長
Murata-*gumi*	村田組

In plain terms the card announced him as the Crime Boss of the Murata Crime Family. He protested to Sugahara that the mug shots of him and his wife had been published without his permission. He added that this kind of adverse publicity could damage his daughter's budding career as a professional wrestler. He said he wanted *"1-pon"* or *"2-hon"* to settle the matter—the "1" in *"1-pon"* was a reference, in yakuza slang, for ¥1 million; *"2-hon"* would be ¥2 million.

It was Kadokawa's corporate policy not to make such payments. On hand that day was another editor, a Mr. Harada, a man who knew Murata from a previous stint in the editorial department of the popular weekly *Shukan Bunshun*. (Murata had made a mini-career of selling his version of the famous fight he had had with Rikidozan to different publications, varying the details each time to enhance the story's value. *Bunshun* had been one of his customers.)

Harada explained to Murata that the law had changed and that demanding money as he was doing was now illegal. Murata eventually tired of arguing, but as he prepared to leave, he turned to Sugahara and said ominously: "Be careful when you use the subway."

Sugahara was a laid-back, good-natured soul who never seemed to let anything bother him. "But that moment," he told me afterward, "was the scariest moment of my life. From then on, for a long time, I was very careful using the subway. I stood as far away from the platform as I could when waiting for the train to come. I really was afraid someone was going to push me onto the tracks in front of an onrushing train."

I felt badly for him, naturally, but I also could not help wondering if and when a similar threat might be coming my way as well. I did not have to wait long.

Shortly after the Murata episode, I received a letter from the office of Ginza Machii—Hisayuki Machii, the feared crime boss of Tokyo, now in his sixties and still going strong. It came in the mail one day, via Kadokawa, in two versions, one in English, the other in Japanese. Both had been written by Machii's long-time male secretary.

Dear Mr. Whiting:
The seasons are changing and we hope this letter finds you in good health. .... However, the Director is very upset about some of the things you wrote about him in *Tokyo Underworld*. Whenever he thinks about it he becomes extremely agitated. He would like to meet with you personally to discuss these issues face to face and to explain his position to you. He requests that you visit our office, the Lumiere in Roppongi, for a frank exchange of views. We are awaiting your reply.

I showed the letter to my longtime friend Kozo Abe, an editor at *Yukan Fuji*, and his face turned white. He said the tone of the letter in Japanese made his blood run cold. "'We hope this finds you in good health' means that you are not going to be in good health very much longer," he said. "This is really creepy."

Gunji-san said the same thing after he had read the letter. He told me that he too had been staying as far back from the edge of the subway platform as he could.

Myself, I started taking different routes home to Kamakura, although there was only one way into my house, which, as you may recall, was secluded and surrounded by trees. I was not worried about the accuracy of what I had written. I had done my homework. I had the police files on Machii and his gang (which I had procured clandestinely for the sum of ¥30,000). They showed that Machii, an ex-boxer, a big hulk of a man at 6'2", 200 pounds, had murdered two men with his bare hands and committed several other violent offenses. (The CIA, with whom Machii had worked closely to suppress communist agitators, had always managed to persuade the Japanese authorities to release him from prison whenever he was arrested.) What I was worried about, of course, was being done in by Machii's thugs.

Now it was my turn to have queasy thoughts when standing on the platform of one of those spotless, gleaming Tokyo subway stations that I was always bragging about to New Yorkers. I wasn't

Tokyo Underworld

2

3

1. & 2. Yoshio Kodama [left] and Hisayuki Machii [above], partners in Showa Era Crime. Machii, the one-time "Crime Boss of Tokyo," was not pleased with *Tokyo Underworld*.

3. A tattooed yakuza, on the rooftop of a Bungeiza street building, Ikebukuro. Tokyo, 1975.

4. Katsushi Murata, captain in the Sumiyoshi Ikka, was not pleased either. "Don't stand too close to the edge of the subway platform," he told my editor. "You never know when someone might push you in front of the train."

4

marveling to myself how clean and efficient it all was. No, just like Sugahara and Gunji, I was looking around to see if there were any suspicious characters lurking nearby, waiting for the opportunity to push me onto the tracks.

"How appealing is Tokyo to you now, Bob?" I asked myself.

After much consultation with the Kadokawa editors and legal team, I finally responded through the Kadokawa lawyer. I wrote that while researching *Tokyo Underworld* I had made repeated requests for interviews to Machii's office, only to be refused each time, so Machii could not say that I had denied him his chance to speak. However, I did also say that I would be willing to meet the Director if I could take a Kadokawa lawyer and a photographer with me, believing that this would guarantee me the needed protection. Machii's office agreed and we set up a time to meet, but then they called back and postponed. Machii's wife had gone into the hospital, seriously ill, and then she suddenly died. Not very long after that, Machii himself fell ill, went into the hospital, and passed on.

It was only later that I found out what the real problem was. It wasn't my research. According to Machii's lawyer, what really bothered him was not that I had written about the Director's crimes, which were all true enough, but that I had not devoted enough space to his contributions to postwar peace in Japan. He and his men had fought communism for the Japanese government hand in hand with the CIA in a devil's bargain during the 1940s and 1950s. Machii had heard that there might be a movie made of *Tokyo Underworld*, and if that were true, he wanted to be portrayed not just as a gangster but also, in equal measure, as a patriot. (The film rights to the book had been optioned out to Dreamworks but would move on to Warner Brothers, where Martin Scorsese would sign on as director, then to HBO with Scorsese and the aforementioned Paul Schrader writing the script, then Amazon, and finally Legendary Global with Terence Winter and Sherry Marsh.)

In fact, the Tosei-kai lawyer showed me a letter that Douglas

MacArthur had written to Machii thanking him for his contributions toward defeating communism. According to the lawyer, whenever Machii went to Hawaii and was stopped by immigration officials because of his history with organized crime, he would pull out the letter from MacArthur and say, "Listen, I am a patriot. I fought the commies for your country. You give those other Japanese yakuza a hard time, but not me."

Reportedly, it worked every time.

Roppongi Hills: Curse of the Dead Souls

There was a saying in Tokyo that change was the only constant. Relentless change that, as the history books will tell you, has been going on in Tokyo ever since the Tokugawa shogunate established its capital there in 1603. As far as I know, this has no parallel among the other great urban centers of the world.

The arrival of the shogun gave sudden prominence to Old Edo in government and trade, precipitating massive landfill projects as the population grew, which today remain the core of the business district between the Imperial Palace and the sea—from Hibiya all the way to Tsukiji.

For all its expansion, Edo remained a town of wooden buildings and as such was under constant reconstruction in the wake of devastating fires. Magnificent Western-style stone structures began to spring up after the shogunate was overthrown in 1868, as the new government, under Emperor Meiji, raced to join the ranks of world powers through a full-scale Westernization program. No sooner had the new Tokyo taken on the semblance of a modern city, however, than the Great Kanto Earthquake hit in 1923, flattening the capital yet another time. Following that came the incendiary bombing of 1945.

When Tokyo's bid for the 1964 Olympics prevailed over that

of competitors like Detroit, at the height of its economic power, and Vienna, with its Old World appeal, it set off a new wave of construction that transformed the city once more. The building frenzy continued right through the "Lost Decade" after the bubble's collapse and continued at a fever pitch as the city got ready for its next Olympics extravaganza, originally scheduled for 2020. No brand came to embody the landscape's transmogrifications and excesses quite like the Mori Building Company. The company had been founded in 1958 by one Takichi Mori, an economics professor, who built his firm into a real estate empire, his projects displaying his name and each building's chronological place in the record: Mori Building 1, Mori Building 2, and so on up to Mori Building 37, built in 1981.

I had always thought it was a cold, unimaginative way to designate buildings. But Mori was just getting started. In 1983 he built the aforementioned Ark Hills, an office towers complex in Roppongi that also housed Asahi Television studios, the Suntory Concert Hall, and ANA InterContinental Tokyo hotel. I belonged to a "high tech" study group organized by prominent business leader Glen Fukushima that met regularly at the tony Ark Hills Club on the thirty-seventh floor. The views were as spectacular as the prices.

In 1991 and 1992, Mori was ranked #1 on *Forbes*'s list of the richest men in the world with a net worth of $13 billion, living simply despite his wealth, it was reported, wearing kimono at work and abstaining from alcohol and tobacco. He came to be known affectionately as Tokyo's "Oya-san," a friendly term for landlord. Upon his death in 1993 his company was taken over by his sons Minoru and Akira, who both went on to make the *Forbes* richest list themselves several years later, producing several more building complexes in the Ark Hills mold.

The family vision was strongly influenced by the controversial French-Swiss architect Le Corbusier, who favored urban designs consisting of a central core of skyscrapers, where business and industry were concentrated, and beyond them a civic center and a ring of apartment buildings.

"Vertical garden cities," son Minoru called them in his book *Mori Building*. "In Tokyo there is only one way to go—up."

The Mori family believed that, in a crowded city like Tokyo, a concrete box in a high-rise was better than a traditional home with a yard. However, critics said the designs the Moris employed were nothing but "human storage spaces" unconcerned with the idea of privacy or comfort. In the Mori view of the world, they complained, there was little room for broad, leafy avenues, open spaces for leisure or art, or anything else except architecturally undistinguished superblocks.

The critics had a point. The unending redevelopment was producing a multitude of sleek, yet faceless, glass and steel towers with seemingly identical shopping malls and vast, sterile plazas, not just in Tokyo proper but in suburban areas and outlying towns as well. What had given Tokyo so much of its energy and charm— the chaotic alleys, the *izakaya* under the tracks, the black-market sites turned legitimate, the hole-in-the-wall nightclubs, and the varied neighborhoods inside and beyond the Yamanote Line (as the Yamate Line had now been renamed)—was giving way to the advance of bulldozers and cranes at an alarming pace.

* * *

I would walk around parts of Shinjuku, Shinbashi, and Roppongi where I had once cavorted in my callow youth and find large swaths of these areas unrecognizable from what I remembered of them in the sixties and seventies. Huge development projects had forced Nicola's Roppongi-based restaurant to move twice, for example, each incarnation diminishing its original appeal. The Club 88 building with its long, canopied entranceway was gone forever. So was the Happy Valley Dance Hall and premises.

My former Komagome neighborhood had completely changed

into cookie-cutter "one-room mansion" studio-apartment blocks. Higashi-Nakano had similarly metamorphosed. The Bokido and the Kawamura Building were both long gone, replaced by high-rises and lookalike convenience stores, *konbini*, as they are called in Japanese. The attempt to sweep away the postwar rubble and impose a top-down, Corbusier-like order on the natural chaos of a big city was destroying that low-rise feeling and character that had attracted people there in the first place.

From a city of a hundred little villages like Komagome, where everyone knew everyone else, residential Tokyo had been transformed into an enormous grid of housing complexes where nobody knew his or her next-door neighbor. The lower one went down the economic scale, the smaller and more uncomfortable the apartments became. It was a kind of "creative destruction," as an acquaintance of mine put it, despite the air conditioning and central heating and protection from the elements and the spanking-new facilities. Along the way it did serious damage to the traditional extended family, with all the implications that carries in a rapidly aging society.

If the city was growing above ground, it was also expanding underground. New subway lines and extensions of existing ones went into operation during the early 21st century and helped solidify the Tokyo subway system's status as the most utilized rapid transit system in the world. Every day, eight million passengers rode the city's 200-mile network of 13 lines and 300 stations. Corresponding underground walkways proliferated, adding to the vast, extensive subterranean system of shopping arcades and pedestrian tunnels. You could walk underground from one side of Shinjuku to the other and from Ginza to Yurakucho without ever having to surface—over a mile in both instances. Some subway lines, like the Chiyoda, ran as deep as 125 feet underground. The Kokkai-Gijidomae Station beneath the Diet Building had five underground levels and is believed to have been designed to double as a nuclear fallout shelter for the Japanese government.

The Kasukabe "Underground Temple."

Plans were made to redo the underground maze beneath Shibuya Station, moving the Tokyu Toyoko Line from the second floor of the Station Building to a newly excavated fifth underground level, as part of a massive redevelopment plan by Shibuya-based firms that also included a brand-new skyline of high-rise buildings. An underground plaza and reservoir underneath the Shibuya River were part of the project.

An eerie addition to this subterranean world was the massive underground tunnel network in Kasukabe just outside the city, 165 feet beneath the surface. Finished in 2006 after thirteen years of construction, it earned the distinction of being the world's largest drainage facility, built to control flooding during Tokyo's monsoon and typhoon seasons. Tokyo sits on the 6,500-square-mile Kanto floodplain, with several rivers running through it. Since approximately one-third of its population lives below sea level, heavy rains can make life miserable in the capital. A flood in 1991 inundated 30,000 homes. The Metropolitan Area Outer Discharge Channel, as this complex is lovingly called, consists of a giant water tank and several massive silos the size of giant sequoia trees that can each hold up to thirteen million gallons of water, which will then be dumped into the Edo River. The "Underground Temple," as it is also known, is so surreal and so unsettling that it has been used as a setting for dystopian movies and is open to adventurous tourists.

* * *

In 1995 my wife was assigned to the Tokyo office of the UNHCR for a five-year term. We rented a three-bedroom Western-style apartment in the Homat Royal Building, directly across from the annex to the exclusive Hotel Okura and two doors away from the US Embassy residence. In the four years we lived there, construction hummed along around us nonstop, high-rise buildings going up all over the neighborhood. Wooden scaffolding and metal pipes lined much of the street all the way to the Iikura Crossing. By the time we moved out, yet another Mori Building complex had gone up.

My wife and I still kept the architecturally distinguished, if aging and molding, wooden-frame house in Kamakura for weekend visits. So when my wife was transferred to Dhaka, Bangladesh, in 2000, followed by a tour of Stockholm that led her up to retirement age in 2007, I returned to my former routine of summers and winters abroad and spring and fall in Kamakura.

Living in Kamakura, I still found it necessary to make the trip to Tokyo two or three times a week for editorial meetings and business dinners. Japanese magazine editors and others in the media differed from those in the United States in the emphasis they put on *uchiawase*, or face-to-face meetings. Instead of just calling you up and saying, "Could you give us a story on so-and so?" or "Could we interview you on such-and-such?" as an American might, they would ask for a sit-down over lunch or dinner to get to know you if they didn't already, to take your pulse as you responded with more or less enthusiasm, and to discuss and prepare whatever it was they wanted you to do. Including the trip to

town and back, it was time-consuming, but that was how business was done in Japan. *Uchiwase* meetings greased the wheels of
all-important harmonious relations. Oh, and money was never
discussed at these meetings. That was considered gauche. When
the publication finally got around to paying you, a month or so
after the piece came out, that is when you found out what your
efforts were worth.

One place I came to frequent in connection with work discus-
sions was the Oak Door restaurant, on the sixth floor of the Grand
Hyatt, a popular hangout for people in media and entertainment,
famous for its open kitchen and Kobe beef steak that was beyond
expensive. You never knew when you were going to spot a Johnny
Depp or a Quentin Tarantino hobnobbing among the wheelers
and dealers.

The Grand Hyatt itself was part of Roppongi Hills, yet another
mammoth Mori Building complex built in 2003, which included
the flagship fifty-four-floor Mori Tower. The whole thing was
nestled amidst a whirl of high-fashion outlets and trendsetting
restaurants. It had transformed a somewhat seedy Old Town
neighborhood of narrow, twisting streets, closely packed wooden
houses, ten-story apartment buildings subsidized by the national
housing authority, and an assortment of bars and cheap eateries
into Japan's most coveted swath of real estate. It came to epitomize
the fame and fortune of its numerous celebrity tenants, including
the multinationals, who couldn't get in fast enough.

For all its glitz, however, Roppongi Hills was also a mess.
Inside it was a maze of escalators, hallways, and multi-level pas-
sages, with warrens of shops and restaurants scattered throughout that were so confusing it was difficult to know where you were
at any one time, or even what floor you were on. It reminded me
of a modern-day kasbah: easy to enter, hard to get out of. It did
nothing to enhance the aesthetic feel of Roppongi. My wife, calling on the diplomatic tact she had acquired in years of service in
the United Nations, said, "They should drop a bomb on it."

Roppongi Hills with Tokyo Bay city center in the distance.

It also had more than its share of problems, among them faulty revolving doors that caused injury to a number of people and the death of a six-year-old boy in March 2004, when his head was caught between a rotating door and the outer frame. Three Mori Building Company executives were indicted for professional negligence and received three-year suspended sentences.

In the beginning, Roppongi Hills had been seen as a symbol of the end of Japan's Lost Decade. Goldman Sachs and Lehmann Brothers had their Tokyo headquarters in the building. Young stock traders, American and European as well as Japanese, lived and worked there. Many of Tokyo's wealthiest denizens had moved into its apartments. One of its more famous tenants was a controversial upstart internet entrepreneur named Takafumi Horie, who defied Japanese business convention by wearing jeans and T-shirts to work and trying to introduce the practice of hostile takeovers in Japan.

But then some of the residents fell afoul of the law over insider trading, fraudulent business practices, and/or tax evasion. Horie himself would be indicted and imprisoned for insider trading and securities and accounting fraud. He wound up serving two years and three months in prison. Lehman Brothers was the victim of a massive fraud scheme by representatives of the Marubeni Corporation, prompting Lehmann to file a $350 million lawsuit against Marubeni in March 2008. That of course was nothing compared to the Wall Street meltdown that was looming on the horizon. Six months later Lehmann's New York headquarters filed for bankruptcy, triggering a global market crash known as the "Reiman Shokku" (Lehman Shock) in Japan, which suffered devastating consequences along with the rest of the world, and required a $700 billion taxpayer bailout by the United States government.

The fallout galvanized right-wing purists, who had long been critical of the era's excesses and the inroads of individualistic, "me-first" Western values. Among other things, foreign traders received death threats and warnings to "get the hell out of Japan."

There was still more. One of the Roppongi Hills apartments was busted by the police for running an illegal underground casino, and there were highly publicized incidents of substance abuse in other residences, including one that caused the demise of the girlfriend of well-known actor-singer Manabu Oshio in the summer of 2009. A high-end Ginza nightclub hostess, she was found dead and naked in a luxury Hills apartment used by Oshio. The official cause of death was an overdose of ecstasy. The thirty-three-year-old celebrity was arrested and convicted of possessing the drug, supplying it to his girlfriend, and neglecting to care for her after she fell ill. He was sentenced to four years in prison.

Media observers digging for clues to the spate of misfortunes uncovered the fact that Roppongi Hills stands on the very ground where ten of the famous forty-seven *ronin* samurai committed ritual suicide after avenging the death of their lord and restoring the honor of the Ako clan. The tale, the aforementioned *Chushingura*, has been told and retold in Japan's classic Bunraku puppet theater, books, film, and TV and held up as a mirror of *bushido* fealty and sacrifice.

In order to start construction on the Roppongi Hills buildings, the graves located on the site had to be moved, but rumor had it that only the headstones were relocated while the bones remained in the ground. It was now whispered that the complex's continuing misfortunes were the result of a "curse of the dead souls." Others blamed bad feng shui. As writer Mark Schreiber put it, quoting a "spiritual journalist" identified only by the initial Y in an article in the magazine *Jitsuwa Knuckles*:

> The many shrines and temples in Monzencho—as Roppongi was called in olden times—were situated to ensure the proper flow of *ki* (spiritual energy), and with the *kimon* (devil's gates) aligned—north, south, east and west—so as to direct bad spirits from the area, but they were successively demolished to make way for new redevelopment projects that have upset the balance. It's the changes wrought by the disappearance of the temples that are enticing more people to commit crimes.

Another troubling aspect was the manner in which the massive complex had originally been put together. Architectural change in Tokyo encompassed more than just design. The underlying nature of real estate development often required clearing the land of its inhabitants, whether they wanted to be cleared or not.

Through an acquaintance I had gotten to know a certain stalwart member in the Roppongi wing of the Yamaguchi-gumi who had helped persuade recalcitrant landowners bent on staying to change their minds. The introduction was made by a professor I knew who had the young man in one of his classes. "This is a guy you might want to meet," the scholar advised me. His nickname was Smoky. He was an American college student from Oklahoma, part Cherokee, a tall guy with Olympic-level martial arts skills and a lot of repressed anger. That combination and his fluency in Japanese had made him an ideal candidate for the local gangs. He had been a bouncer at international nightclubs, often escorting foreign hostesses from their Roppongi apartments to their places of employment and back, and on behalf of his employers sold drug distribution rights to international gangs from Australia, New Zealand, Russia, Brazil, the Philippines, and Thailand. On one occasion, he explained to me matter-of-factly what his role was in the development of Roppongi Hills:

> We, the guys in the gang, all Japanese except me, would go into a restaurant or snack bar in the area where the owner did not want to sell, he was holding out for a higher price. So we would sit there and order one drink and stay until closing, making as much noise as we could. We could come back later in the night and put a dead cat on the doorstep. Or a bag of shit. We kept it up until the guy agreed to sell.

The story had an unpleasantly familiar ring.

Smoky liked the money but hated his job—not, as he explained, because he was doing violence to people who didn't deserve it— but because to do it right you had to take a lot of speed to stay awake, then, at the end of the work shift, drink a lot of alcohol and take more drugs to get to sleep. Everyone chain smoked. That lifestyle was why yakuza in Japan were always so ill-tempered, he said—a fact I had noted long ago with my friend Jiro and his Sumiyoshi-kai associates in Higashi-Nakano.

I almost wrote a book about Smoky in 2003. After all, it wasn't every day that you met an American who actually belonged to a yakuza gang. And he seemed eager to cooperate. Yakuza in Roppongi in the post-Zappetti era seemed a logical hook. I was ready to sign the papers when, out of the blue, he asked for the addresses and phone numbers of my wife's relatives.

"Insurance, Mr. Whiting," he said. "Insurance that nothing goes wrong."

Whoa.

I called him the next day and told him I was going to have to back out. As chance would have it, I had in fact been offered a contract to do a book on Ichiro Suzuki for publication in the United

States (*The Meaning of Ichiro*) and I told him I was going to do that instead. I never saw him again, although I heard later that he had been kicked out of the gang for stealing and went back to Oklahoma to work in "private security."

However, I did bring up Smoky's work, for lack of a better term, at a speech I gave about underworld corruption in the city to a group of Japanese and international businessmen at the China Room in the Grand Hyatt. In the talk, sponsored by the Hong Kong–based Crédit Lyonnais Securities Asia, I described the role the yakuza gangs played in the construction of Roppongi Hills and Ark Hills and before that, all the way back to the 1964 Olympics and beyond.

The audience found it enlightening, especially those foreign banking and real estate executives associated with the Roppongi Hills development and property transfer who had previously believed that everything had been on the up and up. Apparently, they had missed, or had chosen to ignore, newspaper reports of yakuza trucks "accidentally" plowing into corner shops in the neighborhood before the Hills went up.

The Nomo Effect

Occupying office space in one of those new Tokyo skyscrapers, the thirty-seven-floor Shiroyama Trust Tower in Toranomon, was the second coming of the Black Ships, in the form of the MLB Headquarters. They were there to expedite the transfer (theft, the Nippon Professional Baseball owners would say) of Japan's top baseball stars and market the telecast of MLB games featuring those players to the Japanese public.

Evidence of their unanticipated success, and one of the most striking visual symbols of the era, were the Jumbotron screens proliferating across the city at the busiest train hubs like Shibuya and Shinjuku displaying MLB highlights and live coverage of games from the USA featuring Japan's homegrown heroes. It was a craze that gripped the city, and the entire country, from the mid-nineties on.

Postwar visits by American professional baseball teams had helped revivify Tokyoites during their low moments. Oh and Nagashima were the heroes the city needed during the era of high GNP growth and internationalization. But now, in a way not even the best prognosticators could have foreseen, the game took Tokyo, and the nation of Japan, to new, undreamed-of heights.

It had all started with the shocking defection of star pitcher Hideo Nomo, who left the Kintetsu Buffaloes to sign a contract with the Los Angeles Dodgers in February 1995, after he found a way around the rules that had kept Japanese players under lock and key at home since 1965. Said rules were the result of a battle between the Nankai Hawks and the San Francisco Giants over the services of a pitcher named Masanori Murakami, the first Japanese to play in the Major Leagues (1964–65).

In a land where paternalistic regimes and their authority are seen as the keepers of social equilibrium, Nomo's rebellion shook the nation. Baseball executives, media pundits, and fans alike painted Nomo as a traitor, an ingrate. Even his father stopped speaking to him.

A reporter I knew called the Nomo Defection the third great tragedy of 1995, after the January 11 Kobe earthquake that had devastated the city, causing over 5,200 deaths and leaving 300,000 people homeless, and the deadly Sarin Gas Attack on the Tokyo subway system of March 20, perpetrated by a shadowy doomsday cult, Aum Shinrikyo, leaving 13 people dead and many others writhing in agony on subway platforms and stairs, some of them with blood gushing from their noses or mouths. Cult members had dropped five plastic bags of liquid sarin in subway cars packed with rush-hour commuters, piercing them with metal-tipped umbrellas.

But then Nomo started winning and everything changed.

"Hey that's our boy over there," I would hear people say as they stood watching Nomo pitch on the giant station-front screens. "He's showing up those Americans. Can you believe it?"

The energy in the air when Nomo took the field as starting pitcher in the 1995 MLB all-star game was charged in a way I hadn't felt in the city since the 1964 Olympics. What I heard so many older people say at that time with awe and delight about the New Otani Hotel, the Shinkansen, flush toilets, and Ginza's neons—へ～！長生きしてよかったな～ (I'm glad I lived this long)—was being heard once again.

Prime Minister Tomomichi Murayama called Nomo a "national treasure." The *Asahi Shimbun* deemed Nomo's MLB success a "catharsis" for Japanese fed up with constant US carping about Tokyo's trade policies. Wrote the *Mainichi Shimbun*, "Nomo's impact will be so great as to recast the image of the Japanese people in the American imagination."

By the time Nomo had won the ESPY Breakthrough Award for his 1995 MLB debut season, the great gates of Nippon Professional Baseball had been irrevocably torn down. The game's biggest stars would follow in the path he had paved—to far greater financial rewards and wider recognition than they had ever dreamed possible.

Orix Blue Wave's flashy batting star Ichiro Suzuki migrated to the Seattle Mariners and was voted the AL MVP in 2001. He then broke the single-season record for hits with 262 in 2003. Hideki Matsui, the former Yomiuri Giants slugger, nicknamed Godzilla because of his superhuman strength and a bad acne condition, became the Yankees most reliable clutch hitter over a seven-year period, culminating in his selection as the World Series MVP in 2009. It all served to create a huge wave of interest in Major League baseball in Japan that continued to grow as star players like Yu Darvish, Masahiro Tanaka, and the remarkable Shohei Ohtani—who, as a pitcher, could throw a baseball at 100 miles per hour and, as a batter, hit one 500 feet—traveled abroad to occupy center stage.

The exploits of these stars on MLB diamonds dominated Japanese media sports coverage from the mid-nineties on, far eclipsing reportage of the local Nippon Professional Baseball League.

All of this had special significance for Tokyo-based prize-winning jour-

Nomo pitches for the Los Angeles Dodgers.

nalist Midori Masujima. According to her, Japan suffered from an inferiority complex when it came to sports. The cause, she wrote, was the general failure of the country's athletes to prevail in international competitions—except for the rare marathon or judo triumph (Japan's dominance in figure skating was still years away). Japan could produce world-class products, she said, but not world-class human beings.

"We've never been a member of the world community, not in the Edo period, not in the Meiji period, and not today," she wrote in a memorable magazine essay.

Because of this, she said, there was a great craving for overseas approval. The sudden and unforeseen success of Nomo and the others fed that craving and appeared to disprove the notion that Japanese were not "physically or experientially ready for world competition." It amounted to a vindication of Japan itself.

Midori, in her early forties at the time, also wrote a column for *Yukan Fuji*, so my editor Abe-san arranged a dinner for us at an *izakaya* in Ueno. She was impressive—quick and articulate—and living testimony that female journalists could be every bit as good as or superior to men in the male-dominated society that was Japan. She also strongly believed that Japan should take a more assertive role in international society. She reminded me of my wife, Machiko, with one difference. My wife was one of the few living Japanese who did not like baseball.

For a large chunk of the population, watching Major League games in the early morning—as early, sometimes, as 4 or 5 a.m.—before going to work became the norm. Some twenty-five million people watched Ichiro break the single-season hits record in 2003. One out of every two Japanese watched Samurai Japan win the final game of the inaugural World Baseball Classic played in San Diego in March 2006. (Water pressure in Tokyo dropped by 25 percent each time fans made bathroom runs between innings.)

My next-door neighbor in Kamakura, a kimono-clad woman in her mid-eighties and a person in whom I had never remotely detected an interest in baseball, had the starting lineups of the Dodgers, the Yankees, and the Mariners memorized. While waiting with her for the bus to come at the Daitonomiya Station next to the Kamakura Shrine, she would invariably discuss baseball with me.

"Whiting-san," she would say in Japanese, "Matsui belongs in the #5 spot in the batting order, don't you think? Move Posada to #6. It's much better. *Desho?*"

"Don't you think Matsui could hit more home runs if he learned to pull the ball at Yankee Stadium? The right field stands are so close."

I thought she was quite observant. I urged her to write a letter to Yankee manager Joe Torre and offered to translate, but she demurred.

"Torre-*kantoku* is very busy, I'm sure, and I don't want to intrude," she said.

One could argue that the "Nomo Effect" was a factor in other changes that were taking place in Japanese society, including in business, science, and the arts. I did in fact make this point in an essay for a book entitled *Reimagining Japan*, published by McKinsey and Company in 2011. Hallmarks of Western-style individualism, from job-hopping to litigation and even bleached-blond hair, all taboo in the pre-Nomo era, gradually became an accepted part of the culture. Even Japan's stay-at-home ballplayers caught the spirit: Inspired in part by Nomo's confrontational stance, they launched Japan's first (and, as of this writing, only) player strike when, in 2004, the owners threatened to reduce the number of teams.

In the corporate world, perhaps the most notable example of change was the case of Shuji Nakamura, who invented the blue LED in the early 1990s while working for Nichia. The company made a fortune from his invention. All Nakamura received was the company's thanks and a ¥20,000 (about $250) bonus. Initially press reports both in Japan and abroad cited this humble reward as an example of the superiority of the team-oriented Japanese business model. A few years later, however, in the new Nomo era, Nakamura left Nichia to become a professor at the University of California, Santa Barbara, and sued his former employer over the minuscule bonus. He was eventually awarded ¥840 million (more than $9 million at the exchange rate at the time). It was the largest settlement ever paid by a Japanese company for an invention. The rough parallel to the spirit of Nomo's behavior—leaving an entrenched Japanese institution to claim his individual rights—was hard to miss. Several similar lawsuits at other firms followed.

Perhaps the biggest evidence of the Nomo Effect is that when Nomo left Japan in 1995, going to the MLB was the worst sin a Japanese player could commit; however, a decade later, it had become a highly respected ambition. The Japanese baseball world came to think that it was a badge of honor for a top star to play in the Major Leagues.

In fact, in 2013, fans of the Japan champion Rakuten Golden Eagles would practically demand that the Eagles' flashy young billionaire owner Hiroshi Mikitani allow his ace Masahiro Tanaka, who won twenty-five games with no defeats, to go to the US and show what he could do in the MLB. Japanese pride required it. Mikitani would eventually consent, selling the rights to Mikitani to the New York Yankees via the posting system established in 2001. It was said that Mikitani was afraid that if he did not let Tanaka go, fans would rebel, customers would stop using his product—a vast online shopping mall—and his stock price would fall.

All in all, it was a remarkable shift in attitude.

Although Japanese fans and media followed the MLB games passionately, it might be noted that there was little interest in players not from Japan. News reports invariably focused on the Japanese star in the lineup: "Ichiro gets two hits in Mariners loss." The hits may have been dribblers past the mound that Ichiro beat out when there was no one on base and the team was behind half a dozen runs, but the plays would be analyzed and reanalyzed as though a world championship hung in the balance. Often the media coverage did not include the game results at all. Nobody really cared, unless the Japanese player had contributed to a victory.

NPB executives fumed at losing their players to the Americans and at the advertising billboards that dotted the city with Japanese stars in MLB uniforms, endorsing products. But they would later change their attitudes with the advent of heavy multimillion-dollar "posting" fees paid to them by MLB teams for releasing their stars.

The self-important executives at Yomiuri, led by my former star English pupil, the now all-powerful Tsuneo Watanabe, were blindsided by the MLB's hijacking their players—and fans. Watanabe initially compared the American MLB's plundering of Japan's baseball talent to the forceful opening of Japanese trade by the American commodore Matthew Perry and his Black Ships in the 1850s. Yet, he and the other owners ultimately swallowed their defeat and, with their fingers placed squarely on the pulse of the Japanese public, successfully capitalized on the turn of events and organized historic official season openers played by Major League teams at the Tokyo Dome: Chicago Cubs and New York Mets in 2000, New York Yankees and Tampa Bay Devil Rays in 2004, Boston Red Sox and Oakland A's in 2008, and the Seattle Mariners versus the A's in 2012, all to capacity crowds and nationwide TV audiences, while simultaneously working in as many exhibition games with the Yomiuri Giants as possible during the visits. This was in addition to biannual post-season exhibition tours that featured MLB all-star squads playing against their Japan counterparts and were also sponsored by Yomiuri. All of this created a substantial stream of revenue for the media monolith, partially compensating for the Tokyo Yomiuri Giants' drop in Video Research ratings.

A new paradigm had clearly been formed and, for me, it proved to be a powerful and sometimes amusing lens for viewing, and participating in, Japanese society of the post-bubble era.

The opportunity to write a book on Ichiro Suzuki and the other new wave of baseball migrants would provide a much welcome reprieve from the underbelly of Japan and subway platform angst and bring me back to my first love. It would represent the closing of a circle that had begun with *The Chrysanthemum and the Bat* and continued through *You Gotta Have Wa*. It would also reflect the start of a new era in US-Japan relations, as described previously, and the appearance on the scene of a new, boldly assertive generation of young Japanese.

My preparation for the Ichiro book led to a number of thought-provoking interviews with Japanese players that were published in *Time* and other periodicals. Hideo Nomo, big, broad-shouldered, and aloof, came to my home at the Homat Royal with Don Nomura, his agent and the man who discovered the loophole that freed Nomo from the chains that had bound him to Japan. Nomo confided to me that his motivation for going to

Ichiro Suzuki had 3,089 hits in MLB, which are Hall of Fame numbers, and 4,367 total hits including his NPB career. He treated his bat like an ancient Shinto treasure.

the United States was not an overwhelming desire to play Major League baseball or to break down barriers but simply that he could not stand playing another season for his manager with the Kintetsu Buffaloes, Keishi Suzuki, whose idea of curing a sore arm was throwing and more throwing and whose motto was: "Pitch Until You Die."

"If Kintetsu had fired Suzuki," Nomo told me, "I would have stayed in Japan."

The hugely popular Ichiro Suzuki sat for an interview in the fall of 2002 at an exclusive deluxe suite high atop the Hotel New Otani, which was attended by a half-dozen members of his entourage. He had been smuggled in from a secret location. It was like interviewing Elvis.

Ichiro was one of a kind. Sui generis, Mr. West Coast Cool, with his Oakley Radar athletic sunglasses and avant-garde fashion sense. He was also a player who treated his bat like an ancient Shinto treasure, positioned in exactly the same spot to the inch on the bench when he wasn't using it, while his pregame workouts were so intense that opposing players invariably stopped to watch in awe. They had never seen a Major League player practice so hard. I found him intelligent, perceptive, and candid. He said that the harsh training his father subjected him to from childhood, much as in the TV program *Kyojin no Hoshi*, the tough-love father-son anime TV series that had transfixed me in my younger days, had bordered on *"gyakutai,"* a Japanese word that means "physical abuse" and has a particularly nasty connotation when its object is a child. His business manager called me the next morning and demanded I not use Ichiro's negative comments about his father. I found myself unable to comply.

I interviewed Hideki Matsui one morning on the bench at Legend's Field in Florida. We were the only people on the entire field. He was just about the nicest person—MLB star or otherwise—you could ever hope to meet. He was also refreshingly candid. He told me that, yes, the Japanese media reports were true, he indeed had a collection of several hundred adult videos.

"Doesn't everybody?" he asked, wide-eyed.

Later, as the camp drew to a close, Matsui did what no other Yankee had ever done. He invited all the New York beat reporters out to dinner and afterward handed out gifts, many of them items from his own personal AV collection, which he had brought from Tokyo.

One of the interesting sidelights of the book tour I made afterward was a letter from the president of the United States, George W. Bush, and his wife Laura, telling me how much they had enjoyed reading the copy of *The Meaning of Ichiro* sent to them by a supporter in Jackson, Mississippi, where I had given a speech. It was difficult to imagine the first couple sitting in the West Wing residential quarters in the evening, sipping tea and discussing the early life of Ichiro Suzuki. Nevertheless, I would count it as my second presidential endorsement after Bill Clinton's recommendation of *Wa*. He had been asked during a TV interview in 1992 what he was reading and *Wa* was the book he mentioned, gifted him by campaign aide Derek Shearer.

Support for my work crossed party lines at the highest levels.

FCCJ: "Drunken Brawls"

The move from Kamakura to Tokyo's Toyosu neighborhood was a stroke of genius, entirely conceived, planned, and executed by my wife in 2009 upon her retirement from the UNHCR, before the area came into prominence as the planned site of the 2020 Olympic Village. With many athletic venues like the existing Ariake Sports Center in the immediate vicinity, not to mention its selection as the location of the massive new Tsukiji Fish Market, the real estate value skyrocketed.

Also, it was good once again to be living in the center of the city, where Tokyo's legendary energy and discipline showed no signs of abating, although men now wore makeup and skinny suits. It was striking that despite the presence of fast-food outlets everywhere—McDonald's, Shakey's, Wendy's, et al.—the city's denizens somehow managed to avoid the obesity epidemic that had hit the United States, a country that was more and more being defined by overweight people, potholed highways, and vending machines that didn't work.

From our high-rise residence we had a spectacular view of the spanking-new Sky Tree (2012) in neighboring Sumida. It is the tallest broadcasting and observation tower in the world (and second tallest structure after the Burj Khalifa). A three-stop subway ride took you from Toyosu on the Yurakucho Line to the Ginza, with its high-end stores and moneyed Chinese tourists. I bought my first iMac and MacBook Pro at the flagship Apple store there. iPhones, tailored for Japan by Softbank, were all the rage, shoving Panasonic and other domestic flip-phone manufacturers out of the market. Half the pedestrians on the street were now checking email and texting on iPhones as they walked.

Easy access to the Foreign Correspondents Club of Japan was another of the pluses of living in Toyosu. I had become a member decades earlier, and the club had played an important role in both my work and social life. I even served on the Board. I particularly liked the Main Bar, located on the twentieth floor of the Yurakucho Denki Building, which offered a panoramic view of the Tokyo skyline and ringside seats to many a drunken argument between journalists. Now it was just four stops and a one-minute walk away, which meant I could join in the fun every night.

Established in 1945 by and for journalists who landed in Japan at the end of World War 2 with Douglas MacArthur, the Club provided essential services to facilitate the task of transmitting the news of Japan to the world when no such facilities existed in war-torn Tokyo.

At the time, except for a few magnificent Western-style buildings and the Imperial Hotel, which survived the incendiary bombing in the last days of the war, there was barely an identifiable street remaining. With the help of the Occupation authorities, the journalists had quickly secured some living and workspace in a ramshackle former restaurant, moving in five to a room, not counting their new live-in Japanese girlfriends, using sheets for partitions. This annoyed BBC correspondent John Morris, who prudishly insisted that the sex act was meant to be performed in private.

"Drunken brawls were frequent," wrote Morris in a memoir entitled *The Phoenix Cup*, "and there were times when firearms were discharged in the club. It was a cross between a waterfront sailors' bar and a brothel."

The FCCJ quickly became the hub of the international community that reemerged from the ashes of war. Unlike the US servicemen and members of the Occupation Headquarters, who had privileges to procure American supplies at the military exchanges, most journalists in Tokyo had to make do shopping at local stores, which rarely carried what they wanted. Any kind of half-decent whisky, cheese, or ice cream was very hard to come by. Club members, who hailed from all over the globe, wrote home to family and friends for recipes. Japanese cooks working at the

With MLB Commissioner Rob Manfred. 2017.

FCCJ were given survival courses for making pizza and hamburgers, which they had never seen, much less tasted.

Before long the regulars congregating each day in the bar were a Who's Who of the region's most celebrated writers—including Pulitzer Prize winners who had covered the front lines of World War 2, Korea, and Vietnam—as well as politicians, entertainers, royalty, and Asia's busiest spies.

James Michener would be holding court in the dining room, talking about his latest novels to be turned into hit movies in the years since his breakaway blockbusters *South Pacific, Sayonara,* and *Teahouse of the August Moon*, all of which of which deeply influenced the world's view of the Asia-Pacific region. Ian Fleming could also be seen at the FCCJ night after night in 1962 with former colleagues from the *Sunday Times*, doing research for *You Only Live Twice*. Every businessman and spymaster of note needed to be there, such was the convergence of news and deal-making at the club. Walls were covered with photos of famous individuals who had made appearances: Muhammad Ali, Gina Lollobrigida, Ronald

Reagan, Willie Nelson, the Emperor and the Empress of Japan, a young and surprisingly articulate Donald Trump, Roger Moore, George Soros, Rachel McAdams, MLB Commissioner Rob Manfred. The Crown Prince and Princess Michiko danced together at the Club's fortieth-anniversary party. A famous prize-winning Italian journalist made history late one night by entertaining a young lady on the nineteenth-floor Club pool table, completing his task despite an unexpected interruption by a Club employee. The flustered employee bowed, apologized for the intrusion, and quickly exited. The journalist bowed back from his semi-prone position and resumed what he was doing.

The FCCJ played a central role in coverage of major news events throughout the 20th century and into the 21st, including the Olympus and Nissan scandals, both of which illustrated the perils of being a foreign executive in a Japanese company. Olympus appointed England's Michael Woodford as CEO in 2011, but he lost his job shortly after he disclosed a major accounting fraud. Woodford was fired, and the scandal led to the resignation of the company's entire board and the arrest of several senior executives, but he was later awarded £10 million in an out-of-court settlement with Olympus over his dismissal. Woodford had abandoned an earlier proxy fight to take control of the company after it became apparent Olympus's institutional investors were uncomfortable with the Englishman's combative style. Lebanese Carlos Ghosn became hugely famous in Japan, first for leading the restructuring and revival of struggling Nissan Motors in 1999, then later for his arrest in the winter of 2018 for allegedly understating his compensation, a circumstance brought about by his enemies within the corporation. Ghosn spent months acquainting himself with Japan's criminal justice system, undergoing interrogation several hours every day without his lawyer present and sleeping in an unheated cell with the light on all night. Eventually granted bail, which cost him more than ten million dollars, but denied permission to see his wife, Ghosn fled to Beirut, smuggled out in a box from Kansai Airport.

In the midst of a national press corps that ranked last among G7 nations in the annual Reporters Without Borders' World Press Freedom Index, the FCCJ remained resolutely independent, giving a voice to political protestors and refugees frequently turned away from Japan's National Press Center, including the Dalai Lama.

Nightmare in the City of Ghosts

I was at home in Toyosu sitting on our new high-tech john on Friday March 11, 2011, when the Tohoku earthquake struck. I was used to quakes, dating back to childhood in California, and experienced any number of them living in Japan. There'd be some shaking, sometimes violent shaking, and then it was over, usually in a matter of seconds. No reason to panic. But this one was different. It refused to end. There was a dramatic swaying back and forth, punctuated by sudden, huge horizontal jolts and the sound of creaking walls that went on and on and on. It lasted an excruciating six minutes.

When I emerged from the bathroom, no books had tumbled from the bookcase in the room I used as office and no lamps or vases had fallen over. Everything was still in its place. The new tower my wife and I lived in, sitting on reclaimed land, had incorporated the latest in earthquake-resistant technology—its builders had taken the trouble to mix the sand and dirt beneath with concrete—and the building emerged unscathed, save for a couple of easily repaired cracks in stairwell walls.

But the scene in cities and towns in the Tohoku area 150 miles to the north, telecast live on the flat-screen Aquos TV set in my office, was one of chaos and horror. Buildings everywhere had collapsed. Roads and railways were damaged, and fires had broken out in many different places. At a magnitude of 9.1, announcers were saying it was the most powerful earthquake ever to hit Japan and the fourth most powerful earthquake ever recorded on earth since measurements began in 1900. It was later discovered that Honshu, the main island of Japan, had been moved 8 feet to the east and that the axis of the earth had been shifted several inches. The quake triggered tsunamis, arriving an hour after the initial tremor, of over 130 feet in height, tidal waves that traveled as far as 6 miles inland upriver, in some cases carrying with them vehicles, buildings, fishing boats, and debris. In the process, they destroyed highways and other infrastructure, wiping entire towns off the face of the earth. Thousands of smartphones were capturing the hellish scenes.

The assault by nature left what would later be calculated as 15,894 dead—more than 90 percent by drowning—including several hundred school children. The Okawa Elementary School in Ishinomaki, Miyagi Prefecture, lost 74 children and 10 teachers who were caught by a wave while attempting to flee to higher ground. The scope of the tragedy overwhelmed morgues and crematoriums, forcing mass graves to be dug. A total of 2,562 went missing, never to be found, and thousands more were injured.

More than 200,000 would be left homeless, including 80,000 forcibly evacuated from their homes due to concerns over radiation leaks from Fukushima's damaged nuclear reactors. Many of them were forced to live for months in cramped, crowded evacuation centers, often with no running water or other basic amenities of life. The radiation, along with hundreds of very substantial aftershocks, exacerbated their fears.

The enormous scale of destruction—in all, about one-third of Japan was crippled by the disaster—dwarfed anything that had gone before. Some residential houses and condo buildings built on reclaimed land in Chiba Prefecture sank or tilted due to ground liquefaction and had to be abandoned. Roads, railways, and dams suffered structural damage.

In Tokyo, the harm was less severe, if still significant. Sidewalks had buckled in spots and there were cracks in the facades of some buildings. Bridges were closed and trains were stopped as engineers checked for problems, while power outages and reductions dimmed the world-famous neon signs of Ginza and Shinjuku. The surrounding suburbs suffered rolling blackouts.

The FCCJ was housed in the north tower of twin buildings that were designed to "roll" to mitigate the effects of a quake, so the Club, perched on the top floor, experienced violent motion. Glasses filled with water literally flew off the tables. From its superb vantage point, members were witness to a large explosion at a liquid propane storage facility to the east in Chiba, which subsequently went up in flames.

My wife was shopping in Hibiya at the time of the quake, about to enter the Hibiya Line subway station. The station was immediately closed, and she came home by bus. My wife's niece, who worked in Tokyo, could not get back to her home in the suburb of Omiya and had to sleep at our apartment, after making a three-hour hike in high heels from the Toshiba Building in Hamamatsu-cho where she was employed, all the way around the shoreline of Tokyo Bay, to Toyosu.

Super Viva Home, just down the street from our apartment, closed for the weekend to check for repairs, as did Aoki Supermarket in Lalaport. The office buildings in the area, including the NTT Tower across the way, reduced their power consumption.

There were many scary moments during those early days—mostly from the major aftershocks (which were announced twenty seconds in advance on our apartment building's intercom system) and also from the reports of radiation clouds in the morning hours after the quake, prompting a state of emergency to be declared in the Tohoku area. People living within 12 miles of the Fukushima reactor sites were ordered to evacuate, while those living between 12 and 19 miles from the plant were told to stay indoors due to fears of exposure to radiation.

On that evening, a Saturday, Hiroki Allen, a friend of mine formerly in US Military Intelligence, emailed to say there was a

A local reporter in Miyako City survives the killer Tohoku tsunami on March 11, 2011.

radiation cloud "on its way to Tokyo." The message read: "Leak has been going since last night and it is still not under control. If you absolutely have to go out, wear a mask, and a hat if possible. Take a shower immediately after you return home and wash your clothes."

Another friend, a Tokyo-based management consultant named Mitch Murata, brought over some KI, or potassium iodide pills, as well as something called Prussian blue in the case of contamination from cesium, a notably hazardous form of radio-activity. He also brought along some Isojin, a PVP-iodine used for gargling, available at any local pharmacy, and some ordinary iodine for cuts as a topical antiseptic.

"Swabbing the skin with a tincture of iodine," said Mitch, one of those people with an encyclopedic grasp of any number of subjects, "may be an effective home remedy to prevent serious radioactive contamination of the thyroid gland from iodine-131, which will be emitted in the event of a major nuclear reactor breakdown."

The Japanese government and the Tokyo Electric Power Company initially denied, but then admitted, that greater problems existed with the nuclear reactors and that the numbers of radiation-poisoning victims in Fukushima were steadily increasing. The total stood at 160 two days after the quake. This prompted many foreigners to start leaving Tokyo.

That Sunday, on the advice of their top nuclear scientists, the French government sent emails to all French citizens living in Tokyo recommending that they leave the city, citing the risk of further earthquakes and the uncertainty about the situation of the damaged nuclear plants in Fukushima. The German and Australian embassies followed suit. A number of Tokyo-based foreign companies also ordered their charges out of the city and, in some cases, out of the country.

In London, Britain's Foreign Office advised against all nonessential travel to Tokyo and northeastern Japan. So did the US State Department in Washington, DC. Air China canceled all flights to Tokyo from Beijing and Shanghai.

By Monday, foreign residents were shelling out thousands of dollars to fly to Hong Kong, Singapore, and other points considered safe. Concerns about a potential nuclear holocaust were not helped by hyperbole and fearmongering in press reports out of Japan. The BBC's website ran photos of commuters wearing facemasks, or "radiation masks" as they called them, implying that they were trying to protect themselves against radiation when in fact the simple white surgical masks were also what a great many people in Japan wore in the early spring as a preventative measure against pollen allergies.

CNN continually ran alarmist banners along the bottom of the screen. "Nuclear Cooling Has Failed. Radiation Cloud Could Reach US Friday," went one. The station reported fewer people in the streets of downtown Tokyo, attributing the decrease to a "mass exodus" from the metropolis—people "fleeing" rather than perhaps just staying home as a result of transportation difficulties or on instruction from their places of employment.

Neal Cavuto of Fox's *Your World with Neal* showed a screen graphic depicting two nonexistent nuclear power plants in Japan, including one in the densely populated Shibuya quarter of Tokyo called the "Shibuya Eggman," which was actually a nightclub.

But perhaps the most hysterical was a story in the March 17 edition of *The Sun*, six days after the quake and tsunami, headlined "Nightmare Warning to Brits as Nuke Crisis Continues, Get out of Tokyo Now." It featured a telephone interview with a Tokyo resident, a British woman, who described Tokyo as "a city in fear of nuclear catastrophe—with food, water, and fuel running out and radiation levels from Japan's stricken nuclear reactors reaching ten times normal."

Subtitled "My Nightmare Trapped in City of Ghosts—in Tokyo," the article quoted the woman as saying, "I'm stuck in a part of the city that resembles a ghost-town. Normally the streets bustle like nowhere else on earth. But I look outside now and they are completely deserted. It's like London in the zombie movie *28 Days Later*. The streets are silent. We live near the center of Tokyo and yet there is no movement at all. . . . There is no petrol, no water, no food. . . . What if every day the radiation continues to double?" This was followed the next day (March 18, a Saturday) by a Reuters wire service report that said millions in Tokyo remained indoors on Friday, fearing a blast of radioactive material.

I found such reporting surreal because on the day cited in the "City of Ghosts," I had taken the Yurakucho subway line from Toyosu to Yurakucho for a dinner meeting at the FCCJ. Life seemed pretty normal to me. Boys were playing baseball in the park across the street from my home as I passed on my way to the subway station. The Yurakucho Line was operating at 80 percent capacity, but the cars were as crowded as they always were, and so was Bic Camera, the multistoried electronics store in front of

The most powerful earthquake ever to hit Japan triggered tidal waves of over 130 feet in height, wiping entire towns off the face of the earth.

Yurakucho Station, although the indoor lights were somewhat dimmed. The schools were open (if on a voluntary-attendance basis) and *salarymen* were at work. There was no rationing at the Lawson convenience store on the ground floor of the Yurakucho Denki Building, except for batteries, and the lights were all on at the twentieth floor Main Bar of the FCCJ, the reporters swapping tsunami stories on their way to getting hammered.

"Did you see this bullshit Reuters report," boomed Karel van Wolferen as I walked in. "I can't believe the bullshit these bullshit reporters put out. Doesn't anybody look out the window for Christ's sake?"

None of us could find any evidence of an imminent doomsday blast of radioactive material. In fact, the radiation in Tokyo that day was 0.053 microsieverts according to the *Asahi Shimbun*, which ran daily readings, a figure that was lower than the annual average of 0.078.

* * *

Like many other foreigners living and working in Tokyo, I was deluged with messages from relatives and friends abroad, wondering if my wife and I were all right and asking when we were going to evacuate, suggesting strongly that it was time for us to fly back to California.

But leaving was out of the question. We had family and relatives in the city and its environs who needed our help. My wife's brother was in the ICU at the hospital after an automobile slammed into his bicycle, his artificial respirator running on an emergency generator. We never really considered leaving.

The aforementioned Hiroki Allen helped put the weird disconnect in perspective. Hiroki, a big, robust West Point graduate and former special ops officer, was then working in Tokyo as an equities trader, but, as a member of the US Army reserve, he moonlighted as a liaison and interpreter between the US Military in Japan and the Japan Self-Defense Forces. He also knew his nuclear reactors, having been trained during his Army days to sabotage them.

He pointed out an interesting fact he had discovered: When Hiroshima was hit with an airburst atomic bomb attack in August 1945, radiation effects on the city of Kobe 170 miles away were minimal, and not recorded. When Nagasaki was hit with a plutonium bomb, Fukuoka, less than 200 kilometers away, did not suffer radiation effects either.

"Some people with no background in physics, engineering, or military training, they might freeze at the word 'radiation,'" he said. "They believe radiation is some kind of death ray that kills upon contact. Not so. High-intensity gamma rays, perhaps. Windblown radioisotopes, no way. Cigarette smoke is proven to be a nastier carcinogen than radiation at these current levels. The air in Hong Kong is filled with other nasty smoke such as sulfurous fumes from Chinese factories, heavy-metal vapor from industrial activities in Guangzhou, and a lot of automobile exhaust as well as cigarette smoke. Anybody who evacuated to Hong Kong from Tokyo to avoid health issues made the wrong choice."

Of course, no one yet knew about the long-term effects of radiation in Fukushima. It was too early. Although there was some preliminary evidence that the incidence of thyroid cancer among children in the Fukushima area, normally something like one in a million, had gone up by double-digit numbers, medical authorities have denied that the cause can be traced to radiation. We would all just have to wait and see.

The US Embassy in Tokyo initially advised American residents to remain calm and stay the course. However, when it was discovered that one embassy official had quietly sent his family out of Japan, alarm bells went off among embassy dependents, so a decision was made that those who wanted to leave would be provided with a charter flight out of the city.

The disaster did have discernible effects in Tokyo, making life somewhat inconvenient and disrupting the normal course of business. Periodic electricity stoppages affected the public transport system for employees commuting in and out of central Tokyo. Then there was the reduction in electricity usage that caused escalators and elevators to stop running; perhaps the biggest inconvenience I suffered was having to walk up six flights of stairs to our apartment. Subway station lights were also dimmed—a queasy circumstance for anyone who had been under threat from the yakuza—but nothing untoward occurred. There were also temporary shortages and rationing for certain items—AA batteries, bottled water, bread, rice, toilet paper, and fuel. Another concerning factor for the "*fly-jin*," as the non-Japanese escapees were called, was the lack of information coming out of the power company (TEPCO), lending credence to some of the scariest of the rumors. It was some time before the company finally admitted that a meltthrough had occurred in Reactor 1.

But it was Fukushima where life was truly miserable: Vast

crowds of people huddled in shelters without food, heat, or water, sleeping on a hardwood gymnasium floor or a city-center hallway and depending on donations for hot meals and warm jackets and other necessities of life like toilet paper and sanitary napkins. That was where the living hell was. Not Tokyo. Nevertheless, people continued to leave the capital. Records show that from March 19 to April 8, a total of some 210,000 non-tourist foreigners departed the city.

Many of them eventually made their way back but, as of this writing, almost ten years after the catastrophe, tens of thousands of Fukushima residents are still homeless, living in shelters or temporary refugee housing, and tens of thousands of others have moved away to other parts of Japan, unlikely to return to their former homes.

Through it all, the fabled honesty of the Japanese persisted. In the five months following the disaster, more than $78 million in lost cash was turned into the authorities.

A Lid on Garbage

The 2020 Olympics may have been awarded to Tokyo in 2013 but the topic du jour in Tokyo throughout much of the decade was fish. Namely, the move of the world famous Tsukiji Fish Market, formally known as the Tokyo Metropolitan Central Wholesale Market, to my part of the city in Toyosu. The Tsukiji market was an icon. It dated back nearly a century and its colorful early-morning tuna auctions drew tourists from all over the globe. The size of forty-three football fields, it employed 60,000 people, most of whom reported for work between 3 and 11 a.m. every day to prepare and sell fish, some local, others caught in global waters, and, like the highly prized bluefin tuna, sometimes worth hundreds of thousands of dollars apiece, flown in from distant airports. "Tsukiji," said one effusive devotee, "is the Vatican of all things piscatorial, the mecca of all who make a living off the global seafood trade."

But the market was aging and overcrowded, and the city fathers decided it needed to be replaced. So the decision was made to move everything to Toyosu. The new and larger Toyosu Fish Market would accommodate hundreds of licensed fish wholesalers who would process and auction off freshly caught fish, as well as a variety of restaurants, many of them to be set in a recreated Edo-period compound with green roofs and all powered by solar panels.

Toyosu had been chosen as the new location for the market by Governor Ishihara's administration, but the specific relocation area, a huge tract of industrial land that was the former site of a mammoth gas plant owned by the Tokyo Gas Company, was highly controversial due to toxic contamination in the soil, residue of the former operations of the plant. A condition of the land's purchase was that the company would remove the remaining toxins and the move would take place in late 2016.

But then in August 2016 newly elected Tokyo governor Yuriko Koike, the first female governor, postponed the move, informing her constituents that recent testing by the city had revealed substantial quantities of benzene (at a hundred times the safe limit), arsenic, and other toxins in the water in underground chambers—this despite repeated assurances from previous Tokyo governments that the contaminated soil had been removed and replaced and that everything was perfectly safe. There was also mercury in the air in chambers that were supposed to have been filled in with fresh soil and layered over in concrete. This knowledge did not enhance the pleasure of our morning walks.

Koike, a cosmopolitan lady with an international background that included a degree from the University of Cairo and fluency in English and Arabic, launched an investigation into the famously anti-foreign former governor Ishihara's role in the matter, which

Toyosu Fish Market. 2018.

required him—and others in his administration—to appear before the Tokyo Metropolitan Assembly to answer questions. Some observers saw it as an attempt at revenge, given that during the preceding election campaign the outgoing Ishihara had made disparaging remarks about Koike, saying, among other things, that the job of running Tokyo should not be left to "an old hag who wears too much makeup." However, Ishihara testified that he had delegated everything to his underlings and didn't know anything—and what he might have known he no longer remembered. After all he was eighty-four years old. In the final analysis no one was held to account, although the media got a lot of mileage out of the proceedings.

On March 20, 2017, a panel of experts declared the Toyosu site safe, despite the lingering toxins below ground, arguing that fresh layers of concrete would now protect everything above. Upon completion of all tests, Koike was compelled to drop her opposition and decree that the move go forward. In late 2018 the new Toyosu Fish Market opened for business, with a small portion of the Tsukiji market remaining in operation to keep the "Tsukiji brand" alive. Real estate prices in the old, vacated Tsukiji area immediately began to rise. My friend Hiroki Allen, speaking from his position as a financial analyst, viewed the entire exercise with suspicion. "They spent five-and-a-half billion dollars total on the move when that money could just as well have been spent on modernizing the old place. But this way, certain interested parties are going to make a fortune on the sale of the vacant Tsukiji land. And then there is the money Tokyo Gas made selling the toxic land in Toyosu in the first place. The Japanese have a saying, 'putting a lid on smelly things,' 臭いものには蓋をする. In this case, it really applies."

2020 Games: A "Mild and Sunny" Summer

In preparation for 2020, the LDP-controlled government of Shinzo Abe, on his way to become the longest-serving prime minister in the history of Japan, wrapped its new pro-tourism policy into the Tokyo Olympic Games program—the go-to catchphrase being *"omotenashi"* (hospitality), with the nation's major corporations allowed to attach the name "Tokyo 2020" to their advertising in exchange for extravagant donations to the cause. At the same time, the Abe government pushed an unabashedly pro-nationalist agenda, one that involved new antiterrorism laws limiting public protests, the muting of criticism of Japan's wartime excesses, and a sustained effort to revise Japan's constitution, which bans the maintenance of a standing army (Japan's Self-Defense Forces are already the eighth-largest military in the world).

Seldom mentioned by Abe supporters was the notorious wartime record of Abe's grandfather, Nobusuke Kishi—the slave labor, the opium trade, the forced prostitution—or his brutal use of yakuza to subdue protestors during the 1960 Security Treaty demonstrations. Nor did they seem particularly bothered by the fact that a Finance Ministry official under Abe had committed suicide after being ordered to falsify documents related to a real estate scandal involving the prime minister's wife or that the late official's widow had filed a lawsuit against the LDP as a result—the basis of the suit a suicide note the husband had left in which he recorded instructions from above. Thanks to his loyal supporters, the shrewd, ambitious Abe was able to weather the negative news coverage that followed, as was his long-serving finance minister Taro Aso, himself a former prime minister and whose father had forced Allied prisoners of war to work in his mining company during World War 2. Aso, known for his bizarre love of manga, was famous for his bigoted views, praising Japan for having only "one ethnic group" and criticizing women who do not give birth. Yet not once during his eight years at the helm of the ministry was his job ever in danger, not even during the height of the aforementioned forged document/suicide scandal.

However, with the approach of the Games, as with the run-up to the 1964 Tokyo Olympics, certain other problems emerged that could not so readily be brushed aside. Right from the start preparations were plagued by embarrassing cost overruns, ineffective leadership, finger-pointing at all levels, and widespread doubts that a seemingly inept Japanese government would have everything ready in time. I outlined these difficulties in a five-part series for the *Japan Times* in 2014 and again in a collaboration with the former US Embassy advisor and physicist David Roberts as a feature article in *Foreign Policy*, with a translated version run as a cover story in the Japanese edition of *Newsweek*. Government representatives accused us of undermining the Games.

The biggest headache was the overly expensive centerpiece, a billion-dollar-plus National Stadium seating 80,000. The original stadium design by renowned architect Zaha Hadid was so large—a hollowed-out twenty-story building with a roof three times the size of the Tokyo Dome—that it threatened to dwarf the quiet forested surroundings of Meiji Jingu, a sacred shrine of great importance to the Japanese.

Moreover, its shape, likened variously to a toilet seat, UFO, vacuum-cleaning robot, bicycle helmet, and more, became the butt of jokes. But it was the price tag that caused the loudest public outcry—understandable in a country whose national debt exceeded $11 trillion, approximately 245 percent of GDP and more than twice the percentage of US GDP. The stadium's snowballing expense had morphed from the original estimate of $1.3 billion to $2.1 billion.

I went to a panel discussion at the Foreign Correspondents Club of Japan featuring some of Japan's top architects and heard them conclude that Hadid's national stadium was technically not feasible, as well as ugly and overpriced. I was not surprised when the project was subsequently canceled in July 2015.

The Hadid design disaster pointed out an uncomfortable truth about Japan's preparations for the Games: No one seemed to be in charge. There were enough entities in the mix—the Japan Sports Agency, the Japanese Olympic Committee (JOC), the Tokyo Organising Committee of the Olympic and Paralympic Games (TOCOPG), the Ministry of Education, Culture, Sports, Science, and Technology (MEXT), the Foreign Ministry, the Prime Minister's Office, and the Tokyo Governor's Office—the cost overruns and other problems always seemed to be somebody else's responsibility. When PM Abe announced his decision to seek a new stadium design, former Prime Minister Yoshiro Mori, head of the organizing committee for the Games, held a press conference and hastened to point out that, as a mere user of whatever facility the government would put up, his organization had no hand in choosing the design, but he personally had been opposed to the unsightly thing in the first place.

In December, Tokyo selected a scaled-down, more conservative, and less expensive stadium design—one with a wooden exterior inspired by the 1,300-year-old Gojunoto pagoda at Horyu-ji temple in Nara, the world's oldest timber structure—by charismatic architect Kengo Kuma, who told reporters that seeing Kenzo Tange's "heroic" National Stadium as a boy had prompted him to go into his chosen profession. However, at $1.6 billion it would still be one of the world's most expensive ever, three times the cost of London's Olympic Stadium (and that was on top of the bill for the Hadid disaster). Many worried that even though most of the Olympic budget was earmarked for updating aging infrastructure, costs for the Games would spiral out of control.

They had good grounds for concern. By the end of 2019 the estimated real budget for the Games had ballooned from $6 billion to $28 billion, making it the second-most expensive Olympics in history, after the 2014 Sochi Winter Games, which cost an astonishing $51 billion. It was money, Olympic critics argued, that would have been better spent on the Fukushima survivors.

There were additional embarrassments as the Games grew closer. The head of the JOC had been forced to resign amidst a vote-buying bribery scandal. The choice of the official Tokyo Olympic logo became a national ignominy when it came under allegations of plagiarism and another design competition had to be held. It was also discovered that the replacement design for the new National Stadium did not have an Olympic cauldron. What's more, it was discovered that the water in the Tokyo Bay venues for various water sports contained dangerous levels of bacteria and smelled badly.

Perhaps the biggest problem, however, was the decision to schedule the games in late July and early August, when temperatures can soar into the high 90s, with humidity above 80 percent. The brutal summer weather in the capital was the reason why the JOC had moved the 1964 Olympic start date to October 10 and prompted Mexico City to follow suit in 1968. Playing competitive sports at those temperatures is extremely risky for athletes, especially marathoners. Moreover, thanks to the addition of countless glass, steel, and concrete buildings since then, creating "heat

Prime Minister Abe, in keeping with a long family tradition. 2018.

islands," the temperature in Tokyo has risen by 3 degrees Fahrenheit on average. On July 23, 2018, Tokyo recorded its highest temperature *ever* at 106 degrees Fahrenheit. A year later, during the week of August 6–13, amidst a brutal heat wave, 1,857 people were hospitalized in Tokyo with heatstroke and 162 died nationwide. Of course, in fairness to Tokyo officials, they had had to bow to the demands of global TV. The rights to televise the Games fell to NBC, which did not want to compete with telecasts of the Major League Baseball playoffs and the National Football League season—both of which are in full swing in October. But one had to ask, was it really necessary for the JOC bid document submitted in 2013 by then Tokyo Governor Naoki Inose to maintain, disingenuously, that midsummer weather in Tokyo is "mild and sunny" and "an ideal climate for athletes to perform at their best"? Fortunately for the athletes involved, sanity prevailed and, in the fall of 2019, over the protests of Tokyo Governor Koike, the IOC ordered the marathon and racewalking venues moved to the cooler climes of Sapporo. However, why the IOC did not choose the Mt. Fuji marathon course as a venue, with its invigorating temperatures and closer proximity to the Kanto Plain where Tokyo is located, remains a mystery.

The 2020 Tokyo Games certainly had its opponents. A 2014 *Japan Times* editorial complained that despite the city glitz showcased in *You Only Live Twice*, the Olympic reconstruction done during the postwar era had, in fact, also left large swaths of the capital outside the fashionable city center "awash in ugly buildings, bland public areas and [with] few cityscapes that any tourist or resident would care to look at." Moreover, an economic downturn that happened in the wake of the 1964 Games led to the issuance of J-government bonds, which some critics contended put Japan on the path to perpetual red ink. Some have argued that the 1964 Olympics was the root cause of much of what is wrong with the fiscal situation of the Japanese government to this day, although it should be pointed out that the years following 1964 ushered in an economic boom that lasted fifteen years, at the time the longest in Japan's history.

Partners in Crime

Twenty-first century Tokyo, to return to the subject at hand, had indeed fallen behind other major capitals in some respects, starting with a severe labor shortage. The government was struggling to cope with a severely declining birth rate, attributed to cramped housing, long commutes, lack of nearby family support, and an aging population. Thanks in part to a superior, if increasingly costly, national health care system, life expectancy was now eighty-seven, among the highest in the world. In Tokyo, the decrease in the number of young people had resulted in twice as many job vacancies as applicants. To deal with this problem, the government brought in 40,000 Southeast Asians to work at 7-Eleven, Lawson, and other convenience stores and also loosened requirements for those foreigners with needed professional skills. As a result, by the end of 2019 the foreign population of Japan had reached 2.93 million, with 567,000 in Tokyo, both all-time highs. In fact, 1 out of 8 eight residents in Shinjuku was a foreign national. Mass emigration from rising economic superpower China had served to triple the number of foreigners in the city. As of January 1, 2020, 367,000 Chinese immigrants were living in Tokyo, doubling the combined total of South and North Koreans, who had previously been the largest minority. The percentage of Americans in the foreign population living in Tokyo had consequently halved since 1985.

A dramatic rise in tourism simultaneously accompanied the new influx of foreign residents. In response to a government program to attract visitors from overseas, the number of foreign tourists rose from twenty million in 2012 to thirty million in 2016, with the stated goal of reaching forty million by the start of the Olympics. Well over a third of these sightseers came from mainland China.

There was a good side to this. Twenty-first-century Japanese were certainly more receptive to foreigners in their midst then the previous generation had been. In 1988, the government-run Japan National Character Institute began asking the question in its periodic surveys: "Suppose your child said: 'I want to marry a foreigner.' Would you approve or disapprove?" In that initial survey, only 29 percent said "approve." By the 2013 survey, 56 percent said they would approve of such a union.

However most Japanese resisted the idea of mass immigration, pointing inevitably to the inability of the *gaijin* to adjust to Japanese ways, starting with the fine art of garbage collection and other important social etiquette and ending with the unfortunate fact that the more foreigners the country admits, the more narcotics use increases. China and Mexico had come to rival North Korea as prime suppliers of crystal methamphetamine and fentanyl, and by the dawn of the third decade of the 21st century, according to police, there was more cocaine in Tokyo than ever before. In November 2019 police discovered an astonishing 400 kilograms of cocaine in a ship container in Kobe, at the time an all-time record for Japan. It was said to be worth over $75 million on the street. In February 2020, to cite one of a number of such high-profile cases, a Canadian citizen was arrested on suspicion of smuggling 240 kilograms of illegal stimulant drugs, hidden in boxes of frozen shrimp aboard a ship from Vancouver that had docked in Tokyo's Odaiba waterfront area. It had a street value of $140 million. Two months later, customs authorities in Yokohama seized a mind-blowing 700 kilograms of cocaine with a street value of about $130 million. The cocaine was hidden in a shipping container on a vessel docked in the harbor, nestled amidst boxes of bananas and other items. A Finance Ministry official declared that Japan had now become "a major market" in the world of illegal drugs, noting that street prices for stimulants were higher than those overseas. Police in Roppongi adopted a policy of stop-and-frisk for narcotics. A lawyer friend of mine, a man from Vancouver, stopped to watch one such early-morning frisking by a group of four policeman and was himself searched because the lead cop thought he was "acting suspiciously."

Yakuza gangs eagerly participated in the illicit international drug trade—one gangland shooting in 2019 was carried out with an M16, the US military's standard service rifle, indicating cooperation between Americans stationed in Japan and Japanese in the underground arms business. Moreover, despite new anti-organized-crime laws restricting underworld access to bank accounts, office space, and respectable business channels, which served to deplete the formal ranks of the yakuza from a 1963 high of 180,000 (an outgrowth of the postwar black markets) to less than 30,000 in 2020, financial fraud cases and money-laundering crimes involving underworld figures had spiked. It went without saying that the traditional underworld sources of income, gambling and prostitution, did not suffer declines either.

It was not, one might argue, the environment Olympic organizers might have hoped for in which to stage their huge international event.

As Tokyo geared up for the Games, observers noted still other areas in which the capital remained behind the curve, including the availability of international ATMs and public Wi-Fi. The country that invented the Walkman was losing the battle on communication tools and apps. Japan still had its inventors, but except for game programmers, manga and anime producers, and robotic engineers, they were not going out into the world as Honda and Morita had once done to earn global recognition.

All these worries were disrupted by the sudden appearance of a killer virus that swept the world. It caused the Olympics to be postponed and quarantines to be imposed on travel in and out of Japan, adding an entirely new dimension to the discussion about globalization and the loosening of national borders.

The Rojin

Tokyo and the Coronavirus

COVID-19, the novel coronavirus that originated in China, did not impact Japan in the same way it did other harder-hit countries, including Italy, Spain, the UK, and the United States. While Japan mishandled a huge influx of tourists from Mainland China during the Chinese New Year, allowing them in the country with no checks, and did a poor job of containing the virus on the *Diamond Princess*, a cruise ship docked and quarantined in Yokohama, the nation, nonetheless, ranked far down the list in terms of cases of infection and deaths. In Tokyo observers had expected the total to be much worse given the densely packed conditions in the city, the crowded commuter trains that workers endure twice a day, and the fact that a quarter of Japan's population was over the age of sixty-five, but the country's habit of wearing facemasks to prevent the spread of colds and influenza (the typical Japanese goes through forty-three masks a year) as well as the custom of bowing instead of shaking hands, kissing, or hugging, not wearing shoes in the house, and using special slippers in the toilet, appeared to have made a difference, as did the practice at restaurants of providing hand wipes, usually in the form of wet towels.

The general cleanliness of Japanese society, which included spotless subways and armies of old people cleaning public bathrooms, was a decided plus, as was, some speculated, the country's BCG vaccination policy.

As an added precaution Prime Minister Abe closed the nation's schools at the beginning of March and limited traffic in and out of the country. Preseason professional baseball, sumo, and other large sporting events closed their arenas to spectators.

A spike in Tokyo cases occurred after students on spring break abroad returned home ahead of an announced quarantine. This was accompanied by a report in late March that a nightclub hostess had infected three players from the Hanshin Tigers, which was then followed by the death of beloved comedian Ken Shimura from the virus a few days later. Tokyo Governor Koike went on TV to urge Tokyoites to stay out of the city's restaurants, bars, nightclubs, and any institutions of ill-repute, and work from their cramped houses and apartments as much as possible. On April 7, Prime Minister Abe declared a state of emergency for Tokyo and six other highly populated prefectures, instructing that all nonessential institutions and businesses close down and that people self-isolate for a full month, later extended to two.

Interestingly the office of Japan's prime minister did not have the power to order all this to take place, a state of affairs arising from the country's postwar constitution, which was written to prevent the kinds of abuses of power that led to the rise of Japanese militarism and the Pacific War. That would have required a parliamentary resolution. However, Tokyo's citizenry, much to their credit, complied. Seemingly overnight, supermarket shelves were picked clean of all meat, most dairy and eggs, bread, and instant ramen, giving you an indication of the dietary habits of modern-day Japanese. The city's entertainment areas transformed into ghost towns. The government pledged donations of money to those in need, including bar girls and other employees in Tokyo's red-light districts, then later announced a sweeping ¥100,000 handout to all residents. On April 17, Abe extended the state of emergency to the entire nation. Travel during the Golden Week holiday, one of the busiest times of the year, fell by 78.9 percent in Tokyo, according to cellphone data collected by government officials. Major festivals, concerts, and sporting events, including the start of the official pro-baseball season, the summer sumo tournament, and the all-important National High School Baseball Championship at Koshien Stadium in August, were all canceled, along with the shelving of the 2020 Olympics. Estimates put the cost of the Olympics postponement at as much as $6 billion, with most of the cost borne by Japan, requiring budget cuts. (Professional baseball and sumo eventually resumed but to limited fan attendance, with the festivities periodically interrupted by COVID-19 outbreaks. The Japan Series wasn't played until the last week of November.)

The shutdown offered underworld scam artists new ways of bilking people out of their money. Online fraudsters pretending to be city officials offered nonexistent masks and other protective equipment at bargain basement prices, enticing people to surrender details about their bank accounts and My Number ID cards. Predictably, *pachinko* shops owned by those with underworld and North Korean connections refused to abide by the government directive to close down, hindering control of the spread of the virus.

The virus scare also exposed weaknesses in Japanese technological readiness. Whereas the country had once led the world in technological advancement, it was not well prepared to deal with certain aspects of the shutdown. Only 5 percent of Tokyo students, for example, had the equipment necessary for home schooling. It took the government months to issue emergency-aid payments of ¥100,000 to its citizens because of the hard-copy paperwork required. This stood in contrast to the US, where payments of $1,200 to each citizen were made by the federal government in a matter of weeks, mostly through digital direct deposit to individual bank accounts. Poster boy for the out-of-touch LDP was

Tokyo Governor Yuriko Koike urges Tokyoites to stay home as much as possible, eschew crowds, and avoid close contact with others. April 7, 2020.

Yoshitaka Sakurada, the sixty-eight-year-old former deputy chief of the government's cybersecurity strategy office and minister in charge of the Olympic and Paralympic Games; he had provoked astonishment in a 2018 parliamentary hearing when he confessed he had never used a computer in his professional life and did not know what a USB drive was. (On the other hand, Japanese scientists did manage to send a space probe, Hayabusa 2, on a successful six-year, five-billion-mile journey to a remote asteroid to collect earth samples, returning home in 2020, so there is also that.)

Overall, however, when the national emergency rules were finally lifted at the end of May 2020, the fatality rate from COVID-19 in Tokyo was far lower per capita than in Manhattan, Madrid, Rome, Berlin, or London. And despite the enormous financial loss, the shutdown of businesses had a positive side. For the first time I could remember, on my morning walks I saw normally workaholic fathers out playing with their children in public parks. It was revolutionary—as were the newly instituted social distancing measures, which eased congestion in the city, if temporarily. As for me, the lockdown provided my wife and me with an opportunity to

During the coronavirus shutdown, traffic on Tokyo streets, like this Shibuya main drag, had dropped by as much as 90 percent.

catch up on the latest series on Amazon and Netflix as well as to mine the considerable Amazon Japan library for classic Toei yakuza movies starring Ken Takakura. My wife thought they were great. When all was said and done, the seasonal flu rate had declined by more than 60 percent over the previous year, an obvious tribute to the exceptional hygienic practices of the people, which went into hypermode during the coronavirus crisis.

However, a second wave hit in late July, three weeks of nonstop rainfall adding to the misery, with infections rising to as many as 467 in one day in Tokyo. A third wave arrived in November, with numbers hitting an alarming peak of 2,477 in January 2021, thanks to an extremely ill-advised government-sponsored travel and eat out campaign. It caused the city's hospital alert system to be raised to its highest level ever and the government to order another state of emergency. Bankruptcy and suicide rates surged. By March, a vaccine was finally in the works, but would take long months to deliver. Yet, given the low overall death rate (about one thirty-fifth of New York City's), the Tokyo Governor's Office could still cite with some justification a survey by Global Finance published in late November 2020 that had ranked Tokyo as the best city in the world to live in based on metrics including economic strength, accessibility, and Covid-19 health conditions.

A feature of pandemic life in Japan was the willingness of the populace to conform, unlike in the United States, which put a premium on "individual liberty" and led the world in COVID-19 fatalities. Widely reported in the Japanese media was an August 2020 survey by a team of psychologists at Doshisha University that found that the top reason people wore masks during COVID-19 was that everyone else was doing so. Relieving anxiety and preventing infection were far, far behind,

Japan's underlying allergy to foreigners also revealed itself during this period, as the government banned re-entry to foreigners who were permanent residents of Japan and happened to be caught abroad—including many taxpaying homeowners—while admitting Japanese nationals from overseas. It was not until late summer that residential status holders were allowed back into the country.

No one knows exactly why Japan did not record the disastrous levels of infection and death seen in Western countries. Some Japanese scientists have suggested there may be a genetic "factor x" that inhibited the disease, or perhaps some kind of historical immunity that developed over time. The aforementioned cabinet minister Taro Aso, in one of his more memorable foot-in-mouth remarks, attributed the low COVID-19 rates to the "superior quality" of Japanese people. It would be hard, however, to credit the curious responses of the government, which was fixated on "economics" and holding the Olympics instead of using the empty Olympic Village, for example, as a quarantine facility to house the 10,000 Covid patients now waiting to get into hospitals.

Prime Minister Abe had resigned in late August, citing ill health. He was sixty-five years old and had served nearly eight consecutive years. His approval rating stood at 34 percent; the accumulation of scandals involving his administration, his critics said, had proven too much for even him, the latest a vote-buying scheme that led to the arrest and indictment of Abe's former justice minister and his wife, a member of the House of Councilors. It was in keeping with the long family tradition. Moreover, his government's measures to deal with the pandemic faced criticism, such as over the distribution of washable cloth facemasks, which arrived too late and turned out to be too small.

However, as the noted Japan legal expert Lawrence Repeta put it, the Abe administration did achieve success in expanding police power, passing legislation LDP leaders had sought for decades: expanded wiretapping authority, formally recognized plea bargaining, expanded state secrecy powers, and legislation creating the crime of "conspiracy."

"The Abe team managed to achieve all this," Repeta said, "despite opposition from the bar associations, much of the news media and public intelligentsia, and tens of thousands of protesters that repeatedly gathered before the Diet. This is a tremendous record of achievement."

TOCOPG chief Mori resigned when his observation that female Olympic board members talked too much caused an international uproar. He was replaced by a woman, a former Olympian.

The Most Organized City in the World

I've lived in major global cities—New York and Paris, among them—and I have come to the conclusion that Tokyo ranks at the very top. I sometimes like to stand in Marunouchi where the new Foreign Correspondents Club is located and just watch the people go by on their way to and from the train and subway stations. I'm invariably impressed by how content Tokyoites appear to be. You see a lot of smiling faces, in contrast to midtown Manhattan where pedestrians, whenever I am there, always look angry to me. There is a joke people tell about asking directions from passersby on New York sidewalks: "Excuse me, can you tell me the way to Times Square, or should I just go fuck myself?" In Tokyo, the passersby might well drop everything to take you to your destination. There is something else. While NYC is not as dangerous as it used to be, it is also not as livable as it used to be, if that makes any sense. It has lost that neighborhood, working-class feel in the process of becoming, as one journalist in 2019 described it, "the largest gated community in the world with a few cupcake shops here and there . . . no longer a significant cultural entity." On every other block in Manhattan it seems there is a Duane Reade or a Starbucks, but neighborhood bars where you can pop in and have a drink are decreasing in number. This decrease was, of course, exacerbated by the events of 2020, which bankrupted many food- and drink-based establishments and negatively impacted the quality of life in the city. And it is a huge contrast to Tokyo, where every station hub in the city has its warren of pubs and cafes, all identified by warm and inviting neon signs in *kanji* sticking out into the street as if to grab you and pull you in—the negative effects of the Coronavirus notwithstanding.

Paris is a beautiful, historic city, oozing architectural class, and it is a repository of great art, but it is also very dirty; trash is everywhere and the Metros reek of urine. San Francisco, where I often visit from my home on the central coast of California, three hours away via highway 101, in dense traffic, is even worse. One of the wealthiest metropolises in the world, it is the product of a failed civic system. Aggressive beggars in the streets, the smell of urine in the air, people openly defecating in spots, shooting up opioids. Tokyo, by contrast, is a city that works. Its streets are clean and virtually crime free. (Metropolitan police in the aggregate fire an average of four or five bullets a year.) Even in the midst of economic downturns in Tokyo, you had to look hard to see the effects on the city's streets.

I like Los Angeles. My wife and I frequently fly in there from Tokyo to visit with Derek Shearer and his wife Sue Toigo, who live in Santa Monica. Derek, who worked on all three

Clinton campaigns, teaches at Occidental College and invites me to guest-lecture there from time to time. But the traffic in LA can drive you nuts. In Tokyo, there are trains and subways everywhere. No one needs a car.

I also like Stockholm, which rivals Tokyo in many ways. But unless you prefer long, dark winters, it is not a place to live year-round. Tokyo, as Japanese love to remind you, has four distinct seasons, with only the "mild and sunny" summer months being hard to take.

Most important, perhaps, is the honesty of the average Tokyo-ite—in stark contrast to the country's politicians. Once I left my wallet on the densely packed Yokosuka Line with the equivalent of a thousand dollars in cash in it. A few days later it was returned to me in the mail with a note from the person who had found it, saying, "Dear Whiting-san, Please be careful of your wallet."

There are countless stories like that. According to the Tokyo Metropolitan Police, the citizens of Tokyo annually turn in millions of dollars found on the street or on subway seats to the Lost and Found Center or the local *koban*, as the neighborhood police box is called. According to a TMPD report in 2018, to cite one example, $32 million in cash was reported lost the previous year, three-quarters of which was returned to the owner. That's in addition to the multitude of lost gloves, scarves, umbrellas, keys, and eyeglasses also turned in. Japanese are taught from an early age to "think of the trouble the person who lost the item must be in." Unlike in just about every other major capital of the world, you can leave your laptop computer on your table when you visit the restroom at any Tokyo Starbucks—the franchise that began invading the city in the 1990s—with 100 percent assurance it will still be there when you get back.

The conundrum of a culture that features ordinary citizens noted for their honesty and crooked politicians is often remarked upon and usually explained by references to the country's long feudal past, where behavior was strictly controlled from above, as well as allusions to the influence of the imperial system as a symbol of absolute and blind obedience to authority. Whatever the reason, the integrity of the average Tokyoite is a major attraction of the city.

Another great thing about the Tokyo of today is how well organized it is despite being the most crowded city in the world, with 35,000 people per square mile. It has the most extensive train and subway system in the world, as well as the cleanest, used by forty million people a day in Greater Tokyo. It is impossible to get lost in it. Signs, instructions, and maps posted to guide even a neophyte commuter are ubiquitous. A melody is played inside each car to notify riders before each stop and trains are invariably on time, to the second.

Pedestrians on Tokyo's streets walk in an orderly fashion, following arrows that guide them up and down stairs and along sidewalks. The Scramble Crossing at Shibuya is perhaps the busiest intersection in the world with its convergence of ten car lanes and five crosswalks, yet over 2,000 people somehow weave effortlessly across the diagonal at every stoplight change without even looking up from their smartphones. It has become a tourist attraction in its own right.

People on escalators invariably stand stationary on the left side. It is a courteous gesture that leaves the right side open for people who may be in a hurry to go up or down. Old Edo had a lot of samurai with swords, worn on the left, the explanation goes, so people learned to walk on the left to avoid bumping swords. (This is also said to be behind Japan's choice to adopt right-hand-drive cars despite the country's first cars being imported from the USA, not Britain.)

Tokyoites seldom cross against a red light even when the street is deserted; they never jump queues and will wait in line for long periods of time. Taxi doors are opened and closed by the driver, not by the passengers. People exiting elevators often push the close button to shorten the wait for other passengers. Women do not wear heavy perfume in public, especially in confined areas, as

Shibuya Scramble Crossing: the busiest intersection in the most organized city in the world.

it is regarded as an imposition on other people's olfactory organs. Such niceties make one of the world's most crowded cities a pleasant place to be.

People sweep the streets in front of their homes or shops, usually daily, and often wash away dust and dirt with water to maintain cleanliness. Alcohol hand-sanitation stations can be found all over the city, in shops, train stations, and offices (this was so even before COVID-19). On daytime excursions Tokyoites take their trash home if there are no usable trash bins available, instead of dumping it on the street as is the practice in some other capitals. Garbage collection is divided into eight categories—raw garbage, glass bottles, steel or tin cans, aluminum cans, plastic containers, burnable paper, and other non-burnable items. There are different days designated for the different categories. If you put a certain type of garbage out on the wrong day, the designated neighborhood watchperson will likely bring it back and deposit it at your front door—usually with a note attached, bearing instructions as

to when the designated item is to be set out. That has happened
to me more than once. Neighborhood rules have also changed
over the years to prohibit the use of black trash bags and require
transparent ones so that the contents can be identified and traced
back to the owner. In some neighborhoods, residents are required
to put their phone number and address on their trash bags. The
neighborhood watchperson will make sure that everything is in
order.

The organizational gene in the Japanese DNA is evident everywhere. In schools, classes are regarded as platoons and every class
is broken down into 班, or "han," which are squad equivalents.
Students clean the schools instead of janitors, a way of teaching
them to be more responsible members of society. School sports
clubs like baseball and volleyball, where practice is required year-
round, every single day, for several hours each day, are organized
in strict age-based hierarchies, where underclassmen are obliged
to show respect for upperclassmen by serving meals, doing their
laundry, scrubbing toilets, keeping the field spotless, and using
honorific language. There is a famous and revealing story about
the time when former Seibu Lions and Yomiuri Giants star
Kazuhiro Kiyohara was a sophomore in high school in 1980. He
cracked the starting lineup and hit a home run in his first at bat.
Instead of being mobbed by teammates when he returned to the
dugout after rounding the bases, he was slapped in the face by
the team captain, a senior, who barked, "Don't think you're special just because you hit a home run. You're still only a first-year
player."

In most companies there is also a strict hierarchy, a pecking
order for serving tea, for boarding elevators, for speaking up in
meetings. The higher one's rank, the deeper the bow that has to
be accorded you. Being on time means arriving ten minutes early.
Company trips might be planned with schedules in fifteen-minute
increments, freeing the participants from the burden of having to
decide for themselves what to do with their time.

Even the fans at baseball games are organized. Those who want to watch in silence sit in the infield seats. Those who want to cheer sit in the outfield stands in organized cheering groups led by volunteer cheerleaders who follow highly scripted chants and routines for each player. Applicants take screaming tests and are assigned seats on the basis of their vocal abilities.

* * *

Then there is the construction industry that operates unceasingly throughout the densely crowded city. Among the more remarkable structures are the fifty-four-story Midtown Tower and thirty-eight-floor Shin Marunouchi, which opened in 2007; the Mode Gakuen Cocoon Tower at fifty floors, which opened in 2008; the fifty-three-floor Kachidoki View Tower in 2011; the new Tokyo Station, completed in 2012, its facade completely restored to its original 1914-opening state; and the fifty-two-story Toranomon Hills in 2014. It never stops. Forty-five new skyscrapers, mostly residential apartment buildings, went up in the four years preceding 2020, while entire train station complexes, like the major hub of Shibuya, were torn down and completely remade, the work often hidden behind huge canvas barriers, without ever disrupting the daily flow of traffic and commerce. In 2019 Mori Building Company, the developer behind Tokyo's landmark Roppongi Hills, unveiled plans for a new urban-redevelopment complex to open in 2023 that will feature Japan's tallest skyscraper at sixty-four floors, a raft of shops and residences, a luxury hotel, an international school, and 24,000 square meters of greenery. It is located in Azabu-dai, sandwiched in between Roppongi Hills and the Toranomon Hills. Plans are also afoot to tear down the unsightly expressway over the Nihonbashi bridge built for the 1964 Games and construct a new express route underground, with construction to follow the 2020 Olympics, restoring the original view and bringing the landmark bridge full circle. It is part of an overall renovation of the historic Nihonbashi area that also features the thirty-five-story Tokyo Nihonbashi Tower, the deluxe Mandarin Oriental Hotel atop the thirty-four-story Mitsui Tower, and the elegant, ambitious shopping complex known as the Coredo Muromachi, featuring traditional crafts and gourmet foods from all over Japan. More changes will certainly come.

The Summing Up

In October of 2019, to celebrate my seventy-seventh birthday, my wife, sister-in-law Yukie, and two nieces, Kyomi and Yuko, took me out to lunch at the posh Ventaglio, an Italian restaurant in the aforementioned Mandarin Oriental. I could not imagine what the bill was, but I assumed it was the rough equivalent of the monthly salary the girls received at their downtown Tokyo office jobs. We dined on prosciutto, sliced Parmesan, assorted pasta, meat, and fish dishes, prepared by a world-famous chef from Naples, polishing off several drafts of beer and glasses of wine in the process. My birthday present was a box of chocolate and a bottle of sake. Gazing out at the panoramic view of Nihonbashi that stretched below, so much had changed that I could not recognize anything I encountered a half-century earlier, save for the ugly expressway that passed over the famous bridge. It occurred to me over our gelato that there is very little left in Tokyo that is older than I am, given how this city keeps on renewing itself.

After my birthday celebration I had stopped off at the Foreign Correspondents Club, now in Marunouchi, to complete an errand. On my way there, for some reason, I took special note of the tiny *o-inari-san* shrine (the *inari* are fox deities believed to have protective powers, and their shrines and mini-shrines are found all over the country) that stands near the entrance to Yurakucho train station, just to the side of the entrance to the Yurakucho

Denki Building and a few steps from the Rose and Crown British Victorian pub, which blares Beatles music all day. Such shrines, dating back centuries in some cases, have been miniaturized and marginalized in the rash of new skyscraper construction. Not a few shrines that once occupied the ground before these edifices went up were scaled down and relocated on building rooftops. The gods have been downsized, but at least they're still around, which is important since people in Japan see the involvement of the gods in everything and will often visit the shrines to consult with them on matters great and small.

It made me think again of all the other things that have changed and of those that haven't. When I first got here in 1962, attempting to make an international phone call was a trying experience. You had to make a reservation at a special phone through an international operator at the one company that held the monopoly in order to make an exorbitantly expensive call, and when you finally got the connection you could barely hear the other party through the background noise on the line. Now, of course, you pick up an iPhone and have instant audio-visual connection to anywhere in the world.

Another change is that the lifetime employment system has started to crumble. I think back to the unshakable dedication to their companies of the *salarymen* that I once tutored in English or got to know in other venues. It is now no longer rare to change companies, and performance has come to be valued almost as much as seniority. However, it is still very difficult to fire an employee under Japan's protective labor laws. And despite the current debate on revising labor law, there have been a number of *karoshi* (death from overwork) lawsuits in recent years, prompting Japan's corporations to tone down their demands on their employees, at least publicly. After a young female employee of the Dentsu Advertising Corporation, unable to handle a crippling schedule that forced her to log 130 hours of overtime per month, committed suicide in 2016, the advertising and promotional monolith was

The twin towers of the Tokyo Metropolitan Building, or "Tocho" as it is known, and other striking high-rises of Shinjuku face Mt. Fuji and pay their respects.

named "the most evil corporation in Japan" by a panel of journalists and labor rights activists.

The shift away from lifetime employment has also reached into the Imperial Household. Hirohito's son, Emperor Akihito, eighty-four, who reigned with the kind of self-assured, honest dignity that his father could never muster, became the first emperor since the Meiji Restoration of 1868 to be allowed to retire, paving the way for his son, Naruhito, to take over as emperor in April 2019.

Students don't look to study abroad the way they used to. The cachet of a graduate degree from a top US university is not what it once was. Perhaps it is the rising tuition fees or concern over the high crime rates in America reported in the news. Or bad experiences on the part of those who returned from overseas study only to be assigned demeaning work or shunted aside because they were "too different" from the rest. Others point to a general insularity among the young in contrast to the perpetual fascination with the world the postwar generation displayed. Still others point to a rising sophistication among the younger generation, an acknowledgment that in a city that has as much to offer as Tokyo, overseas travel is just not that important anymore.

Fewer people in today's Tokyo speak English well—this despite a billion-dollar English tutoring industry and continuing noise from the Education Ministry about revolutionizing the way the language is taught. College entrance exams still emphasize grammar and writing over communication skills, although that is what the ministry has been promising to change. With the advent of the 2020 Olympics, however, people once again began to brush up their language skills in preparation for volunteering as guides, as many did at the first Olympics more than half a century ago. Uniformed information attendants on stand-up two-wheeled electric scooters began patrolling the central areas of the city in teams, offering help to befuddled tourists in preparation for the great influx of visitors for the Games. "May I help you" once again became the most frequently heard expression on the city's streets. In addition, taxi drivers and train conductors began addressing foreign visitors in English.

It might be noted at the same time that on Coming of Age Day in 2019, the second Monday of the New Year, one in twenty of all new adults were foreign, and in Tokyo the figure was one in eight. In Shinjuku Ward it was nearly half. Nearly *all* of the employees in 7-Eleven, Lawson, and other *konbini* stores were from Southeast Asia. That is progress. But unlike New York City, which has certification tests in twelve different languages, all immigrants have to learn Japanese. Moreover, Japan continues to rank low on the list of countries by the number of refugees allowed to enter. It fully accepted only 27 refugees in 2016, out of a total of 10,901 applicants.

Finally, I would like to note the long, slow disappearance of smoking, one of the few vices I managed to renounce some years ago. Tokyo used to be enveloped in a cloud of cigarette smoke, trailing many other countries by years. You could light up in any restaurant or coffee shop and no one would complain, possibly because they couldn't even see you through the thick haze. The government had a monopoly on all tobacco sales in those days, so there was little incentive to ban public smoking. On the contrary, smoking was a patriotic duty that helped build the economy, even though, when mingled with the auto and factory pollution, it was not conducive to a healthy set of lungs. Today, public smoking is illegal in large swaths of the city, including all of Chiyoda-ku where Ginza, Shinbashi, and Yurakucho are located. There are uniformed anti-smoking patrols that move around the city and issue fines of ¥2,000 ($20), payable on the spot, to those found smoking on the street. The air, I might add, thanks to improved pollution controls, is cleaner than ever.

These days no one calls up to me from the street to come down and have a drink at 2 a.m. I can't say that I miss it, but I do look back with nostalgia at some of my old haunts that have since gone under. Life in the old neighborhoods, with its sense of familiarity and community, was a revelation—front doors were often left unlocked, and neighbors and deliverymen simply walked in, announcing themselves with *"gomen kudasai!"* I miss the fellowship, even if some of it centered on unsavory companions.

Many of the people who have populated these pages are also no longer around. My Encyclopedia Britannica and Time Life partner Dwight drank himself into oblivion and died of pancreatitis at the age of fifty-four. His wife Mary, who had divorced him and remarried, is a PhD in upstate New York. Dale and Mary Ann also divorced and went their separate ways, Dale to Ann Arbor and Mary Ann to Scarsdale where she became public schools librarian. I have lost touch with more than a few others as well. I never saw Jiro, my gangster friend in Higashi-Nakano, after I returned to Tokyo from New York. Given his profession and his volatile personality, I assume he did not enjoy longevity. Greg Davis, as mentioned, died in 2005 of liver cancer, and David Halberstam was

No lifetime employment. Emperor Akihito, a most decent man, opens parliament for the last time before he abdicates. 2019.

killed in an automobile accident in 2007. Six years later in 2013, my old *SI* editor Patricia Ryan, the one who helped kick-start my career as a writer, passed away in her home in the Berkshires.

My father died of heart trouble at the age of ninety-two in 2004. Not so long after, my mother failed a dementia test and went into a nursing home. Her ungrateful, doltish children, as she put it, the ones who had taken care of her, were not allowed in to see her at her specific request. She died in 2017 at the age of 104, still complaining about her lot in life and telling everyone, "I never wanted to come to California."

Shigeo Nagashima was still around and so was Sadaharu Oh. Nagashima survived a stroke at age sixty-eight in 2004 that had partially paralyzed his right side, left him without the use of his right arm, and seriously impaired his speech and ability to continue his various public appearances as "Mr. Giants." Oh survived a cancer operation in 2006 at age sixty-five in which his stomach was removed. Restricted to eating only tiny portions of certain foods, he still returned to manage the Softbank Fukuoka Hawks

Whiting-Kondo Family

1

2

3

4

5

6

7

8

1. Omiya family gathering. 1981.

2. With my father-in-law. He liked to quote Hegel in Taisho-period Japanese.

3. Machiko with my mother in Carmel-by-the-Sea, California. 1981.

4. My seventy-seventh birthday at the Mandarin Oriental Hotel. With Yukie, Yuko, Kyomi, Machiko, and me, Kono Watashi.

5. With Machiko. 2012.

6. Whiting family gathering in Salinas, California. 1996.

7. At Akasaka Festival. 1978.

8. With my sister Margo in Pacific Grove, California. 2019.

and later serve as team GM and president. I truly admired the *konjo* (guts) of both men.

Mr. Kusaka, my neighbor and guide during my Komagome days, was transferred to Osaka in the 1970s and I lost touch with him until a surprise email a few years ago, which led to a reunion at the FCCJ. He was in his mid-eighties, still in good health and cheerful as ever, although his wife had died years earlier.

One wintry night in 2015 I ran into Father Beaulieu from the Ochanomizu language school where I taught in the '60s. I had just exited a Hibiya Line subway car in Hiroo Station on my way to a year-end party and was walking down the platform toward the gate when I heard a voice calling me from behind.

"Monsieur Whiting! Monsieur Whiting!" He stood there in his shabby coat, smiling and waving vigorously.

"I have read all your books. They are delightful. I have enjoyed them all tremendously," were the first words out of his mouth. I had not seen him for nearly half a century. But he looked healthy, aside from a slight redness in the nose and cheeks, which I took to be the residue of holiday cheer. He was living at the Dominican headquarters outside Shibuya, he told me. A few days later, he invited my wife and me to dinner at a restaurant in the Shinjuku Odakyu Department Store. It was good to catch up with him after fifty years. He also said he had changed his mind about Tokyo being no place for a young man to live and marry and settle down.

"It's not like that anymore," he said. "Tokyo has become very sophisticated."

It occurs to me that that sophistication, the product of the city's continuing renewals and rebirths, has redefined what it means to be Japanese. Along the way it redefined me as well.

I arrived here all those years ago in the full flush of American cockiness, a sense of superiority and entitlement that was unaffected by my total ignorance of any and all matters—cultural, historical, or practical—that might weigh in the discussion. After all, America had won the war, led in every field of economic endeavor,

View of Tokyo from Tokyo Skytree.

and boasted GNP that towered above the rest of the world, which flocked to see American movies and listen to Rock 'n' Roll. US Major League baseball, football, and basketball set the pace in sports. I thought it was terribly nice of my colleagues and me to be in Japan and share some of our largesse. I have had occasion since to revise that estimation.

I have learned a lot from living in Tokyo, much of it through osmosis. In the beginning I had no knowledge of and little interest in the Japanese arts. Kabuki put me to sleep within an hour. I was not enthralled by the tea ceremony—hard on the knees, and I found the tea itself bitter tasting. But then there were the beautiful prints by Hiroshige, Hokusai, and others, the gardens, the elegant temple architecture. And when I started to read, I encountered traditional writers such as Kawabata and Osaragi—all of which began to change my perspective.

Above all, it was baseball that gave me the window I needed into the workings of the culture. Researching and writing *The Chrysanthemum and the Bat* and *You Gotta Have Wa* helped me organize my thinking about my adoptive home and crystalize my understanding of the cultural differences between Japan and America.

That experience, which helped open my mind and expand my horizons in ways I never could have imagined, also made it possible for me to tackle a project like *Tokyo Underworld*. As seen, the book produced not a little controversy and a few scary moments, but one comment in particular validated the whole process. The president of the Yokohama wing of the Inagawa-kai hailed the accuracy of *Tokyo Underworld* and the research behind it. It was one of the best compliments I have ever had, right up there with my US presidential endorsements.

I was once asked by the aforementioned David Roberts, a Cornell and Oxford grad who had spent most of his adult life as an expat in Europe, Asia, and Africa, and who has now settled in New York, if I actually felt that I had assimilated in Japan. After more than half a century living here in Tokyo, I'm not even sure I know what that means. At different stages of my life I have been called a "Jap Lover," a "Japan Basher," and an "Anti-American." I suppose that signals a certain measure of accommodation to circumstance, although I do not consider myself any of the above. Nowadays I have no problem embracing the fact of being a foreigner, an outsider. I no longer waste energy on resenting slights or complaining that Japanese values don't always conform to the ones I learned growing up in California. I have come to feel grateful, in fact, for the ways that life in Japan has changed me for the better.

Some of my friends will have a hard time swallowing this, but I am a nicer person. I have developed more patience and become far more polite than—for example—when I was living in New York. I think I have become less selfish, as well. I accept jobs from editors without ever asking what the pay is because I don't want the subject of money to intrude on the relationship. That may sound bizarre to Americans—it did to me at one time—but to people living in Tokyo it is more the norm. And it is all right with me.

"Well, don't you ever regret not returning to live in the United States?" David persisted. "Haven't you ever felt lonely?"

Lonely? In a city of thirteen million inhabitants; with a beautiful, clear-eyed wife who tells it to me like it is; with her warm and welcoming family; with good friends on both sides of the cultural divide; editors, translators, critics, and people to interview—not to mention travels to various exotic locations around the world—when the hell would I have time for loneliness?

My health insurance premiums—a universe away from the spiraling costs of healthcare in America—have been adjusted to reflect the venerability attached to my last birthday, but I have not gone out to buy a corncob pipe and a rocking chair. I still run a mile a day without getting winded and I could probably still win an arm wrestling contest with some of the scrawnier yakuza. More importantly, work keeps coming over the transom and there are many more subjects that lure me on to explore and write about. Life here is a continual reminder that there is still much left for me to do.

"Come on," said David. "Looking back, there must be things that you wish you would have done differently."

It put me in mind of a famous quote from Miyamoto Musashi: "Do not regret what you have done. There is more than one path to the top of the mountain."

I'll remember to bring my notebook and a tape recorder when I get there.

Index